Designing for

FOUNDATION PAPER PIECING

DANA E. JONES

Designing for FOUNDATION PAPER PIECING

Creating Custom Quilts with Precision and Joy

DANA E. JONES

SCHIFFER CRAFT
4880 Lower Valley Road • Atglen, PA 19310

Other Schiffer Books on Related Subjects:
Design Then Quilt: A Dynamic Guide to Creating Stunning Modern Quilts, Irene Roderick,
ISBN 978-0-7643-6877-6

The Quilting Power Grid: A Design Skillbook for Beginning Modern Quilters, with 50 Example Projects,
Sandra Sider, ISBN 978-0-7643-6550-8

The Quilting Experience: A Celebration of Community and Patchwork Patterns, Victoria Findlay Wolfe,
ISBN 978-0-7643-6807-3

Library of Congress Control Number: 2026932887

Designed by Christine Stuermer
Cover design by Lindsay Hess
Type set in Gravita GEO/Archer
Edited by Kaylee Schofield and Karla Rosenbusch
Endsheet design and background images on pages 1, 13, and 154 courtesy of Cherrywood Fabrics
Illustration scanning and editing for Chapters 1 and 2; quilt photography for pages 6, 9, 11, 17, 18, 19, 26, 28, 35, 81, 110-127, and 142; and color correction for these illustrations and photographs by Assist Art Services. Photography by David Chambers. Illustration scanning, editing, and color correction by Sean Tracey.
Artwork for block and quilt patterns by Joyce Robinson.
Computerized illustrations, pages 87 and 95-103, by David Espy.
Photo of author, page 157, by Tom Nicol of Tom Nicol Photography.

ISBN: 978-0-7643-7241-4
ebook EAN: 978-1-5073-0759-5
Printed in China

10 9 8 7 6 5 4 3 2 1

FSC www.fsc.org MIX Paper | Supporting responsible forestry FSC® C104723

Published by Schiffer Craft
an imprint of Schiffer Publishing, Ltd.
4880 Lower Valley Road
Atglen, PA 19310
Phone: (610) 593-1777; Fax: (610) 593-2002
Email: Info@schifferbooks.com
Web: www.schifferbooks.com

DEDICATION

This book is dedicated to Andrew "Andy" Robert Fogle, my forever love. Andy reappeared in my life—we were in the same high school class—about the time I began work on this book. As the manuscript and illustrations came together, so did we. August 2, 2025, around the time my manuscript and illustrations were due, we were married.

CONTENTS

INTRODUCTION

When I took my first foundation paper-piecing (FPP) class in the 1990s, I discovered my quilting passion. Even before completing that class project, I launched into designing my first FPP quilt. As I designed *Peace Cranes Over Hiroshima*, I knew I had to draw straight lines and only straight lines. I was faithful to this, but each time I tried to piece the quilt, something in my design didn't work. I consumed rolls upon rolls of freezer paper and spent a small fortune on markers, pencil leads, and erasers, always convinced the latest version of my design was right.

I didn't give up. Finally my lightbulb moment came. Straight lines alone weren't enough. Those lines couldn't turn corners within a foundation or I would be up against the enemy: Y-seams. Once I realized this, I created a design I could piece. It remains one of my favorite designs, perhaps because I spent so many hours with it and because I love the gracefulness of this iconic symbol of peace.

▲ *Peace Cranes Over Hiroshima*, 35" x 49.5", 2006, designed and made by Dana E. Jones

At that time and since, I've searched for books that teach FPP design. I've found wonderful FPP pattern books, and I've gleaned ideas for FPP design from quilt greats such as Ruth B. McDowell and Cynthia England, even though they're not foundation paper piecers. I've studied other people's FPP patterns, and I've drawn foundations for patterns that were not intended for FPP. All this effort has proved invaluable to honing my design process—the process I'm sharing in this book. *Designing for Foundation Paper Piecing* fills a gap in what's available to quilters who want to move from making other people's FPP patterns to creating their own patterns. If you're reading this book, you are likely among these folks.

As someone who seeks order in all things, I began pulling together insights from my work designing for FPP. As the dos and don'ts of FPP design became clear, and as I began teaching these to others, my Paper Police rules emerged. In the quilt world, we remove the "quilt police" from our classrooms and guilds because they hold us back. My Paper Police have a different presence. They are helpers. Their rules are few. If you follow them, you will succeed in designing quilts you can foundation paper piece.

I recommend you work through this book from beginning to end, doing the exercises in the order they appear because that will help you learn—really learn—what does and doesn't work. Like most of my FPP design students, you may want to go straight to designing a pictorial image. I encourage you to be patient. Take time to play with traditional quilt blocks. They have much to teach you. Take time to design and piece one or several blocks. By doing so, you'll practice the Paper Police rules and find out how they can serve you. You may discover a love of blocks you never knew you had as you design blocks unlike any you've seen. You'll discover secondary patterns that appear when you put multiple blocks together and when you twist and turn and reverse them in a multitude of combinations. Then you'll be ready to design from a photograph.

As we move into working with photos, I'll introduce a few more Paper Police rules. While these are not unique to pictorial designs, you need to really understand them as your designs become more intricate. You'll practice these rules, then be ready to tackle your first pictorial design. At this point, you'll need to ignore the urge to race ahead. A slow, methodical approach guarantees success.

I encourage you to work by hand as you begin learning to design for FPP. This is not because I'm a Luddite. I've been designing with computers for years and will encourage you, once you know the Paper Police rules, to design by computer if that is your preference. I've found in teaching FPP design that starting with paper, pencil, and eraser yields the best early results. Research shows that drawing by hand engages more areas in our brains, which, in turn, improves our understanding and memory of what we are learning. This is why many schools that had stopped teaching cursive writing are reintroducing that instruction. Studies show that the value of drawing and writing by hand continues to pay off even as we age. The intimacy of hand drawing, erasing, and redrawing on paper builds muscle memory that will continue into drawing with a mouse or smart stylus. Start out working by hand.

There are numerous computer programs you can use for FPP design. Some of these are free; others can be purchased or rented. There are programs designed specifically for quilters and those used for design in other fields that adapt well to quilting. I've had students use a range of programs based on their familiarity with design software from their vocational and avocational experience. Instead of having you work with software you don't know, I prefer to teach you what works and what doesn't work, then set you free to decide if you want to continue working on paper or computer. I'll let you know when I think it's a good time to computerize your design process, but feel free to go that route when it is comfortable for you to do so.

I thank you for joining me on this journey toward creating your own unique FPP designs. You'll soon be designing quilts that will mystify all who see them. "Oohs" and "aahs" from quilt buds, family, and friends await you. Enjoy the journey.

THE FIRST LUDDITES

The term "Luddite" has its roots in the 18th and 19th centuries' textile industry when the advent of the division of labor threatened textile workers' livelihoods. Kassia St. Clair explains this in her book, ***The Golden Thread: How Fabric Changed History***. She writes that economist William Perry turned the textile industry upside down when he suggested cloth would be cheaper if carding, spinning, weaving, and the other production processes were be done by workers who only did one of these functions instead of all of them.

The response from woolen workers in Leeds, England, was swift, prolonged, and fruitless. They tried to stop the industrialization of their industry to no avail. St. Clair writes: "It was fears such as these that gave rise to the Luddite movement, a wave of violence against machinery by unemployed cloth workers. The term Luddite has since become derogatory, used to signify a techno-dinosaur vainly standing in the way of progress."

As I said, I'm not a Luddite.

GETTING STARTED

FOUNDATION PAPER PIECING IS MORE popular than ever, and more and more, quilters want to create their own designs to foundation paper piece.

What Is Foundation Paper Piecing?

Foundation paper piecing—FPP for short—is a quilting technique that allows for precision, sharp points, extreme angles, and intricate designs. It requires stitching pieces in sequential order as they are printed on paper. Most foundation paper piecers stitch on the lines on the paper and remove the paper later.

The term "foundation" comes from the fact that the paper provides stability to the fabric that prevents it from stretching when stitching and pressing, especially along bias edges. When foundation paper piecers talk about a foundation, they are talking about a portion of a quilt that can be stitched as a single unit.

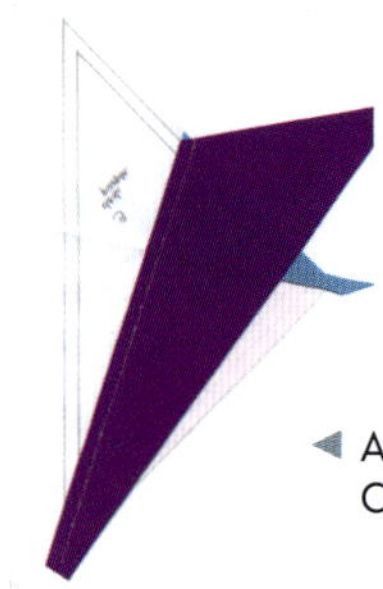

◀ A foundation for Cool Star block

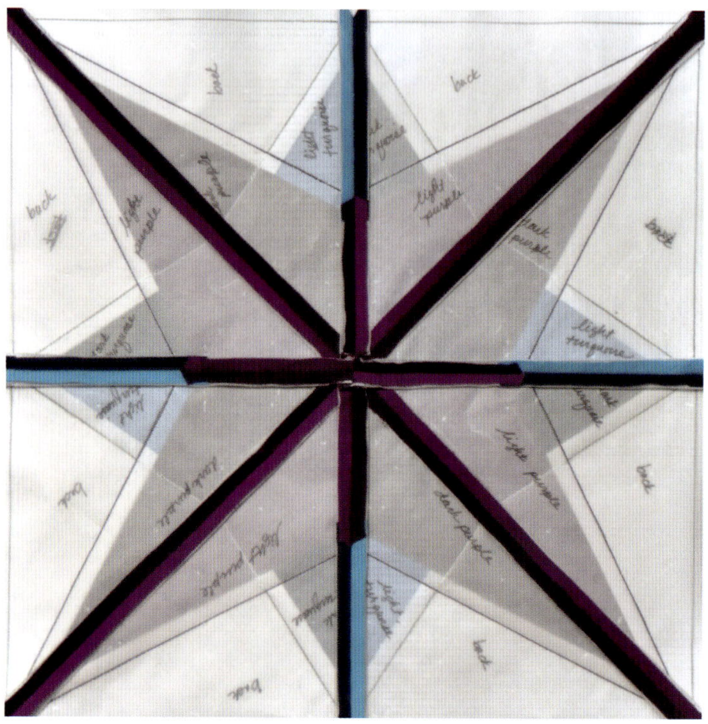

▶ Cool Star block, 12" × 12", designed by Dana E. Jones, shows the precision made possible with foundation paper piecing. It has eight foundations.

While I've made a few large quilts that were just one foundation, such as my *Cat's Meow*, this is not the norm.

Most FPP quilt patterns and many blocks require multiple foundations. The number varies greatly. There are quilt blocks that can be pieced with one foundation, while others call for a dozen or more foundations. Full quilts can require many foundations. For example, my *Peace Cranes Over Hiroshima* has 39 foundations. This book will explain when and why a design must be divided into multiple foundations.

▲ *Cat's Meow*, 58" × 72", 2022, designed and pieced by Dana E. Jones, quilted by Rita Meyerhoff, was done as one large foundation.

Each quadrant of the Cool Star block needed to be divided into two foundations for a total of eight foundations to make the block.

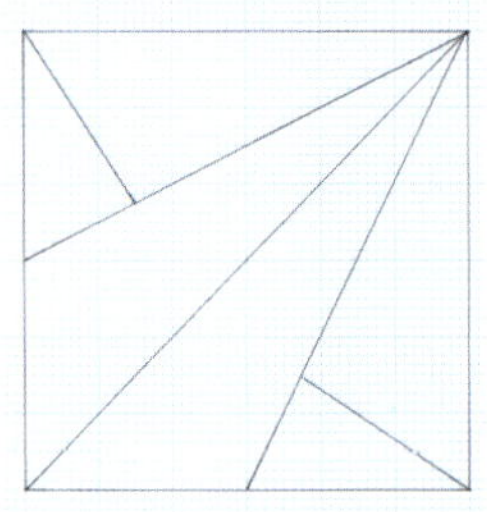

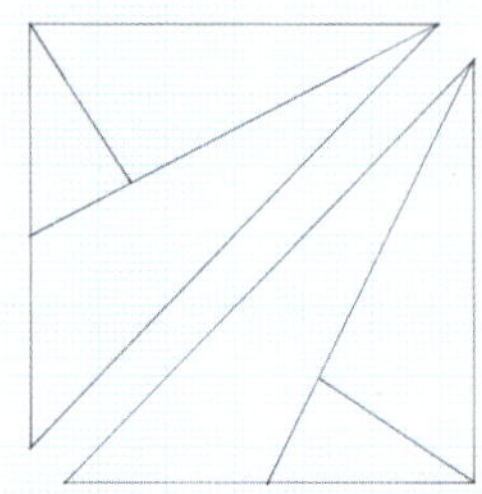

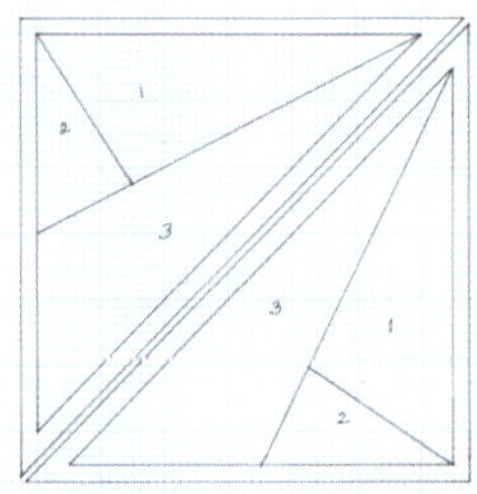

Cutting pieces for FPP is different than cutting them for traditional piecing. FPP pieces are cut larger. While traditional piecing requires adding an exact ¼" seam allowance around each piece, FPP doesn't require such exact cutting. You have to cut pieces large enough to ensure they will cover the intended space on the foundation plus extra fabric for joining the next piece. FPP usually requires more fabric than traditional piecing. The Bonus Tips section of this book, page 102, will show you how to make cutting templates so you can use fabric more efficiently when foundation paper piecing.

FPP stitching lines are always straight lines. While you can suggest curves when foundation paper piecing, this must be done with straight lines.

I've been known to compare FPP to Paint by Number. Once you have your pattern, constructing your quilt is as simple as stitching pieces together by sewing on the lines in the order they are numbered. If getting a consistent scant ¼" seam has evaded you, it's time for you to try foundation paper piecing, because it removes the need to master the perfect seam allowance. Seams are stitched wider and can vary in width over the course of the seam.

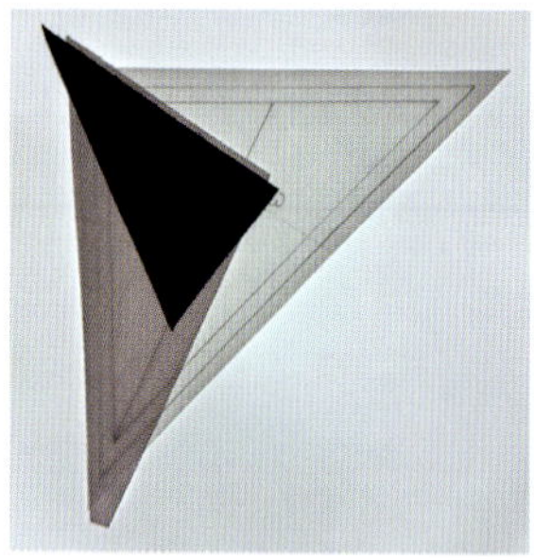

Seams are trimmed to ¼"—narrower when you're working with small pieces—after they are stitched.

FPP can be challenging because the foundations are mirror images of the final piece.

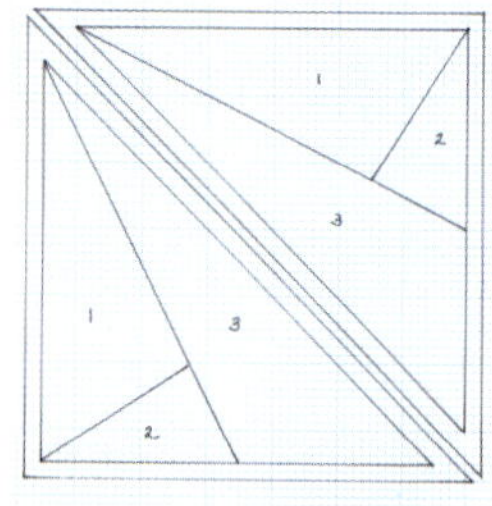

I've found that thinking about this too much is the culprit. FPP is a methodical process. If you learn the method and stay the course, it's likely you'll stop twisting your brain around mirror images. When designing for FPP, mirror imaging isn't a factor. You design your block or quilt as you want it to look. When your design is complete, you reverse it by tracing it from the backside, reversing it in a computer program, or pushing the reverse button on the copy machine. As I say later in this book, you don't have to look in the mirror when designing.

Some quilters don't like removing the paper. I find it a mindless activity that keeps my hands busy while watching TV or sitting in a waiting room. If this is the only thing stopping you from embracing FPP, there are paper and fabric foundation materials that can be left in, and there are some that wash out.

EPP: A HISTORICAL WORD

English paper piecing originated in England in the 1700s and was soon brought to the United States. In the United Kingdom, the technique is known as "mosaic piecing" or "mosaic patchwork." It's unfortunate that U.S. quilters renamed it. Calling it mosaic patchwork would avoid confusing it with foundation paper piecing.

Like other quilting techniques, the popularity of EPP has come and gone and come again. The Great Depression of the 1920s and 1930s brought renewed interest in EPP. A second revival occurred in the 1980s, and the most recent resurgence began about 2010.

While early English paper-piecing enthusiasts designed mostly with hexagons, triangles, and diamonds, today's EPP devotees and several companies that produce supplies, books, and tools for EPP have expanded the range of shapes and provide instructions for piecing the shapes. Quilt groups dedicated to EPP have formed around the United States.

I encourage you to give EPP a try if you haven't, especially if you enjoy handwork. But first, learn to design for FPP, EPP's very distant cousin.

▲ *Grandmother's Flower Garden*, 77" × 93", made by Gertrude Jones, grandmother of Dana E. Jones, circa 1960

▶ *Sparkle*, variation 6, designed by Mickey Depre from *Pieced Hexies: A New Tradition in English Paper Piecing* (American Quilter's Society, 2015), pieced by Dana E. Jones

I'm often asked what the difference is between foundation paper piecing and English paper piecing—EPP for short. When I began foundation paper piecing in 2004, I didn't hear this question. Most of the quilt world called the technique now known as foundation paper piecing simply "paper piecing." Carol Doak, a leading teacher and author of books on the technique, called it "machine paper piecing." Her book *Easy Machine Paper Piecing: 60 Quilt Blocks for Foundation Piecing* (That Patchwork Place, 1994) remains a favorite of mine for the basics of how to foundation paper piece.

When I was hired as an editor at *Quilters Newsletter* magazine in 2009, the magazine was using the term "foundation paper piecing," though it wasn't yet being abbreviated as FPP. Calling the process foundation paper piecing became my default when writing, but when I was teaching, I found I used the terms "foundation paper piecing" and "paper piecing" interchangeably. I confused my students. About 30 minutes into class, someone would ask about the difference in the two terms, and I'd explain they are two names for the same process.

The confusion began multiplying about 15 years ago, when a resurgence of interest in English paper piecing began in the United States. English paper piecing has only one thing in common with foundation paper piecing: the use of paper. Here are the differences:

- Foundation paper piecing is a machine technique. English paper piecing is a hand process.
- When foundation paper piecing, you stitch on the paper or fold it back and stitch along the fold. When English paper piecing, you fold the fabric over paper templates and stitch or glue the fabric in place.
- With FPP, you join multiple pieces of fabric on one piece of paper. With EPP, you have a paper template for each piece.
- FPP doesn't allow Y-seams; EPP delights in them.

In both processes, the presence of the paper under the fabric helps stabilize the fabric and prevents it from stretching.

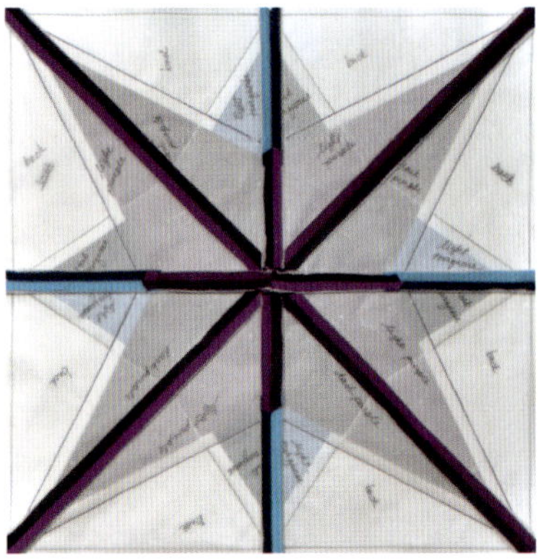

English paper piecing is a wonderful process. I find hand stitching relaxing, and EPP projects are easy to carry with you. EPP is not, however, the subject of this book.

▲ English paper piecing is a hand-stitching process that begins with creating individual pieces like the hexagons (hexies) shown above, then joining them by hand. *Work by Dana E. Jones*

◀ When foundation paper piecing, you machine-stitch on the lines or fold the paper back and stitch right next to the fold.

WHY AND WHEN TO FOUNDATION PAPER PIECE

I love to foundation paper piece (FPP). If you've purchased this book, I suspect you do too, and I suspect you love it for many of the reasons I do. These include the following:

- Foundation paper piecing allows precision and accuracy in matching points and aligning pieces in blocks and pictures. Because you are sewing on lines you've drawn, you know they will line up when you join the foundations.
- You can create and piece designs that have extreme angles that are difficult, if not impossible, to piece by other piecing methods.
- You can create intricate patterns that may require small pieces. For example, I'm a fan of designs that use ¼" strips. These are easy to piece precisely when you're stitching on paper.
- Piecing is easy. You stitch on the lines, adding pieces in the order they are numbered. You work out piecing challenges in the design process, so the only challenge left in piecing is to be sure you're adding pieces cut from the right fabrics in the right order.
- Cutting doesn't have to be precise. Pieces for FPP are cut about ½" larger all around than the finished size.
- You don't have to stitch perfect scant ¼" seams because you trim seams to the desired width after stitching.

Must-Have Design Tools and Supplies

Gathering the tools and supplies you'll need to design for foundation paper piecing means stepping outside the quilt shop in some cases. These supplies are available at brick-and-mortar or online fine-art supply stores. Craft stores are not likely to have what you need. For blocks, you'll need the following:

Gridded Vellum Paper

I recommend using translucent vellum paper because you can see through it, permanent markers don't bleed through it, and it erases cleaner than most other papers. I recommend you use gridded vellum that has eight squares per inch because we most often design blocks in multiples of ⅛". This paper is also good for laying out full quilts to scale.

Transparent Gridded Ruler

I've found these rulers work best because they lie flattest on your paper. That lets you draw more precisely on the grid lines of your paper, exactly where you want your lines. I like working with a 1" × 12" ruler. Quilt shops that carry transparent gridded rulers tend to carry 1" × 6" or 2" × 18" or both. These can be used, but the 1" × 6" may prove too short for many of your designs. I prefer the 1" width over the 2" width because I can handle it better. This may not be true for you. If you can get to a brick-and-mortar store, try each width to see what works best for you. These are not expensive, so if you're ordering online, I'd get one of each width. If you can find a 1" × 18" ruler, get it too. I like to get ones that have red lines because the gridded vellum paper has blue lines. The contrasting colors are helpful.

Mechanical Pencil

You will do a lot of drawing in the design process, so I recommend that you get a mechanical pencil and plenty of extra leads. Having to constantly sharpen your pencil is irritating and wastes time. You can work with an inexpensive mechanical pencil, but you will be more precise with a better-quality one. Go for a 0.5 mm or 0.7 mm HB or B lead. Harder leads will leave indentations in your paper when you erase. These are distracting. Lines drawn with softer leads are too wide, leading to more difficulty sewing precisely.

Eraser

I recommend a pink or white Pink Pearl brand eraser. I've found these erase the cleanest. Store brands that look similar don't work as well. You will need an eraser beyond the one that comes on your pencil.

Fine-Point or Ultra-Fine-Point Permanent Marker

You will draw your final design in permanent marker. Fine-point or ultra-fine-point markers give you the finest lines for the most precision. Sharpie and Micron are two brands to look for. My favorite is the retractable ultra-fine Sharpie because I live in a dry climate where these last the longest. Microns are great markers if you don't have to deal with them drying out as I do. If you are drawing tiny pieces, they will give you the most precision.

For pictorial images, you'll need a ruler or rulers, mechanical pencil, eraser, and a fine-point or ultra-fine-point permanent marker, as described above. You'll also need the following:

Translucent, Nongridded Vellum

Buy this vellum the size of the quilt you are designing or a bit larger. This is available from fine-art supply stores, some office supply stores, and online. You may be able to find only 8½" × 11½" paper. I often design on this, then enlarge my designs before making my foundations. Sheets of vellum larger than 8½" × 11" may be available from office- and art-supply stores and online. For larger quilts, you can purchase a roll of translucent vellum without grid marks from fine-art stores. These are usually 36" wide. For wider quilts, I tape several widths together. I recommend translucent vellum instead of tracing paper because it's often easier to see through, has a smooth surface compared to the textured surface of most tracing paper, won't tear easily as tracing paper does, and erases cleaner than tracing paper.

Copy Paper or Other Plain White Paper

You will need a sheet of white paper the size of the quilt you are designing or slightly larger. You will periodically put this paper between your photo and the vellum to help you see what you have drawn. For large quilt designs, a roll of mural paper will work. You won't draw on this, so it can be reused.

1"-Wide Masking Tape

I find blue painter's tape works best. You can use artist's white tape, but it's a bit pricier. You'll use this to tape your photo to your drawing surface and to hinge vellum over your photograph. You want a tape that holds things in place but is easy to remove without tearing your papers.

CHAPTER 1

MEETING THE PAPER POLICE: RULES *for* FOUNDATION PAPER PIECING DESIGN

WHILE I'M GLAD THE QUILT POLICE have been banned from most quilt settings, there is another set of folks I welcome: the Paper Police. When you're foundation paper piecing (FPP), the paper is often in charge. This can be challenging until you learn that following a few simple rules is the key to success. I recommend making friends with the Paper Police. You'll be glad you did.

Draw Straight Lines Only

When foundation paper piecing, all lines must be straight lines.

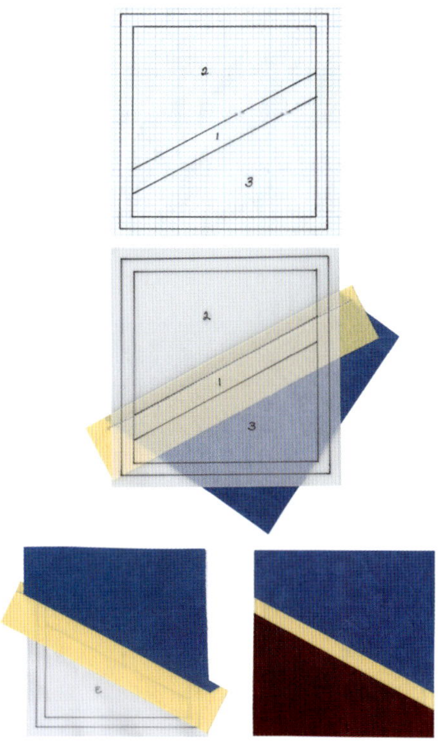

There are no curved lines in FPP. You can stitch a curved line on paper, but you cannot fold the paper back. If you force it to fold back, it will tear.

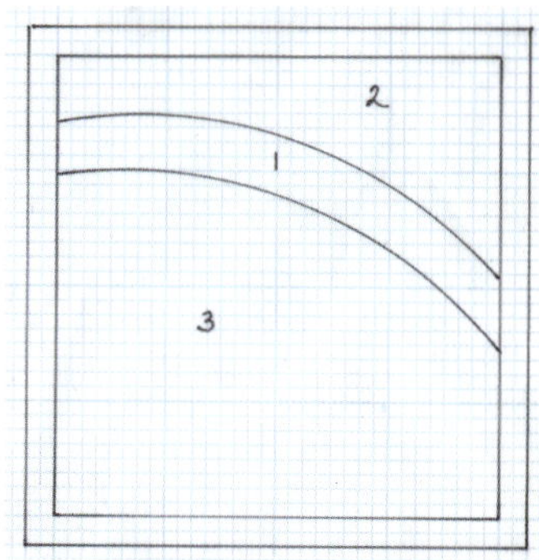

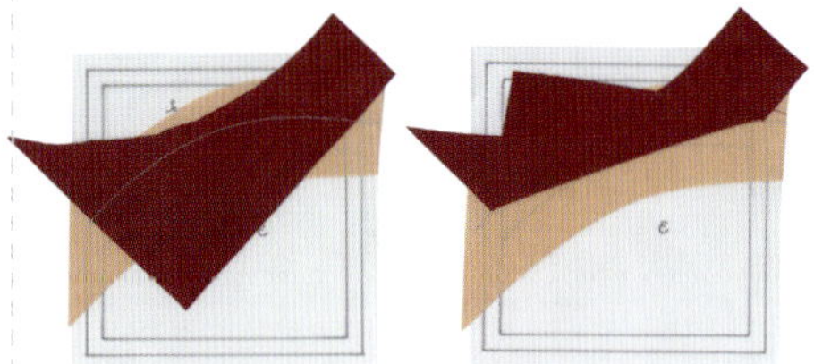

For some designs, such as my *Whose Red Line* quilt, this is easy to see. Using a roll of gridded vellum, I drew my quilt full size, then broke it into long, vertical foundations. I could have made horizontal foundations. That choice was mine as the designer.

Some quilts, such as Possibilities' *Christmas Pickle*, page 18, combine foundation paper-pieced segments with actual curved piecing, which is done after the paper is removed. Foundation paper piecing allows quilters to get consistent, spiky points.

▲ Foundation for *Christmas Pickle*, used with permission from Possibilities

Jaynette Huff turned to appliqué and embellishment to add real curves to her FPP design of a rotary cutter in her book, *Needles and Notions: Paper-Pieced Patterns with a Sewing Room Theme* (Martingale, 2000). She created the blade with appliqué and enhanced

▲ *Rotary Cutter*, designed by Jaynette Huff, pieced and quilted by Dana E. Jones

▲ *Whose Red Line*, 56" × 72", 2018, designed and pieced by Dana E. Jones, quilted by Rita Meyerhoff

the image by adding buttons to suggest the screw and washer that hold the blade in place. The cutter handle and the circle on which the blade rests are made entirely of straight lines, but we see curves.

Working with straight lines in this way takes advantage of the fact that we see what we expect to see. We see a rotary cutter. We know that a rotary cutter has a curved handle and a curved blade, so that's what we see. On closer examination, we realize some of what we see as curves are actually straight lines. Even as you design, think about what embellishments and appliqué can do to help your viewers see curves where there aren't any.

In the chapter 3 subsection "Curves Ahead: Creating an Illusion," page 88, we'll look at how to suggest curves with straight lines.

Don't Turn Corners

When I designed my first quilt for foundation paper piecing, I knew I had to draw the pattern with straight lines. Less obvious was the fact that those lines could not turn corners, because when you turn a corner, you create a Y-seam. To understand this, let's look at a Four Patch block.

I can join pieces 1 and 2 without a problem, but when I add piece 3, I create a corner. I can stitch piece 3 to pieces 1 and 2, but when I try to add piece 4, the corner I created when I added piece 3 is in the way. Adding piece 4 would require stitching a Y-seam, and the paper won't let me do that.

▲ *Christmas Pickle*, 55" × 79", 2019, pattern by Nancy Smith and Lynda Milligan of Possibilities, pieced by Dana E. Jones, quilted by ZJ Humbach

I didn't understand this rule when I first designed *Peace Cranes Over Hiroshima*.

I thought I had to draw the lines of the cranes exactly as they appeared in my inspiration image, and that required turning a corner where the head and neck of the blue crane meet. You know how your GPS tells you to make a slight right turn? That doesn't work when foundation paper piecing. There is no way to fold back the paper even if the turn is slight. If you try to fold it back, it

tears. I had to tear the paper off and hand stitch the Y-seam.

When *Quilts With Style* magazine published a pattern for this quilt, they removed the corner, eliminating the need for the pesky Y-seam. The head is a different shape than the image I worked from, but that's not a problem. If I hadn't pointed out the difference, it's unlikely you'd have noticed it. The cornerless version still looks like an origami peace crane.

If you find yourself thinking you have no choice but to turn a corner that will create a pattern with a Y-seam, step back and take a break. When you come back to your design, you'll find a way to eliminate the corner, and your design will still look the way you want it to look. Like our eyes see curves where there are only straight lines, our eyes will see your image despite the fact you tweaked a few lines to avoid corners.

▲ *Peace Cranes Over Hiroshima*, 35" × 49.5", 2006, designed and made by Dana E. Jones

Add Only Pieces That Align Edge to Edge

This third Paper Police rule is key to avoiding corners. When you add a piece, it must be the same length as the piece or pieces to which you're adding it. Let's look at how this works.

I joined pieces 1 and 2 and pressed piece 2 away from piece 1 without creating a corner because the two pieces are the same length on the side where they are joined.

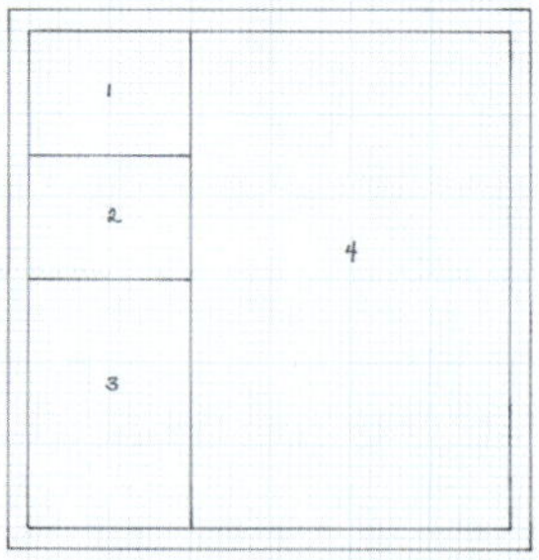

The same was true when I added piece 3.

When I added piece 4 to pieces 1–3, I could press it out without creating a corner because it was the same length as the first three pieces when sewn together.

I made my block more interesting by adding more vertical pieces. After joining pieces 1–3, I could add any number of vertical pieces as long as they were the same length as the combined pieces 1–3. I added three strips.

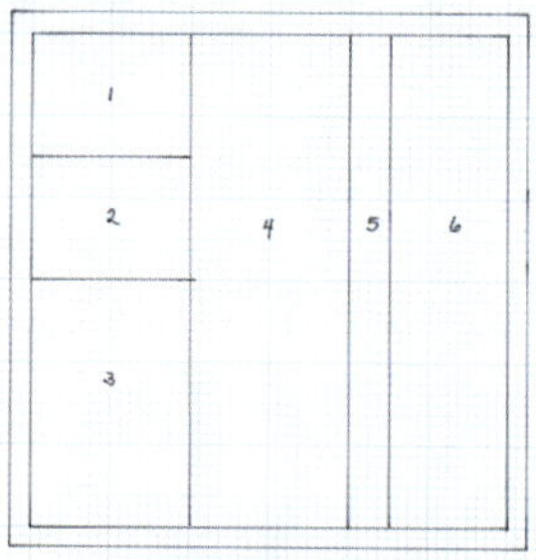

When I wanted to add piece 4 to combined pieces 1–3 horizontally, I encountered a challenge: I created a corner. This happened because piece 4 positioned horizontally is shorter than the length of combined pieces 1–3.

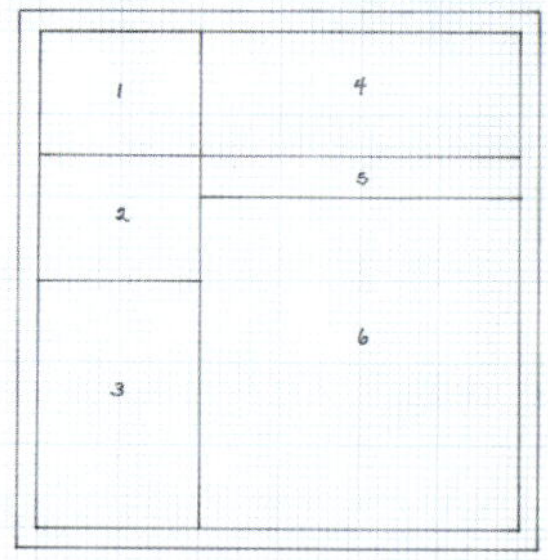

To position piece 4 horizontally, I had to break the block into two foundations. I pieced each foundation, then sewed them together.

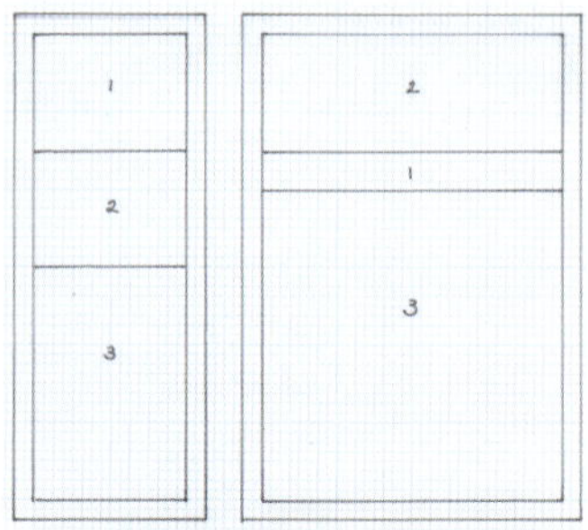

When your design requires you to turn a corner, that's a tip that it's time to draw multiple foundations to get the look you want. Understanding that you can't turn corners can help you know when to divide your block or image into multiple foundations.

Press Seams Toward the Last Piece Added

When foundation paper piecing, you can press seams only toward the last piece added. The paper dictates this. When you join pieces 1 and 2, the paper will force you to press the seam toward piece 2. When you join piece 3, the paper will force you to press the seam toward piece 3. And so it continues.

As an FPP designer, you always have a choice as to which piece is piece 1 and which piece is piece 2. This lets you control the direction the seam between these pieces will be pressed. From then on, the paper is in charge. Having to press toward the last piece added can result in shadows when the paper insists you press a dark fabric toward a light fabric.

When I designed the block below, I made the center piece in the top left corner piece 1 because I planned to use a pale-yellow fabric for that piece. That let me press the dark-green pieces 2 and 3 away from the pale-yellow fabric, thus avoiding shadows at those seams.

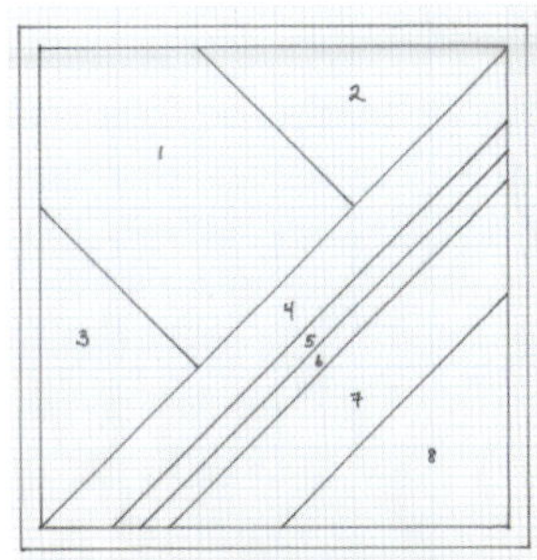

When I added piece 4, I lost control of the direction the remaining pieces would be pressed.

When piece 4 was stitched in place, the seams between pieces 1 and 2 and pieces 1 and 3 became locked in place. Even removing the paper did not allow me to reverse the direction in which the seams were pressed.

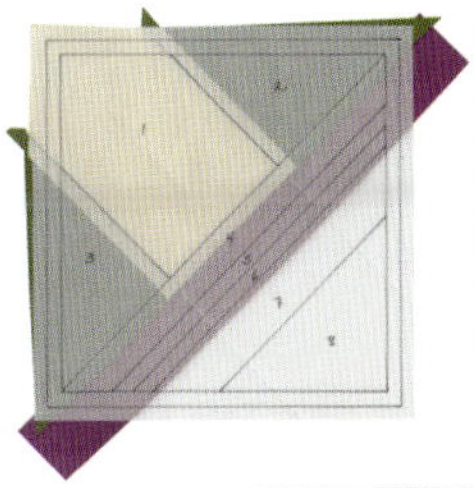

If you haven't stitched over pressed seams, you can press those seams in the opposite direction after you remove the paper. I find doing so tedious, and it is difficult to get as firm a press as when the seams are pressed the correct direction the first time. It's best to consider pressing directions in the design process. Use arrows to indicate the directions that seams will be pressed.

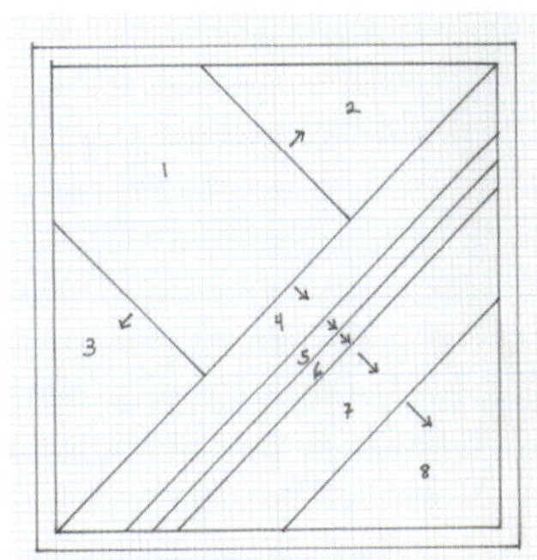

By doing this, you can discover when the directions you will be forced to press pieces are problematic. The solution to this may be to divide your design into additional foundations, because when you join foundations, you control the directions you press seams, and you can press them open instead of to one side to make your quilt top lie flatter.

In the block below, I changed the directional arrows in the bottom right portion of the block to show pressing the seam between the newly labeled pieces 1 and 2 away from the pale-yellow piece 1 and toward the dark-red piece 2.

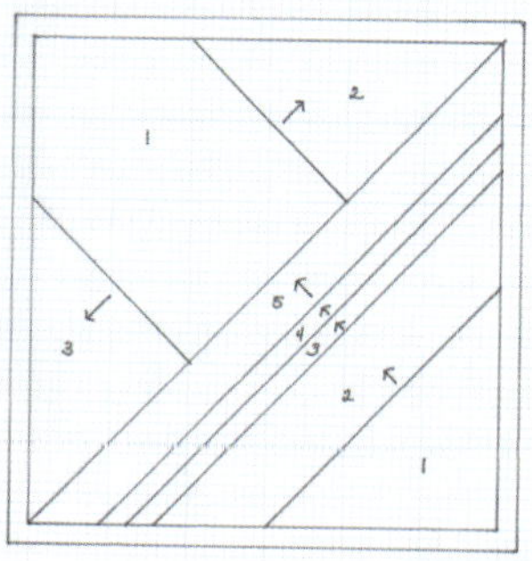

This eliminated the possibility of a shadow under the pale-yellow fabric, but it required stitching two foundations instead of one.

In the one-foundation version, I knew I could press the dark-red fabric away from the pale-yellow fabric once the paper was removed, because I wasn't going to stitch down the seam between the pale-yellow and dark-red pieces. This meant the direction of the seam wasn't locked in place. I could reverse the direction once the paper was removed. I don't like to do this because reversing the direction of seams in this way often doesn't result in as crisp a press as the original direction. The fabric often remembers the direction in which it was first pressed, and it resists the new direction, resulting in a softer press. There are situations, however, where reversing a seam after the paper is removed is the best solution. Be sure to keep a note that you want to do this. It's easy to forget. Once you join two foundations, you may lose the opportunity to reverse seam direction. I make such notes to myself on the foundation so I will see them as I remove the paper.

I chose to divide the above block into two foundations, making what was piece 8 in the one-foundation version into piece 1 in the second foundation.

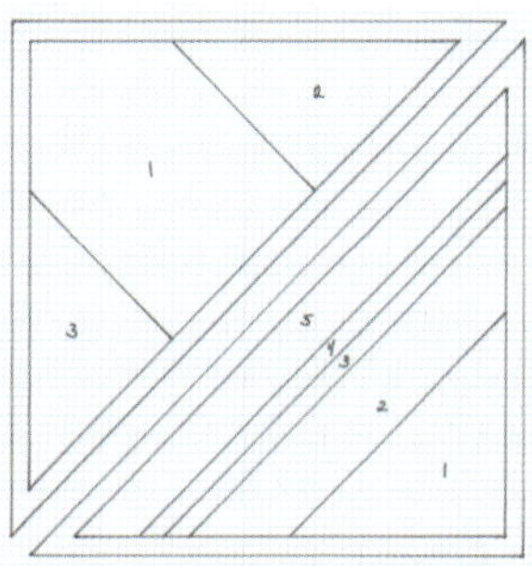

This let me press the seam between pieces 1 and 2 of the second foundation toward the dark-red fabric.

Though I had to make an additional foundation, I didn't have to sew additional seams. I simply sewed the two foundations together after they were pieced.

On a rare occasion, you may decide to clip a seam to reverse the direction it is pressed. Careful planning in the design stage can eliminate the need to do this in most cases. If you plan to clip a seam, make a note on the foundation to remind yourself of this.

Plan Nested Seams

In traditional piecing, you decide which direction you will press your seams after you've stitched them. You can reverse the direction when needed to nest seams for better alignment. This usually is not possible with FPP, so you need to plan for nesting seams as you design.

A Nine Patch block shows how to do this. You want the seams to align at the four points where four pieces meet. The easiest way to do this is to nest the seams. Marking the foundations with arrows will help you number the pieces, so the seams can be pressed in opposite directions for easy nesting when you join the foundations.

I numbered the first horizontal row of the Nine Patch block 1, 2, 3 from left to right. I numbered the second horizontal row 1, 2, 3 from right to left, and the third row 1, 2, 3 from left to right, the same as the first row. This made nesting the seams possible.

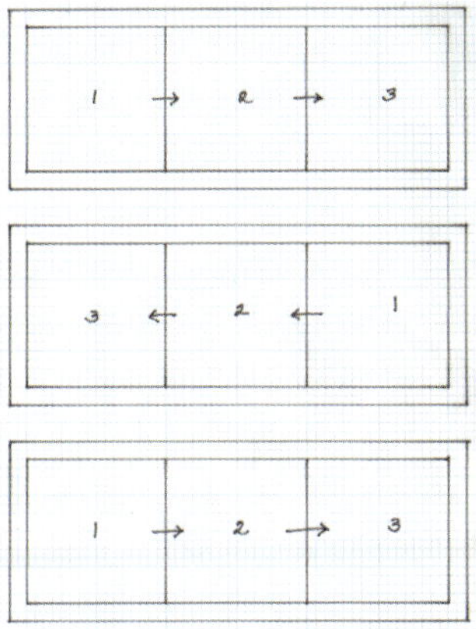

I planned for nesting of the seams when I designed my Clear Creek Shimmer block, which is Block No. 197 in *Quiltmaker's 1,000 Blocks: A Collection of Quilt Blocks from Today's Top Designers* (2015). It first appeared in *Quiltmakers 100 Best Blocks*, volume 3 (Summer 2011) as Block #223 on page 37.

While it's possible to make each of the eight triangles in this block with one foundation, doing so results in the six seams in each triangle being pressed in the same direction for all the triangles. That makes nesting the seams impossible. Aligning seams that are pressed in the same direction is difficult, and there is added bulk at every seam, a nightmare when you quilt the quilt.

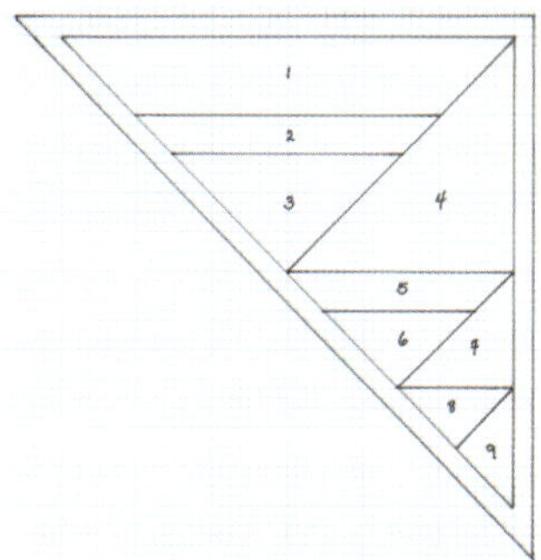

My solution? I divided half the triangles—the lighter-colored ones—into three foundations.

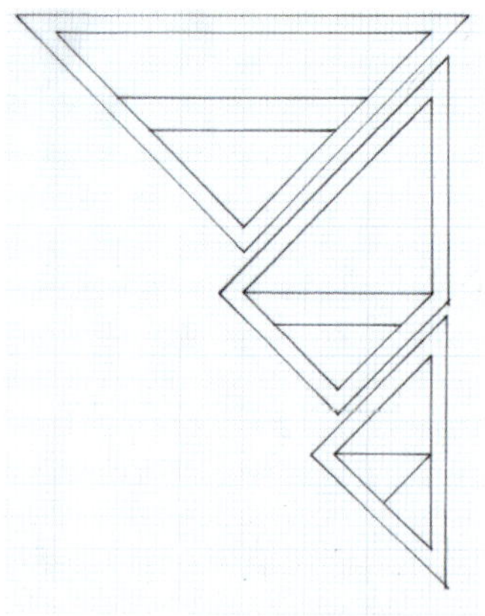

I drew arrows to show the directions the seams should be pressed.

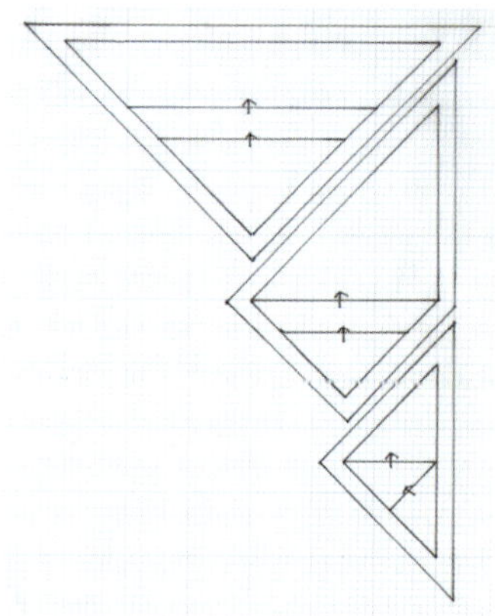

Then I numbered each foundation 1–3.

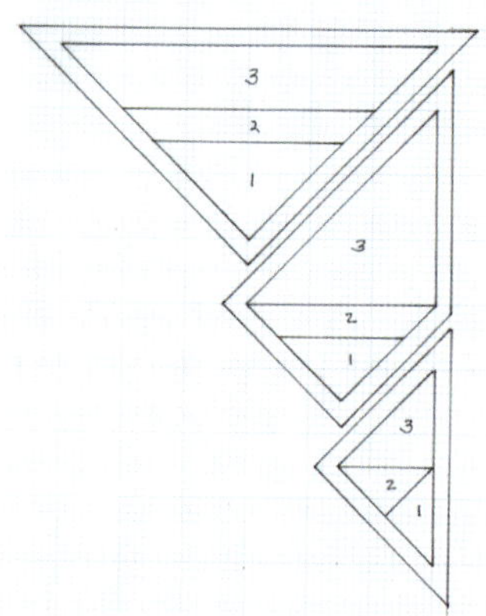

FPP FOR IMPACT

When deciding if you will foundation paper piece a quilt or portions of a quilt, think about what FPP does well. FPP allows you to create and piece designs with extreme angles, sharp points, and small pieces with precision that is difficult to achieve with traditional piecing. Don't shy away from combining piecing methods. My quilts often combine foundation paper piecing with curved piecing, appliqué, or traditional piecing, or a combination of these. When you know how to design for FPP, you'll be able to decide when foundation paper piecing is the best method for you, be it for an entire quilt or portions of it.

◀ I foundation paper pieced the triangles in my Bubbles & Swirls block to get precise, sharp points. I pieced the rest of the block with traditional piecing.

Once the three foundations were pieced, they could be sewn together, then joined to a dark foundation. The seams could nest at the six points where they aligned.

To complete the block, I made four dark triangles, each with one foundation, and four light triangles, each with three foundations. I paired light and dark triangles to make four half-square triangles, then joined four of these half-square triangles to make my block. I loved the block, so I made enough blocks to piece a lap-size quilt.

Striving for as few foundations as possible is often a design goal, but it is not always the optimum choice. By creating the additional foundations for the light triangles, I was able to press the seams in opposite directions, which made it possible to nest the seams, resulting in a flatter quilt top that was easier to quilt.

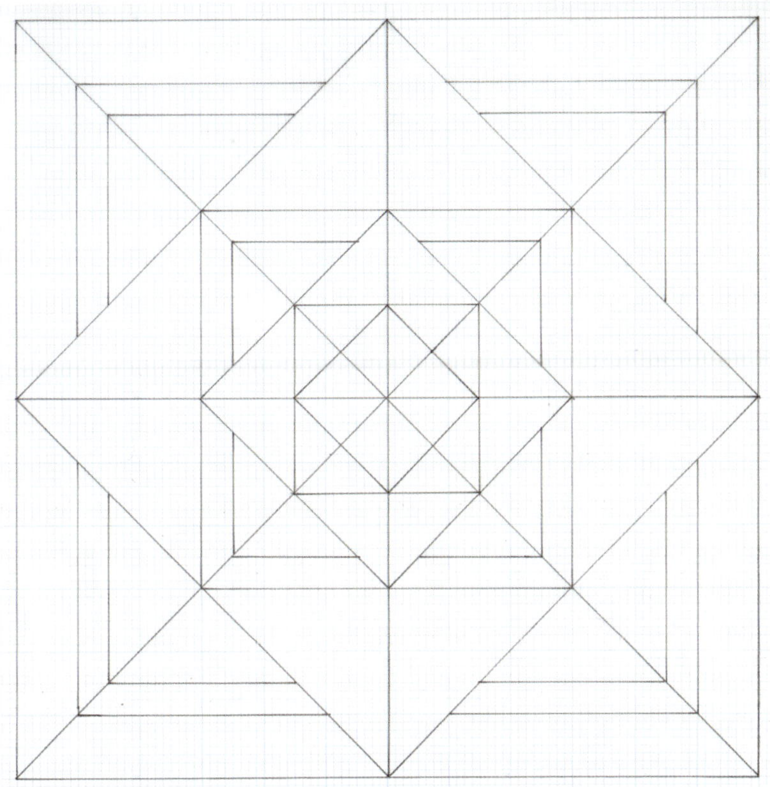

▲ Clear Creek Shimmer block, 12" × 12", 2011, designed by Dana E Jones

BANISH Y-SEAMS

For many FPP designers, Y-seams are the bane of their existence. I often see folks commenting on social media that they had to include Y-seams in their designs. When you find yourself thinking you must use Y-seams, stop and ask yourself several questions:

- Can I redraw one or several lines to remove the Y-seams? Sometimes slight changes in angles of lines are all you need.
- Am I trying to capture every line in my inspiration image? If so, can I drop a line or two or slightly redraw one or more lines to remove the Y-seams?
- Will renumbering the pieces in the foundation remove the Y-seams?

If you want to keep the look created by a Y-seam, you may need to break the foundation into two or more foundations. This will keep the look and remove the Y-seam.

▲ *Clear Creek Shimmer*, 71" × 56", 2018, designed and pieced by Dana E. Jones, quilted by Rita Meyerhoff

ONE FOUNDATION OR MORE?

It's great when you can piece a block or large area of a quilt as one foundation, but there are times when breaking a design into multiple foundations will make joining blocks or sections of a quilt easier. At these times, I remind myself that breaking images into more foundations doesn't mean more stitching. Seams I would have stitched within a foundation become seams that join foundations. When deciding if you will go with more than one foundation, ask yourself the following:

- Can I remove shadows that result when dark fabrics are pressed toward light fabrics by breaking my design into two or more foundations?
- Will it be easier to nest seams if I break my design into more foundations to allow me to press seams in alternate directions?
- Will breaking my design into more foundations add seams that will detract from my design?
- Can I avoid the bulk of many lines meeting at one point by breaking my design into more foundations so I can press seams between foundations open?

WHEN TO REVERSE A DESIGN

Reversing your pattern isn't required if your design is symmetrical left to right or top to bottom. To see how this works, select a block. Draw the block, then place your drawing right side down on a light box or window during daylight hours. Does it look the same as from the right side? If so, there is no need to reverse your pattern.

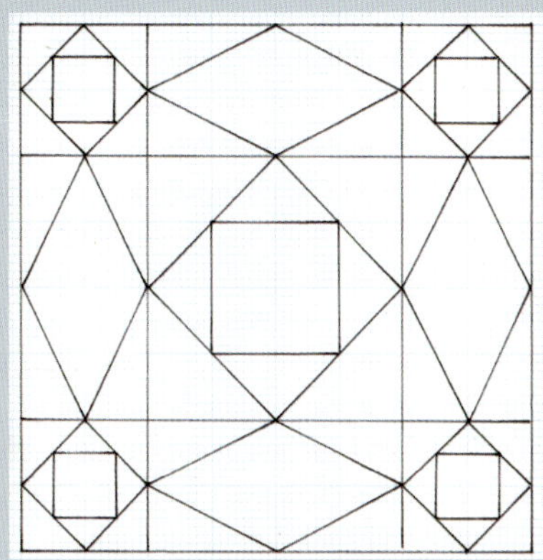

▲ The Storm at Sea block is symmetrical side to side and top to bottom, so there is no need to reverse the design.

Don't Look in the Mirror Yet

The need for the foundations to be mirror images of the finished piece confuses some quilters so much that they decide to never foundation paper piece again. Don't fear. This is not a factor when designing for foundation paper piecing. You will design blocks and images as you want them to look when done. When your designs are complete, you will reverse the foundations to get the mirror image needed for piecing. This is easy to do. You can trace your designs on the back of your drawings, which is especially easy if you've used a translucent vellum paper. A light box also comes in handy here. A window can stand in for a light box during daylight hours. Or you can take your design to your local copy shop, set the reverse button on the copy machine, and make a reverse copy.

▲ *Peace Cranes Over Hiroshima*, designed by Dana E. Jones, pieced and quilted by Laural Hoppes

Because you don't have to deal with thinking in reverse as you design, you may, like me, forget to reverse your finished design. Even this is not the end of the world in many cases. You will end up with the reverse of what you intended, but short of lettering or other images that must read in a specific direction, this isn't a problem. When Laural Hoppes took my Peace Cranes Over Hiroshima class, she stitched on the opposite side of the foundations than was intended. She'd not worked with foundations printed on translucent vellum before. She could see the lines clearly through the paper, so she didn't realize they were reversed. The result was a quilt in which the cranes are flying in the opposite direction from my original. I like it.

Ignore Seam Allowances for Now

When foundation paper piecing, ¼" or narrower seams are created after you stitch pieces together. When you are creating your design, you will draw what you want with no thought to seam allowances until your design is complete and you're ready to divide it into foundations. At that point, you will add ¼" seam allowances around all the edges of every foundation. We will look at how to do this in the chapter 4 subsection "Seam Allowances: Their Time Has Come," page 98.

ADD COLOR TO YOUR DESIGNS

I often color my foundations. I use Prismacolor pencils, which are waxy art pencils that work well on vellum. This helps me see my design clearly and provides a guide as I select fabric. While doing this is not a Paper Police rule, the Paper Police do recommend this. Why not add a bit of color to your design life?

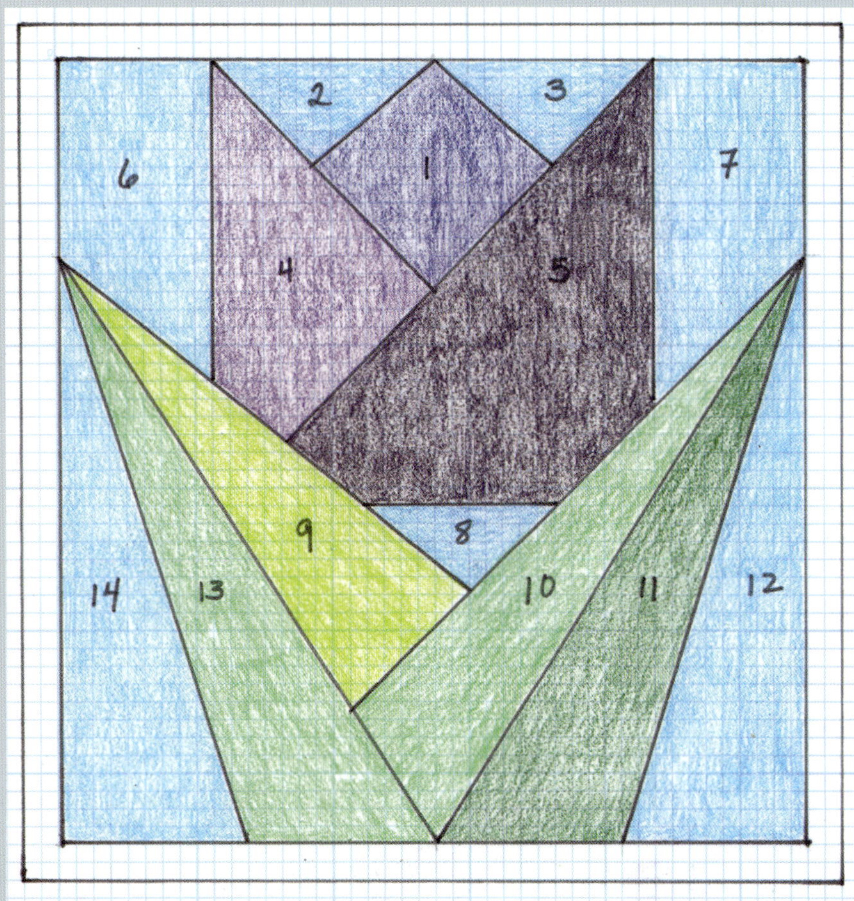

▲ Tulip block, 6" x 6", designed by Dana E. Jones

CHAPTER 2

DESIGNING BLOCKS *for* FOUNDATION PAPER PIECING

When you begin driving, you study the Rules of the Road, then you head out to the largest empty parking lot in your neighborhood to practice behind the wheel. That's where we are in our foundation paper-piecing journey. You've learned the Paper Police rules, and now it's time to practice using them to hone your FPP design skills. I encourage you to work through the exercises outlined here. It's in the doing that you will internalize the Paper Police rules.

Create a Solid Foundation: Working with Traditional Quilt Blocks

Working with traditional blocks is a great place to start learning to design for FPP. These blocks come out of the common canon that quilters share. They are familiar, a gift from our quilting foremothers and fathers. They help us learn when foundation paper piecing is a good choice and when another piecing method will yield better results. FPP can facilitate more precise piecing, but it can also be tedious for blocks that require myriad foundations. Such blocks may be pieced more quickly and more accurately with other piecing methods. Many traditional blocks were designed when most quilters pieced by hand. Some of these blocks defy the Paper Police rules, especially the rule that you cannot turn corners. When piecing by hand, turning corners, also known as stitching Y-seams, is relatively easy. When foundation paper piecing, you have to add seams within these blocks.

In this section, we'll first work with traditional blocks that are simple to foundation paper piece because they require one to three foundations, then we'll tackle blocks that are more difficult because they have multiple corners to turn, so they require four or more foundations. We'll see that FPP can lead to blocks that don't press as flat as they can when pieced using other methods. Whether or not you choose to foundation paper piece blocks with many foundations and those with pressing challenges is your decision as an FPP designer. I love all things FPP, so I have been known to piece blocks with many foundations, but I don't foundation paper piece those that won't lie as flat as possible. The following exercises will help you determine your preferences for FPP versus other piecing methods.

You may never have pieced a traditional block and may never do so in the future. That's okay. Enjoy them as a learning tool. They will prepare you for what comes next—designing pictorial images for FPP. Trust there is a tested method to my madness here.

The Log Cabin Block: One-Foundation Wonder

The Log Cabin block is among the most iconic and widely loved of our traditional quilt blocks. It's a great place to start our FPP design practice. The Log Cabin block is a one-foundation wonder. When piecing a traditional Log Cabin block that has straight-set logs 1" wide or wider sewn around a center square, traditional piecing may be quicker than FPP, but more and more, quilters are embracing blocks with irregular logs, wonky set logs, narrow logs, and more. All these variations are ideal for foundation paper piecing because of the precision of FPP, and because no matter the style of the block, you'll need just one foundation.

▲ Log Cabin block

Let's work with the Log Cabin block. The first step is to draw a Log Cabin block. Use a pencil and straightedge, and gridded vellum paper or other graph paper, and have your eraser handy. You may be thinking you can just trace this block. Don't. I'm having you draw it and the rest of the blocks in this chapter by hand because drawing connects eye, hand, and brain so you will better internalize the Paper Police rules. You will learn how the lines of this block relate to each other, which is key to why it requires just one foundation. Once you know how to use the Paper Police rules, you can continue to work by hand or in a computer design program of your choice.

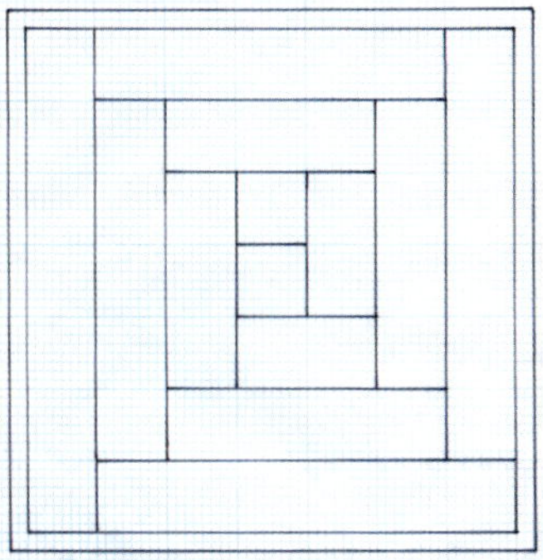

For the Log Cabin block, draw from the middle of the block out to best understand its construction. This means you will start by drawing the inside square.

COMING HOME

An interesting piece of quilt history: If you were stitching the block in traditional colors, the center square would be red, representing the hearth that is at the center of the home.

ALWAYS JUST ONE FOUNDATION

Regardless of the number of logs in your block; regardless of whether your logs are even widths or a variety of widths; regardless of whether the logs are set at right angles or at wonky angles; and regardless of whether your block is a square, a rectangle, or another shape (try a triangle), a Log Cabin block and its cousin, Courthouse Steps, can be made with one foundation.

Number the block you've drawn in the order you would foundation paper piece it, starting with 1. Each log of the block should have a number. If you've made Log Cabin blocks with traditional piecing, think about how you stitched them. The order of piecing will be the same when foundation paper piecing.

When you began numbering, you should have started in the middle of the block. You have a choice in terms of numbering pieces 1 and 2; they are interchangeable. You can begin by numbering the center square 1 and the adjacent square 2 or you can reverse them, making the center square 2 and the adjacent square 1.

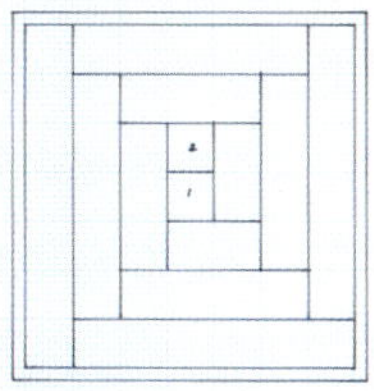

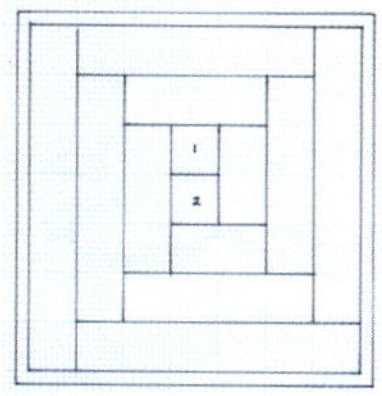

Once you've decided on the placement of pieces 1 and 2, there is just one path around the center if you are going to avoid turning corners.

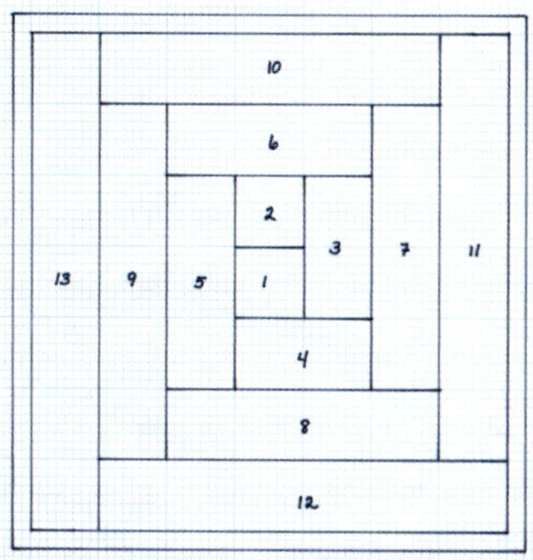

▲ Tulip block, designed by Dana E. Jones

WHEN MORE IS BETTER!

While I'm directing you to number this block as one foundation, designing for the fewest foundations possible will not always be your goal. Sometimes you will need more foundations to get a design the way you want it. When we work with photos to create pictorial quilt designs in chapter 3, "Designing Pictures for Foundation Paper Piecing," page 64, you'll begin to understand when drawing more foundations is the better way to go—when less is not more.

Bloom Bright: Lessons from a Tulip

The work of Carol Doak, known to many as the queen of what she calls "machine paper piecing," inspired the next block we'll work with: a Tulip block.

Draw this block, using a pencil and straightedge. Begin by drawing a square that is 5½" × 5½".

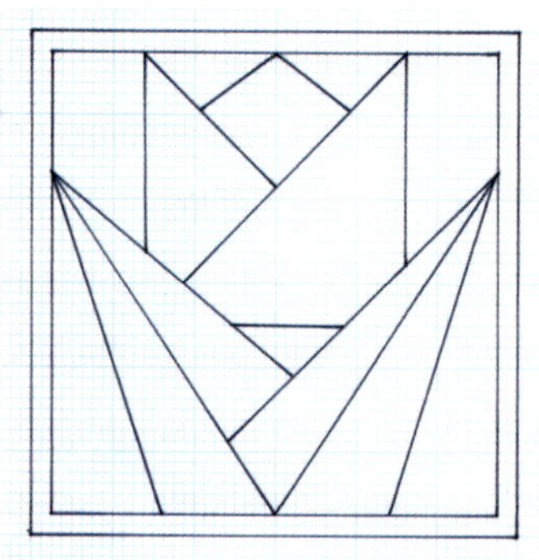

Take a few minutes to study this block, then number it in the order you would piece it. You will discover that unlike the Log Cabin block, this block often provides you with choices as to which piece to add next. With every foundation, there is always a choice when numbering pieces 1 and 2. This block provides choices at other points, but not always. In some instances, you will have only one choice that follows the Paper Police rules. Hint: This block can be pieced with one foundation.

There are multiple right answers to this exercise. When you design for FPP, you often have choices about piecing order. Think about the directions the seams will press. Draw arrows to help you figure this out. Sometimes you can select a piecing order to eliminate or reduce pressing dark fabrics toward light fabrics. This is not always possible, but it's good to do when you can.

You will also want to think about whether there are seams that need to nest, because this impacts piecing order. If nesting and seam direction aren't concerns, you can simply decide which piece you want to add next. Work to find a piecing path that requires just one foundation.

To piece this Tulip block as one foundation, start numbering the pieces in the top center of the block. Any of the three pieces in the top center can be piece 1.

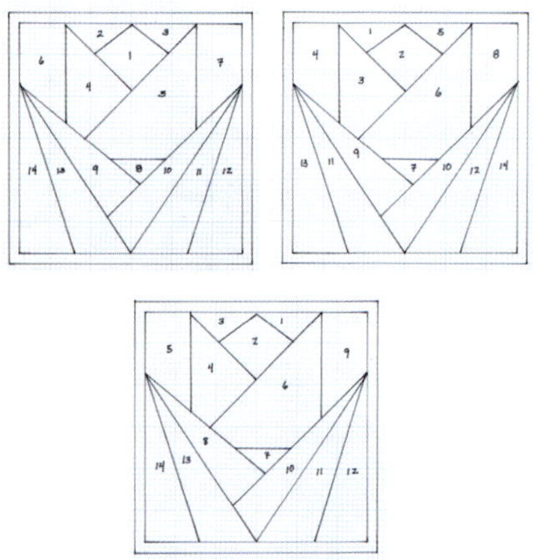

If you start in a bottom corner, you will need to create more than one foundation.

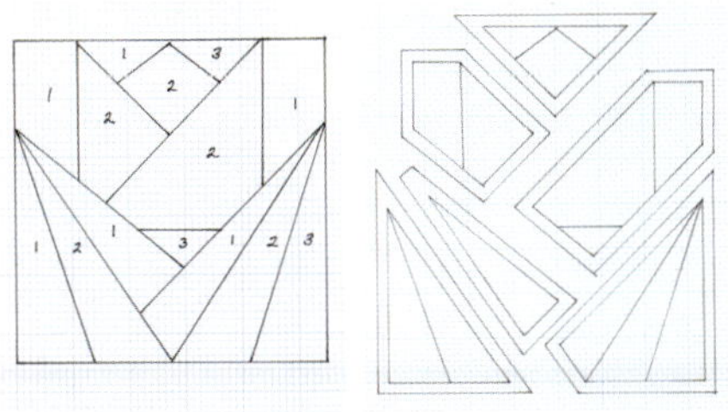

When One Foundation Isn't Enough: From Rail Fence to Necktie Blocks

Many of the blocks we know as traditional blocks entered the quilt world when piecing was done by hand. Y-seams were less dreaded then than they are today, because doing them by hand is easier than by machine. As you work through the next exercises, you'll find there are blocks you'd definitely foundation paper piece, and there are blocks you'd never foundation paper piece. There are some I'll recommend that you not foundation paper piece. Drawing foundations for traditional blocks not only will teach you how to divide your design into foundations and how to number them, but it will also help you learn when foundation paper piecing is the way to go and when it's not.

▲ Rail Fence block

Rail Fence

Our first block is Rail Fence. If you know this block by a different name, it's probably correct too. Blocks often have more than one name, depending on where they were made, when they were made, and who designed them. Similarly, the same name may be used for multiple block designs.

Draw the Rail Fence block, using a pencil and straightedge. FPP requires straight lines, and we can't draw straight lines freehand.

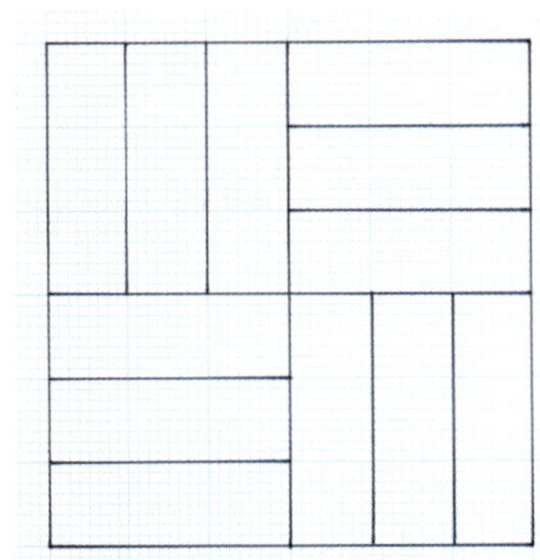

KEEP IT SIMPLE

By now you're seeing there can be multiple right answers for dividing designs into foundations just as there can be multiple right ways for numbering pieces within foundations. My usual recommendation is to search for the fewest foundations needed. Don't create work for yourself unless you have a compelling reason to do so.

Once you've drawn the block, study it to decide how you will piece it, then number the pieces, keeping the Paper Police rules in mind.

I find students often break this block into four foundations, each with three pieces known as rails. This is okay.

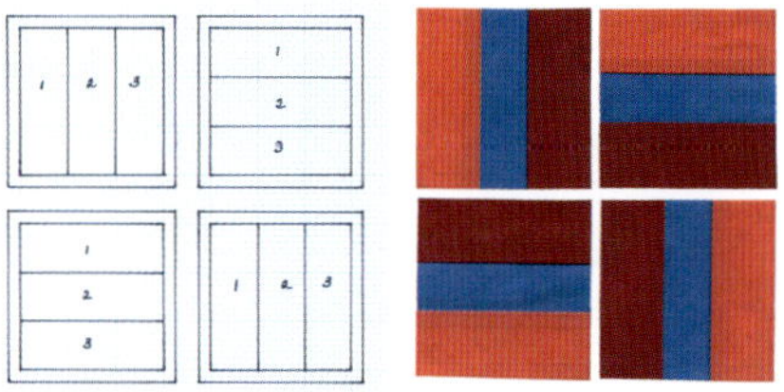

You can also break it into two foundations. As with many of the blocks to come in this section, you can break this block horizontally or vertically. This is your choice as the designer.

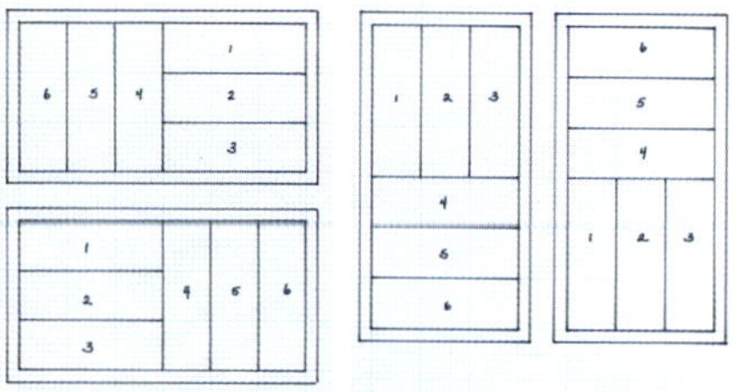

TRADITIONAL BLOCKS BY THE THOUSANDS

Barbara Brackman's ***Encyclopedia of Pieced Quilt Patterns***, third edition (Electric Quilt Company, 2020), is an excellent resource with images of thousands of block patterns. She includes information on where and when each pattern was introduced and what each was named. This is a good resource for your library.

▲ Flying Geese block

Flying Geese

As with the Rail Fence block, draw the Flying Geese block, using a pencil and straightedge.

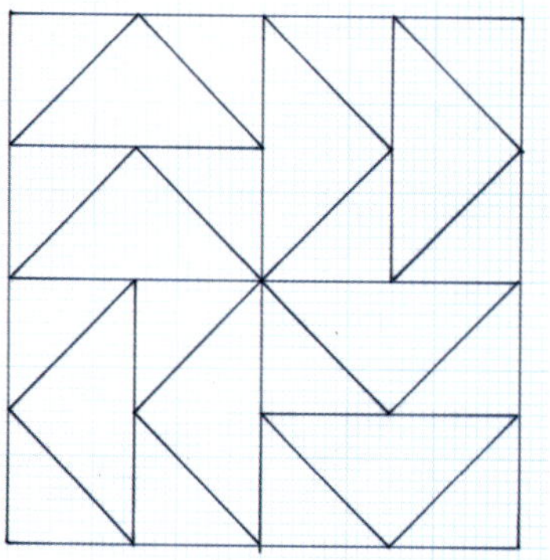

Number it as you would piece it, determining how many foundations you will need. This can be drawn as a two-foundation block.

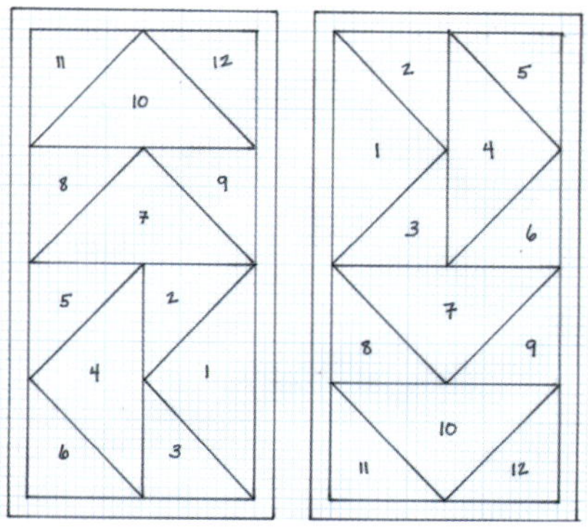

I love Flying Geese. They are a motif I often incorporate in my quilt designs. *Geese Over Manhattan* is an example.

▲ *Geese Over Manhattan*, 49½" × 49½", 2015, designed and pieced by Dana E. Jones, quilted by ZJ Humbach

ALWAYS BEGIN WITH NO. 1

When numbering foundations, start with 1 for each foundation. Let's say your design has three foundations.

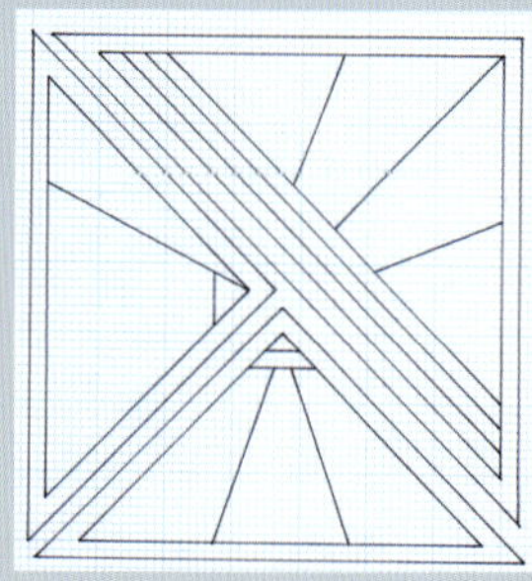

The first foundation has seven pieces. These will be numbered 1–7. The second foundation has three pieces. They will be numbered 1–3. The third foundation has five pieces. They will be numbered 1–5.

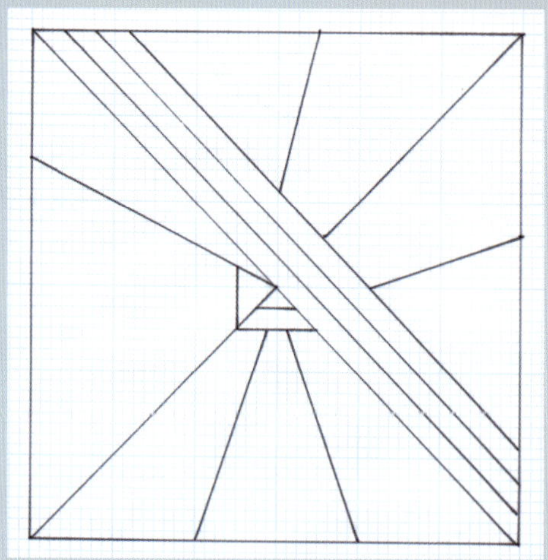

If you're tempted to continue numbering from one foundation to the next, don't. It will confuse you when you start piecing. Each foundation needs to start with piece 1, because each foundation is pieced as a unique entity.

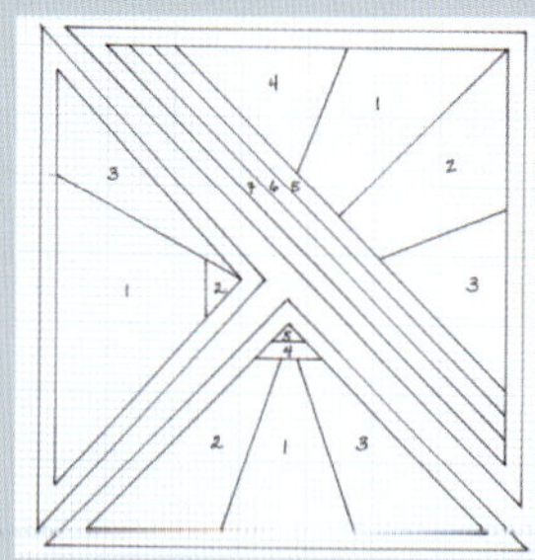

I foundation paper piece Flying Geese because I've found it faster and more precise than the other half-dozen methods I've tried. There's no limit to the chains of geese you can draw for FPP, and it's easy to make irregularly shaped geese and to fill curves with geese. FPP is especially good when you want to make tiny Flying Geese.

▲ Birds in the Air block

Birds in the Air

The Birds in the Air block is aptly named. It reminds me of watching cranes and swans migrating with the seasons. On first glance, it doesn't look like a great candidate for FPP. Let's find out. Draw the block, using a pencil and straightedge.

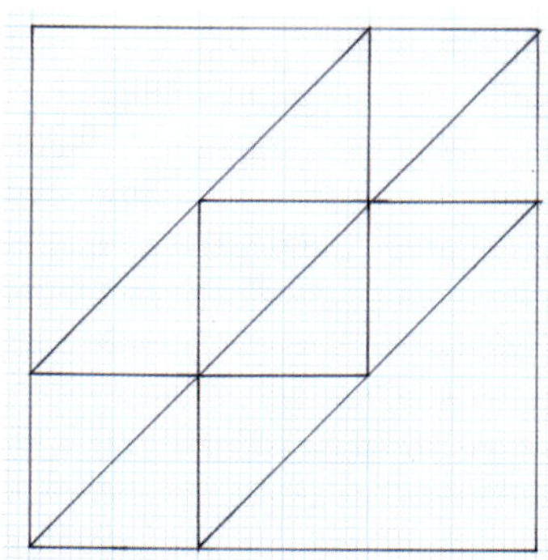

Number the foundations for piecing, determining how many foundations you will need. While it looks more complicated than Rail Fence and Flying Geese, Birds in the Air can be made using just two foundations. It is a good candidate for FPP after all. The key is dividing the block in half diagonally. As you number the piecing order, think about the directions the seams will press. Add arrows to see if you can number the foundations so the seams will nest in the middle of the block. Even though they meet on a diagonal, having the seams going in opposite directions will reduce bulk and make aligning the seams easier.

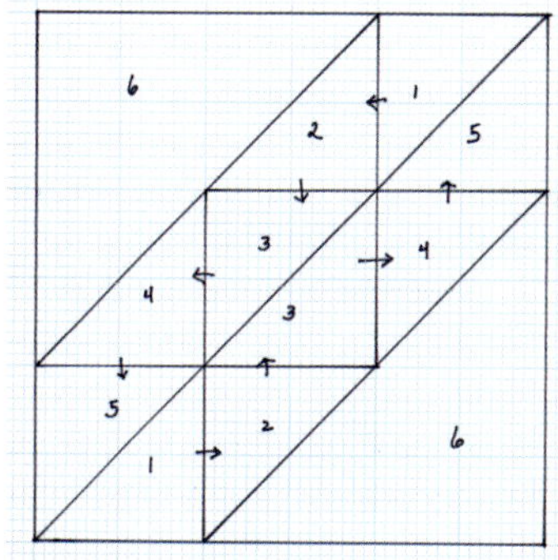

The two sides of the Birds in the Air block can be made with two copies of the same foundation, but note that the colors are reversed. It's easy to get the color placement wrong in this block. I recommend coloring your foundations to avoid this confusion.

Bear's Paw

Bear's Paw is a delightful block. Maybe I believe this because I live in the Rocky Mountains and occasionally have these majestic creatures visit. Draw a Bear's Paw block, using a pencil and straightedge.

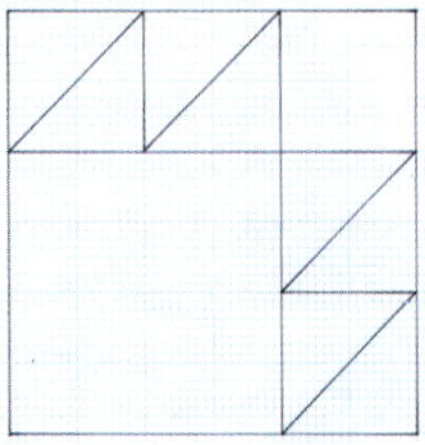

Study this block to decide how you will number it for piecing and how many foundations you will need. You may be surprised to learn this is a two-foundation block.

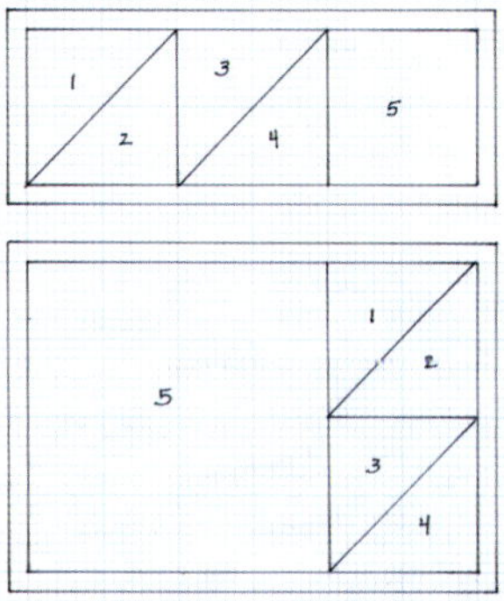

To expand your skills, try your hand at a block that combines four Bear's Paw blocks with sashing between the quadrants and a cornerstone in the center.

▲ Bear's Paw block

Draw this block, using a pencil and straightedge.

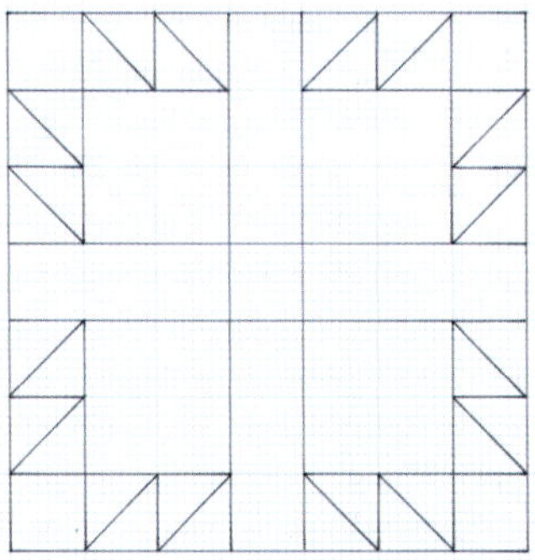

You may be tempted to add a sashing strip to one side of each Bear's Paw unit. If you do this, you will discover that putting the square in the center will require partial seaming, which is best done when you've removed the paper. While this is not a dreaded Y-seam, I would avoid it by adding the strip to the sides of two of the Bear's Paw units and making a separate foundation for a center strip.

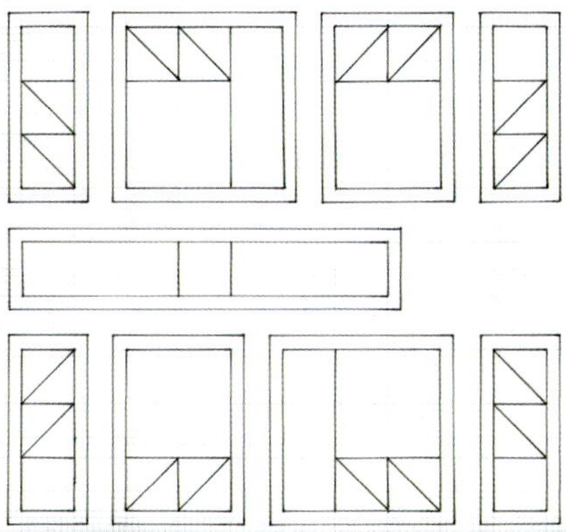

▲ Nine Patch block

Nine Patch

A number of traditional blocks are designed on an underlying Nine Patch grid. Let's start with the basic Nine Patch to get familiar with how it can be foundation paper pieced. Remember, learning how to do this doesn't mean you will want to foundation paper piece Nine Patch blocks, but you may. What you learn from the basic Nine Patch will prove valuable in creating foundations for more detailed blocks that are built on an underlying Nine Patch grid.

Draw a Nine Patch block, using a pencil and straightedge. Use an 8½" × 11" piece of gridded vellum paper for this, so you can easily make all the squares in the block the same size.

Draw a square that is 6" × 6". Divide it vertically and horizontally into 2" squares for a total of nine squares.

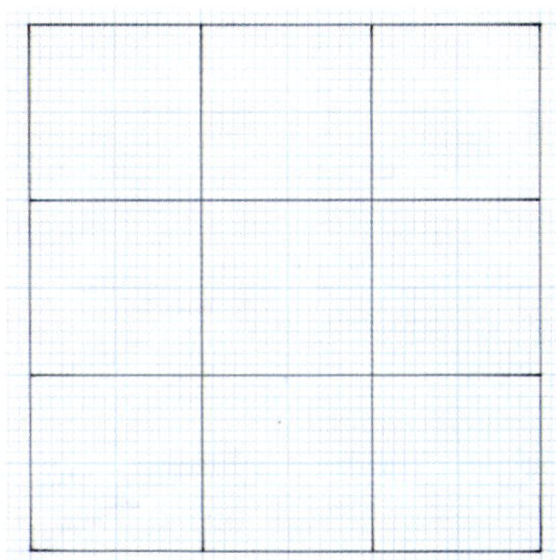

Nine Patch blocks have four nested seams, so pay attention to the directions the seams will press. Remember, the Paper Police demand that you press seams toward the last piece added. Always.

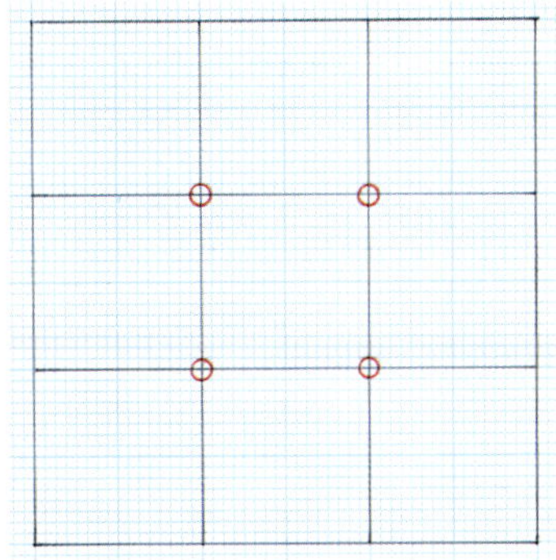

▲ The four red circles show the points where your seams should nest.

This is a good time to practice using arrows to determine pressing directions. The best way to ensure you can nest the seams is to plan for it. At this point in my classes, a student usually notes that with a Nine Patch block, you can reverse the directions the seams are pressed once you remove the paper. True. Do you want to do that extra work? It's okay if you do. I prefer to avoid pressing seams twice by planning seam directions in my design process. I find it is harder to get seams to lie flat when they are reversed after their initial pressing. This is a designer's choice. For now, go with me so you can practice drawing arrows to show the directions the seams will press. Developing this practice will be valuable when you begin designing more complicated blocks and pictorial quilts. In those designs, you'll likely stitch seams down as you add pieces, eliminating the ability to reverse the direction in which they are pressed after the paper is removed.

I drew right-pointing arrows in the first horizontal row. For the second row, my arrows point left, and for the third row, they point right, the same as in the first row.

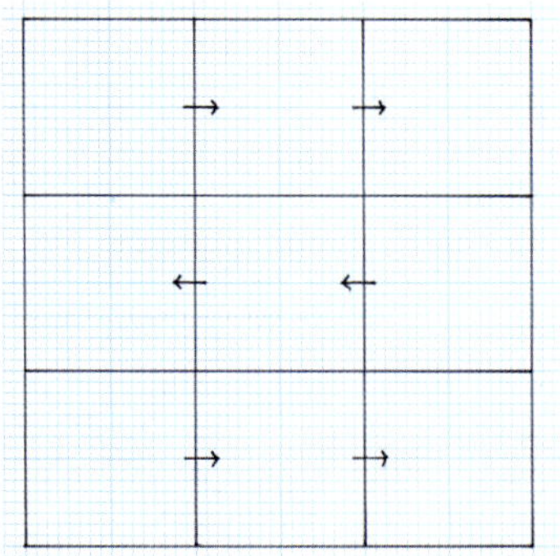

With your arrows drawn, it is time to number the pieces of the Nine Patch. I started with 1 in the top left corner of the block, then numbered the square to the right as 2 and the next square to the right as 3. Is there a piece you can label as 4? The answer is no. Why? Because labeling any piece in the second horizontal row as piece 4 creates a corner, which we can't do when foundation paper piecing.

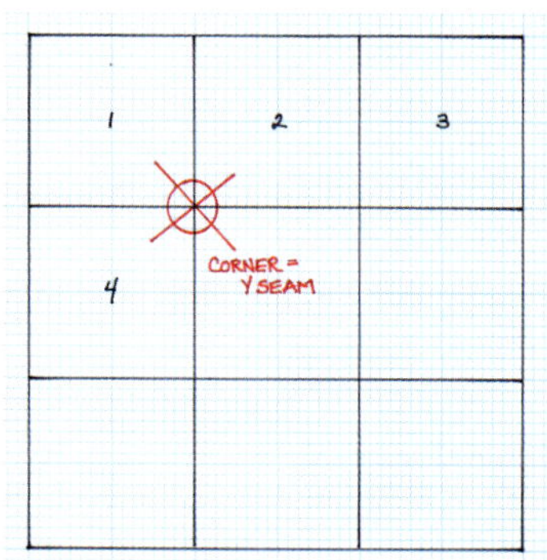

Not being able to add a piece 4 signals the need to break to a second foundation.

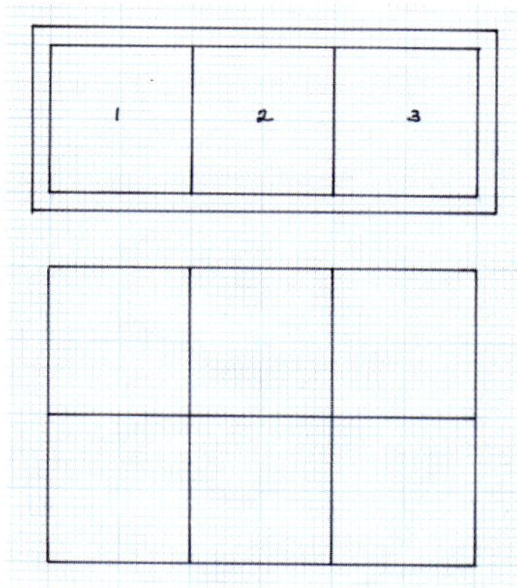

Number the second horizontal row from 1 to 3, reversing the order of numbering by making the farthest right square piece 1. Similar to the first horizontal row, you can't continue to a piece 4.

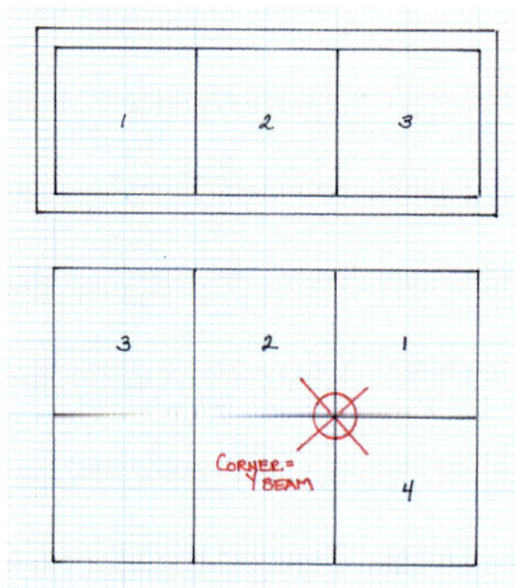

LIVING WITH SHADOWS

While it is good to try to avoid shadows that are created when dark fabrics are pressed toward light fabrics, it is not always possible when foundation paper piecing. Don't lose sleep over this. It's the reality of FPP.

You must break to a third and final foundation. Number the three pieces in this foundation as you did for the first horizontal row: 1 to 3 from left to right.

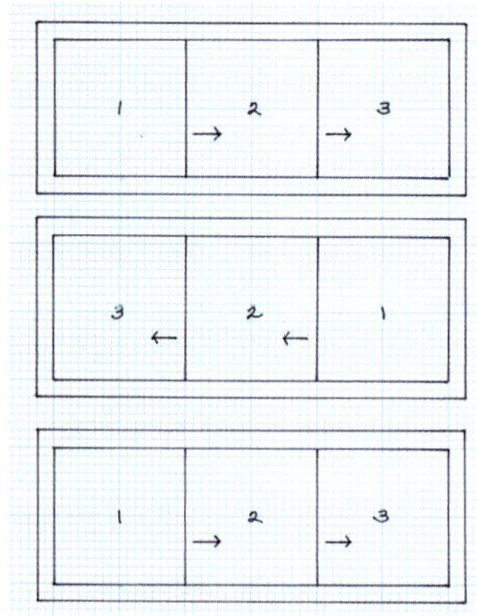

Alternating the direction of the numbering makes nesting the seams possible.

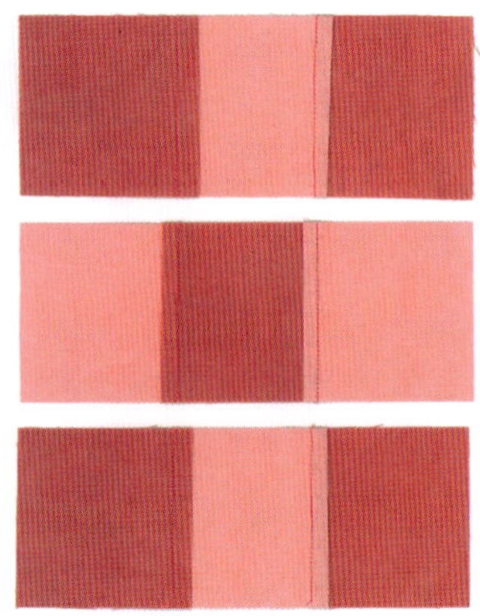

Nine Patch blocks require three foundations. All blocks with underlying Nine Patch blocks require at least three foundations.

Friendship Star block

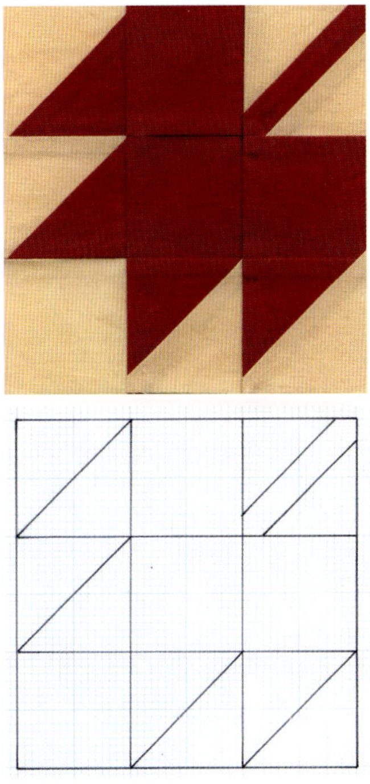

Maple Leaf block

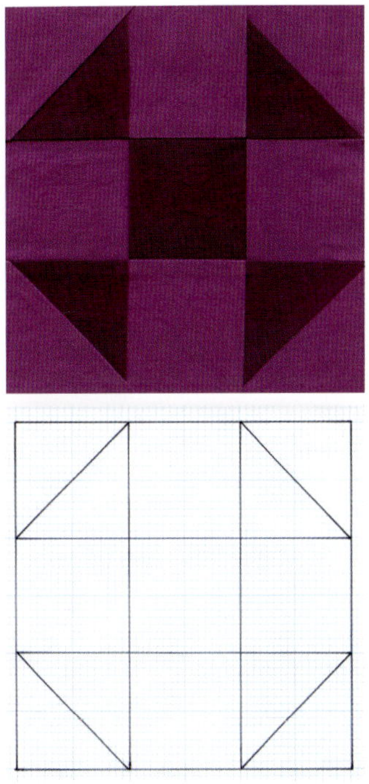

Shoo Fly block

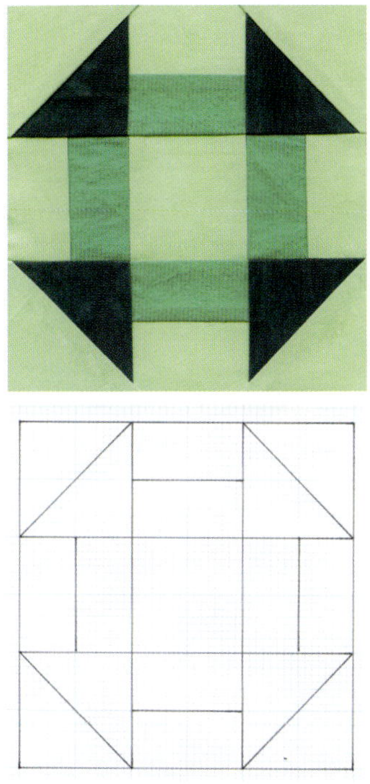

Churn Dash block

Nine Patch Plus

Now that you know how to foundation paper piece a Nine Patch block, try your hand at one or more of the traditional blocks that are built on a Nine Patch grid. These include such blocks as Friendship Star, Maple Leaf, Shoo Fly, and Churn Dash.

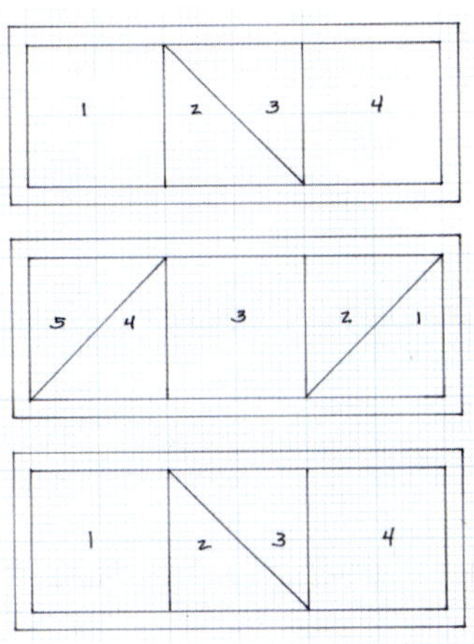

Friendship Star block

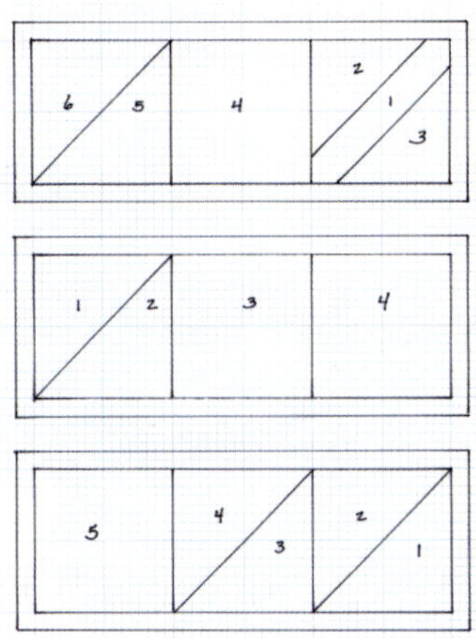

Maple Leaf block

You can piece these in horizontal or vertical rows. Try one block horizontally and one vertically.

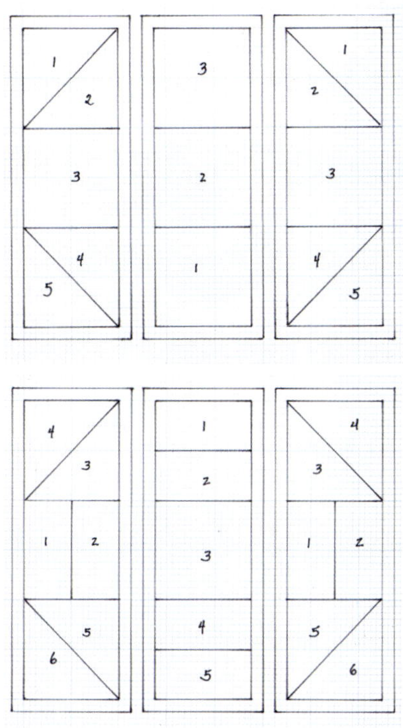

▶ From top, Shoo Fly block and Churn Dash block

Does one direction feel more natural to you? I tend to go vertically, but the only right answer is what works for you.

As you work on these blocks, note when the foundations you create are duplicates of each other. This is true of symmetrical blocks—blocks that are the same side to side or top to bottom or both. For example, the left- and right-side Churn Dash foundations are the same.

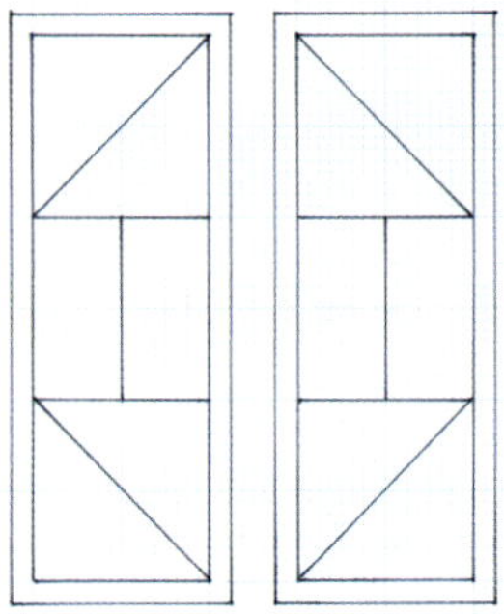

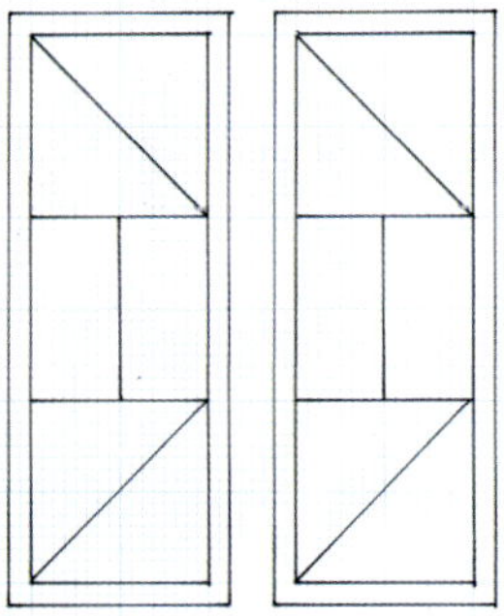

This means you need to draw these foundations only once, then make copies. This saves time and ensures these foundations are identical, which facilitates precision piecing.

Some blocks have foundations that mirror each other. For these, you can reverse them by hand or with a copy machine. Similar to duplicate foundations, reversing foundations that are mirror images by hand or copier saves time and facilitates precision piecing. The English Ivy block is an example of such a block. The bottom right quadrant of the block is a mirror image of the upper left quadrant.

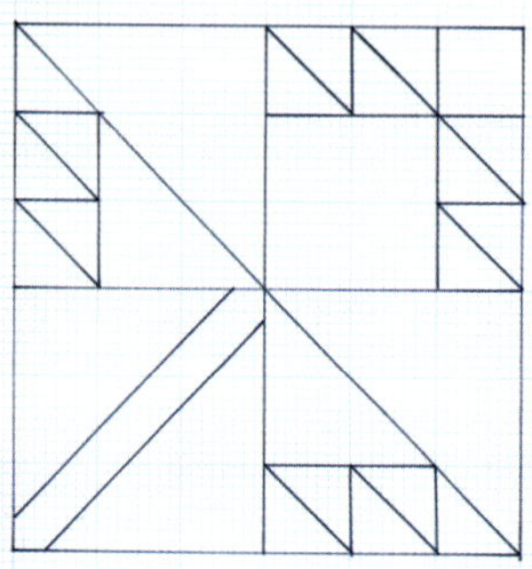

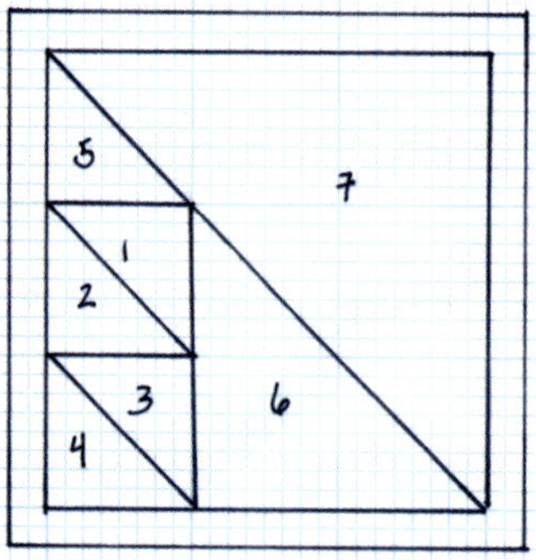

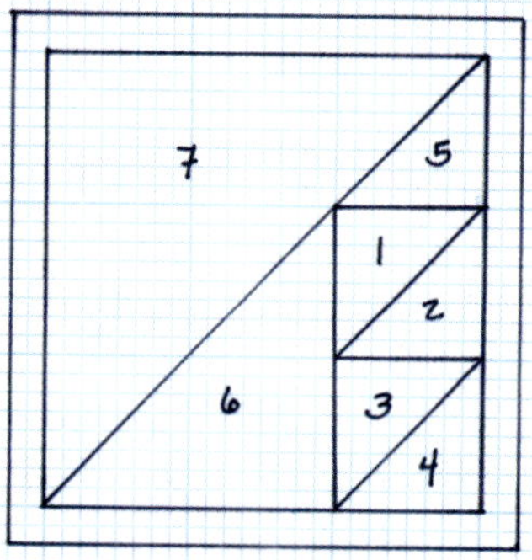

COPY MACHINE TO THE RESCUE

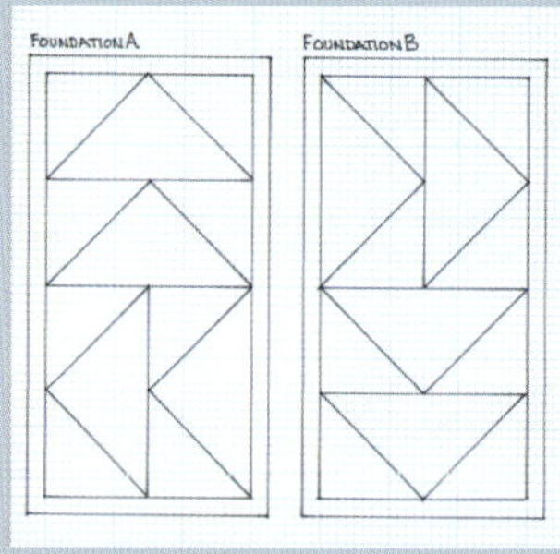

Foundations A and B are the same foundation.

When I say a block requires a certain number of foundations, I'm talking about the number of foundations you will piece. For many blocks, you'll be making two or more of the same foundation and stitching them together. You can make multiples with a copy machine; just be sure the copies are 100 percent to size. Copy functions on some home printers produce slightly reduced copies. Even a fraction of 1 percent can throw you off, so if this is the case with your machine, visit your local copy shop.

Pay attention to whether you're using an inkjet or laser printer or copier. Foundation papers are produced specific to types of printers. If you use vellum, the ink from inkjet printers may sit on the surface and iron off onto your fabric. For this paper, use a laser printer or copy machine. Test your paper and printer before making multiple copies.

▲ Basket block

Basket

Basket blocks are perennial favorites among quilters. There are many styles of basket blocks, some that lend themselves to FPP. Draw this basket block, using a pencil and straightedge.

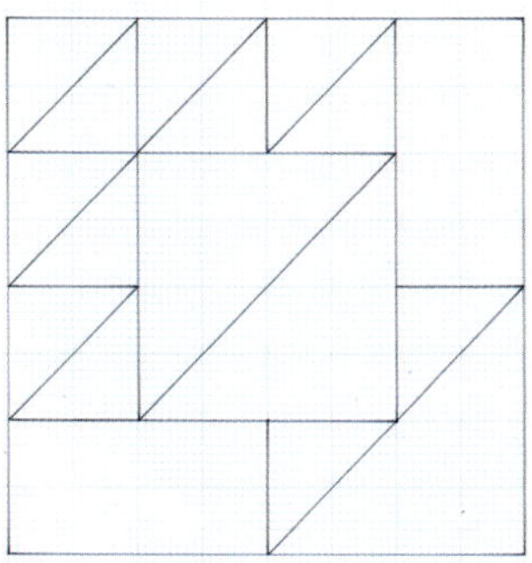

Number the block for piecing and divide it into foundations. Do not add lines that aren't in the diagram above. This is a good time to ask yourself if this is a block you would foundation paper piece.

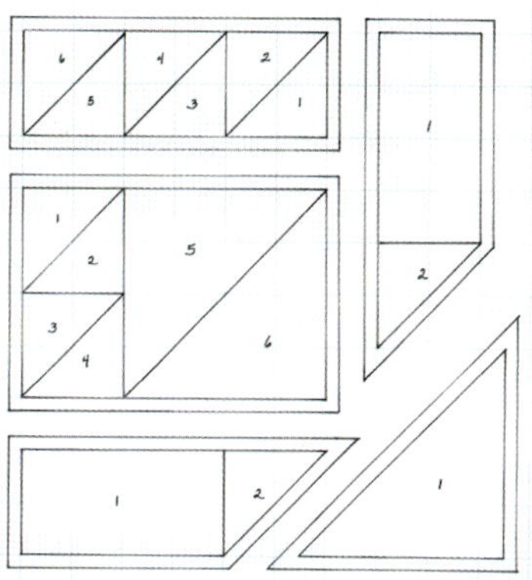

FPP designers sometimes add lines in blocks where they don't exist in the blocks' original designs. Add one or more lines to your drawing of the Basket block to reduce the number of foundations needed. To do this, imagine there is a 16 Patch grid underlying the block. Draw the lines of this grid. Color in the basket because this will help you know where lines are needed for color breaks.

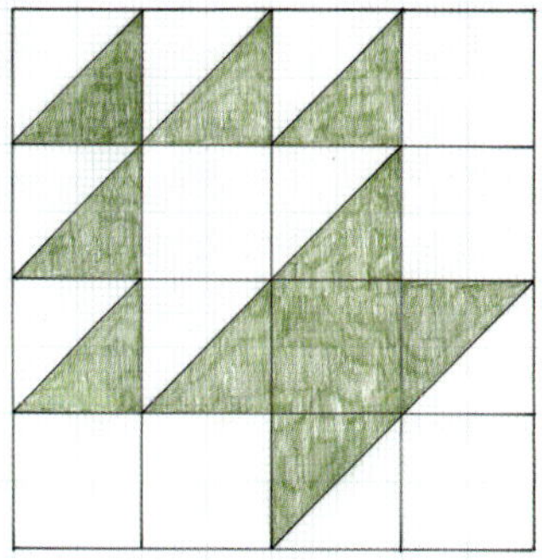

Erase lines that don't reduce the number of foundations needed. Leave the rest.

Do you like the look of the block when the lines are added? This is not a trick question. This is your assessment of whether you find the extra lines acceptable or distracting. Every line you draw becomes a seam. This will be explained in detail in the chapter 3 subsection "Every Line Becomes a Seam," page 77.

SEAMS OR NO SEAMS: YOU DECIDE

Fabric choices can help you decide if you're okay with the extra lines—seams—not traditionally in the block. The seam lines may disappear if you're using small prints or tone-on-tone fabrics, but will likely stand out if you're using large, bold prints or solid-color fabric. They will be more visible on light-colored fabrics than dark-colored fabrics. The best way to see if the seams are visible and to decide if you're okay with how they look is to make a sample block.

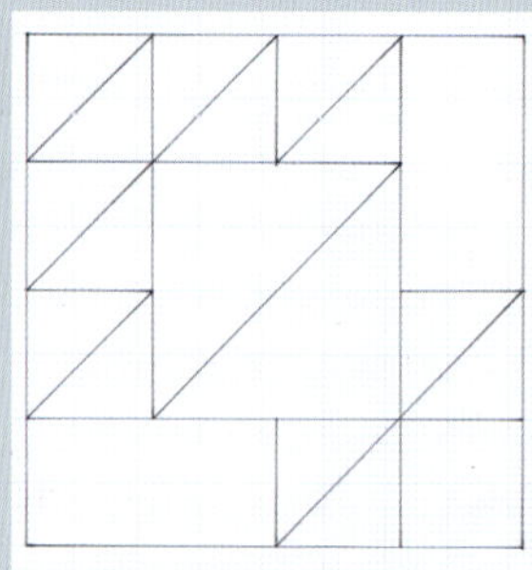

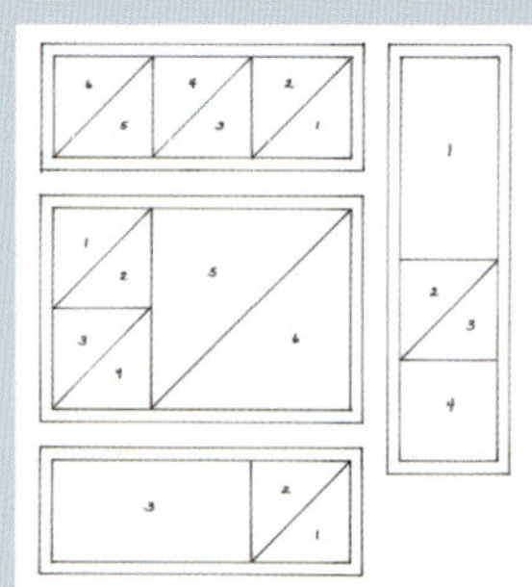

▲ *Bethlehem: Prayers for Unity*, 48" x 63", 2018, designed and pieced by Dana E. Jones, quilted by ZJ Humbach. Portions were foundation paper pieced.

► I foundation paper pieced portions of my *Bethlehem: Prayers for Unity* quilt, including the half square triangles used to make the Pinwheels and the alternating blue and yellow triangles.

▲ Turnstile/Whirlwind block

▲ Pinwheels block

Turnstile/Whirlwind and Pinwheels

Using a pencil and straightedge, draw the Turnstile/Whirlwind block. Note that the underlying grid of the block is a Four Patch divided into half-square triangles to create a Pinwheel.

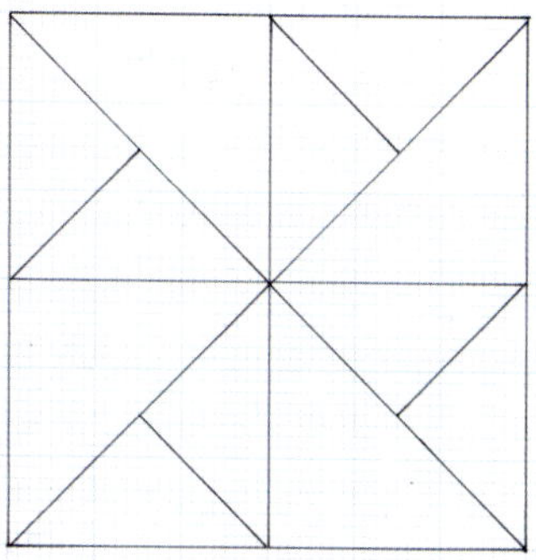

Number the block for piecing and decide how many foundations you will need. You can piece this block with two foundations.

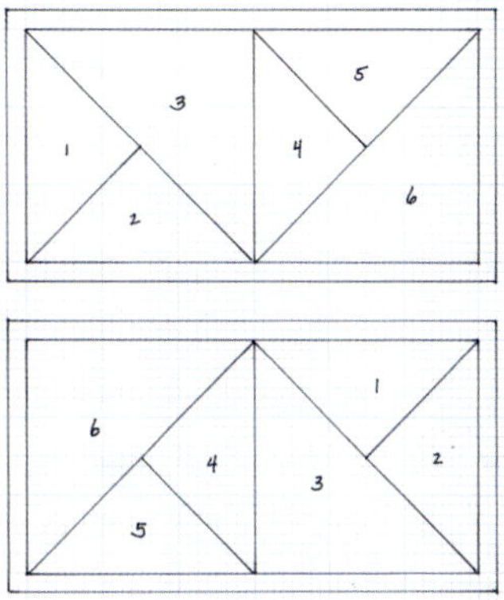

However, you will encounter a problem when you join the foundations. Getting Pinwheels to lie flat in the center of the block requires unstitching the few stitches in the seam allowances at the center of the block and using your fingers to work out the seams to form a tiny Pinwheel in the center back of the block. When you piece this block with two foundations and sew the foundations together, you can't open up the Pinwheel on the back of the block.

I prefer making four foundations—one for each quarter of the Pinwheel—so that when I stitch them together, I can open the Pinwheel on the back and press the block as flat as possible.

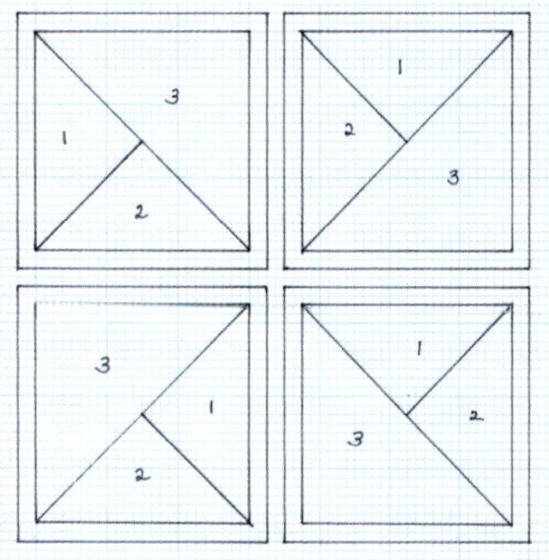

For the Turnstile/Whirlwind block, that means piecing four identical foundations—each one is basically a half-square triangle—then sewing these foundations together. When these are sewn together, it's possible to remove the stitches in the seam allowances and open up the tiny Pinwheel on the back of the block, so the block can be pressed flat.

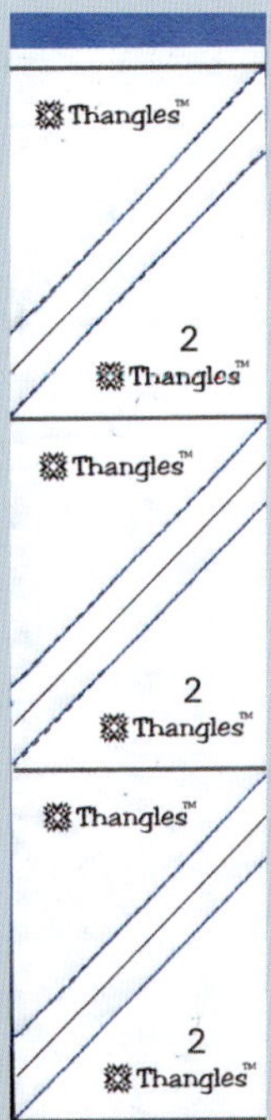

PERFECT HALF-SQUARE TRIANGLES EVERY TIME

For the Pinwheels block, I made 16 half-square triangles and stitched them together. My preferred method for making half-square triangles is to foundation paper piece them. I use preprinted papers such as Thangles or Triangles on a Roll because it saves me having to drawing the foundations. You can find foundations for half-square triangles online, and you can create them by using various computer design programs. Like with the Turnstile/Whirlwind block, this makes it possible to remove the stitches in the seam allowances and open up the tiny Pinwheel on the back of the block, so that it can be pressed flat.

▲ Flying Crow block

▲ Hourglass block

Flying Crow and Hourglass

I have foundation paper pieced the Flying Crow block. It takes five foundations. The reason so many foundations are needed is that the block has four Hourglass units, which can't be pieced as one foundation because seams cross in the middle of the block. Think Four Patch on point.

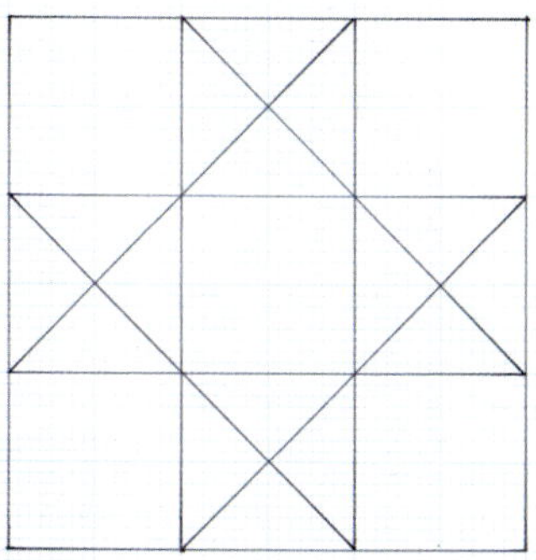

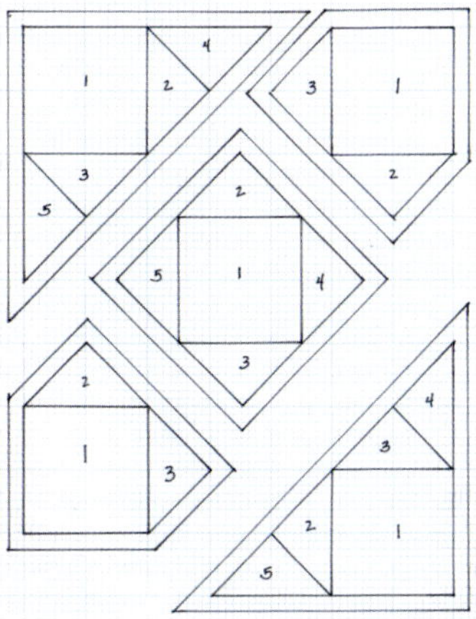

A tried-and-true non-FPP method for making Hourglass blocks starts with layering two squares of fabric. This method, which is explained on page 48, gives you a precise seam match in the center of the block and allows you to remove the several stitches in the seam allowances at the center back of the block so you can press the seams open in a tiny Hourglass. This reduces the bulk in the middle of the block so you can press it flat.

You can accomplish the same thing when foundation paper piecing Hourglass blocks, but I find I have less precision matching the center seams when I foundation paper piece. The non-FPP method described here is my choice when making Hourglass blocks with two fabrics. This method results in two identical Hourglass blocks, one more than you may need, but the amount of a fabric used is about the same amount you will use to foundation paper piece one block.

To make Hourglass blocks by this traditional method, follow these steps:

- Cut, then layer two squares of fabric, right sides together. On the wrong side of one of the squares, draw a diagonal line from the upper left corner to the lower right corner. Stitch ¼" on both sides of this line.

- Cut the layered square into two triangles along the line you drew.

- Open out the two triangles and press the seam toward the darker fabric to make two half-square triangles.

- Layer the two half-square triangles, right sides together, nesting the middle diagonal seam. Draw a diagonal line as shown. Stitch ¼" on both sides of this line.

- Cut along this line.

- Press the block open.

- For a flatter center, press all the seams in the same direction, working around the center of the block and opening out the tiny Hourglass on the back of the block.

- You will have two Hourglass blocks.

When you use three or four fabrics and the common method described above, you end up with four identical blocks. If you need four blocks, go with this method. If not, opt for FPP because you will save fabric by foundation paper piecing the unit. It takes two foundations to piece an Hourglass block. When numbering the foundations, pay attention to the directions the seams will press, so that you can nest the seams at the center of the block.

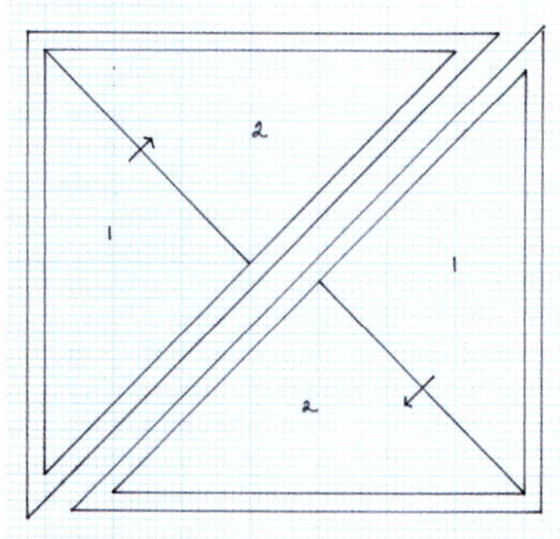

Once you've pieced the foundations, joined them, and removed the paper, you can remove the stitches in the seam allowances in the center back of the block—same as with the traditional method. Then you can open up the tiny Hourglass on the back of the block and press the block flat.

▲ From left, From the Heart block and Star block from Jen Kingwell's *Wandering Wife* quilt pattern, pieced by Dana E. Jones

Jen Kingwell is a hand piecer. I am not. I machine-pieced the hourglass units in these blocks by the method explained on page 48.

▲ Hand-pieced Necktie block

▲ Hand-pieced Empty Spool block

Necktie and Empty Spool

The Necktie and Empty Spool blocks were designed in the days when most quilters pieced by hand. Can these be foundation paper pieced? The answer is yes, but they won't be identical to the traditional design because they require additional seams to foundation paper piece them. Remember, every line you draw will be a seam, and you have to draw extra lines to break these blocks into foundations. You need to decide if the extra seams will detract from the finished look.

Let's see how this works. Start by drawing a Necktie block, using a pencil and straightedge.

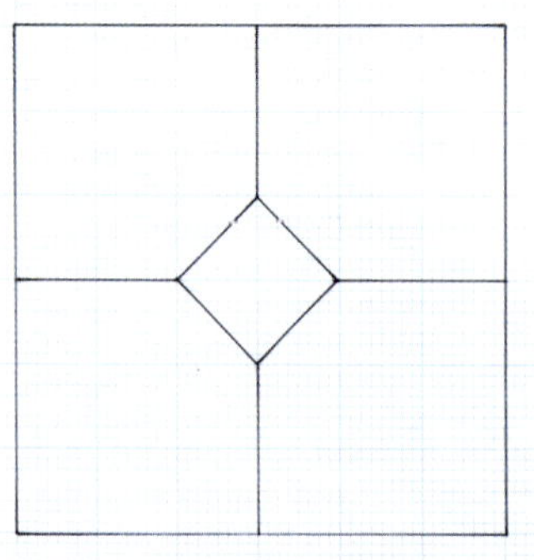

Divide the block into foundations. You can draw lines through the knot of the tie, which results in four foundations.

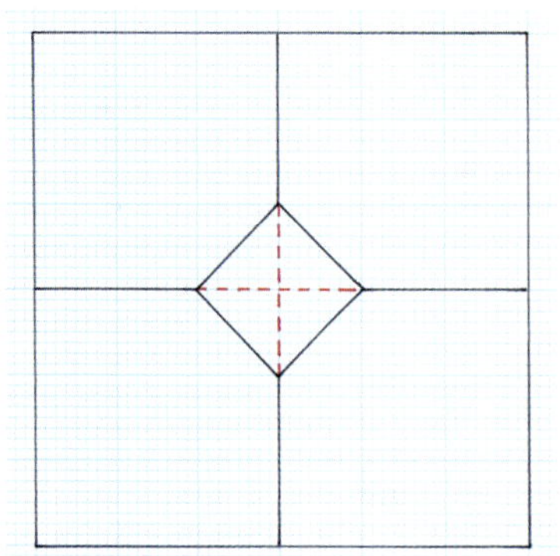

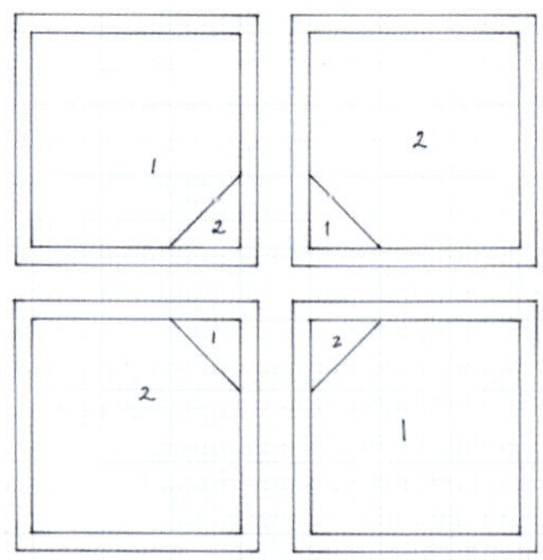

Or you can draw lines through the bow ends of the necktie, which results in three foundations.

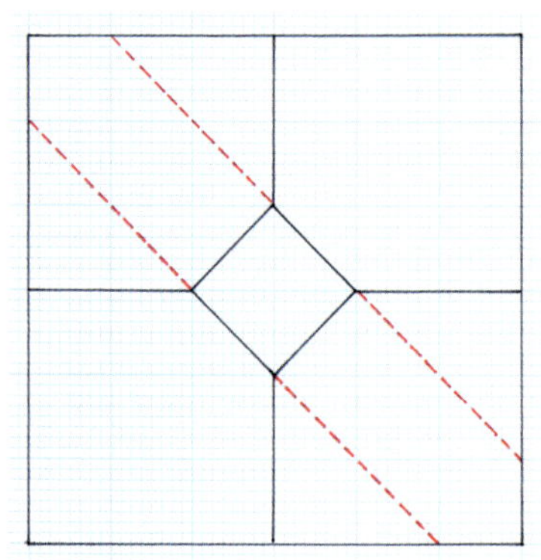

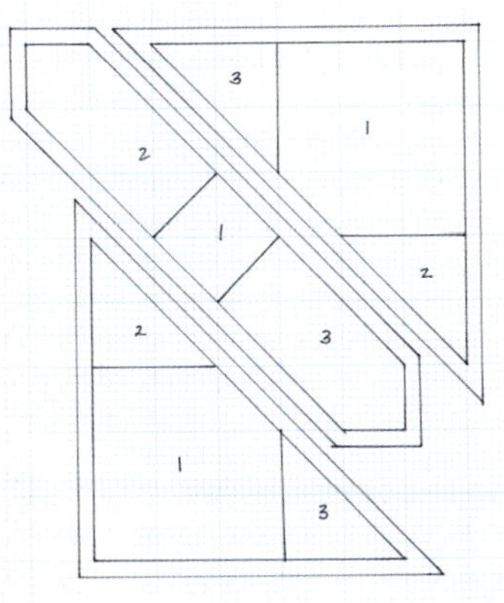

Fabric choices can help you decide if you are okay with the extra seams. The seams will show less when you use small prints or tone-on-tone fabrics. The seams will show more when you use large prints or solid-color fabrics, and the seams will show more on light fabrics than on dark ones.

Whether or not you choose to foundation paper piece this block is your choice as an FPP designer.

The Empty Spool block provides a similar design challenge. Like the Necktie block, this block requires additional lines to foundation paper piece. Draw the block, using a pencil and straightedge.

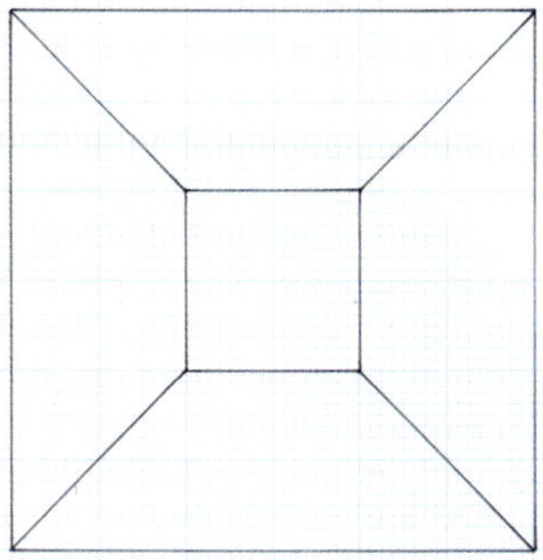

Divide it into foundations, adding extra lines as you design. You can divide it horizontally, which will add seams in the background and will require three foundations.

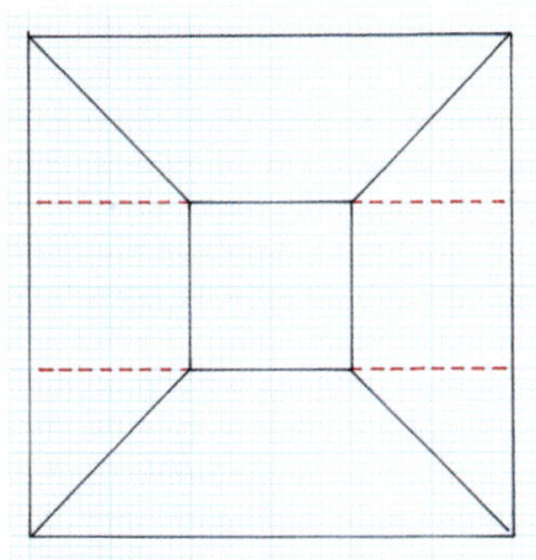

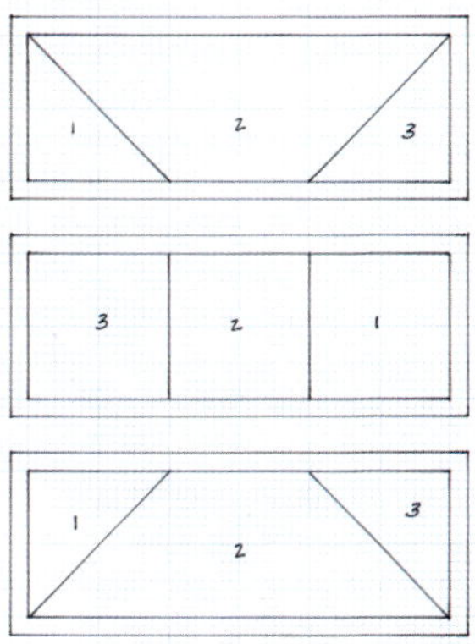

Or you can divide it vertically, which will add seams in the center of the top and bottom of the spool. This will require three foundations.

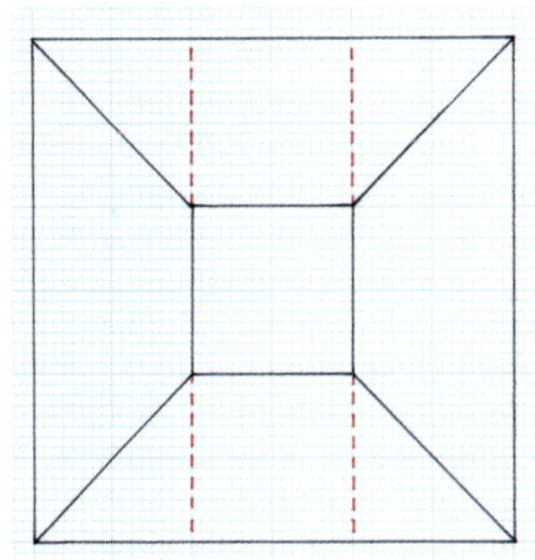

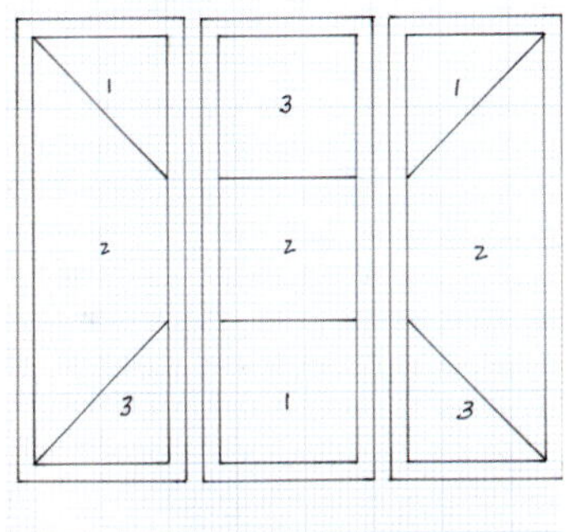

▲ Jacob's Ladder block

Jacob's Ladder

The Jacob's Ladder block is lovely, and not a good candidate for FPP. To figure out why, draw the block, using a pencil and straightedge.

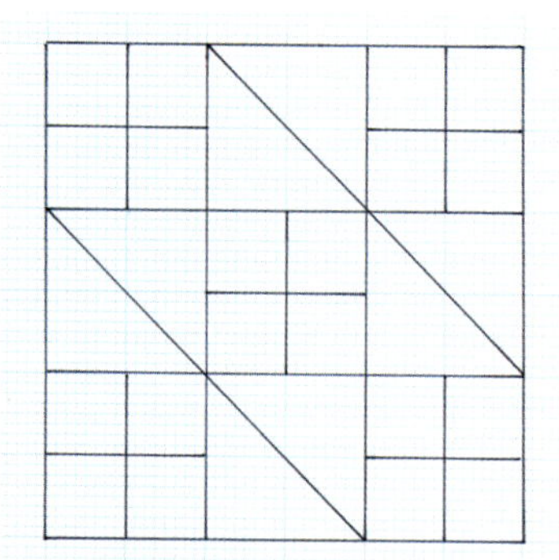

When you divide this block into foundations, you will discover that the Four Patch units within it create the need for a lot of foundations because they include corners that require you to break each Four Patch into two foundations. It's possible to add half of some of the Four Patch units to adjacent pieces, but you can never stitch a Four Patch as a single foundation. Jacob's Ladder can be foundation paper pieced, but you will need to decide if you want to stitch six foundations for one block.

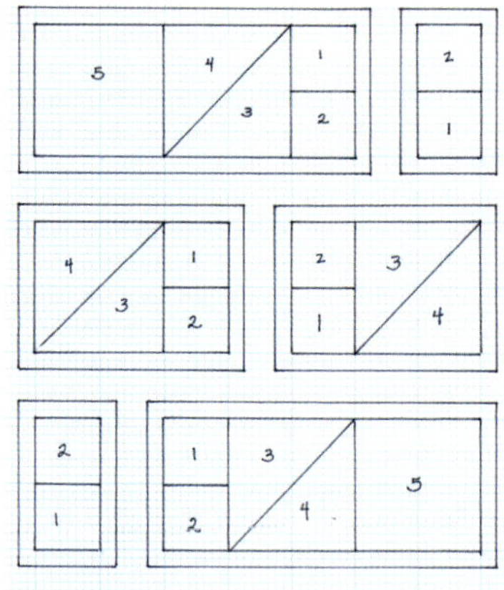

I would foundation piece the half-square triangles but not the rest of the block. This is a designer's choice.

Fly High: Lessons from a Kite

As a child, I looked forward to spring because I would get a new kite. They were simple, one-color Hi-Flier kites. My dad would help me put my kite together, including tying on a tail made from strips of scrap fabric. I'd head down the street to a vacant field, and soon my kite would be flying high, sometimes spinning and dipping in strong gusts. I remember seeing my kites silhouetted against the sky. That image is the inspiration for our next exercise. A kite can teach us much about designing for FPP.

Start Simple: Make a One-Color Kite

It is important that you use a straightedge for this exercise. In addition to your pencil, you'll need a fine-point or ultra-fine-point permanent marker. Draw a 6" × 8" rectangle on a piece of paper, using the permanent marker.

Set the marker aside. You will use a pencil for the rest of this exercise.

The rectangle you just drew defines the edges—the perimeter—of the small kite quilt you are going to design. Your first step is to draw a kite—a.k.a. a diamond—inside the rectangle. Use your straightedge, but don't worry about drawing a perfectly proportioned kite, since we never see them as such in the sky. Your kite can either float within the rectangle or can touch the edge of the rectangle at one point, but one point only, no more. I recommend against touching multiple edges because you'll get more experience applying the Paper Police rules when the kite is mostly or completely floating in the background of your rectangle.

There are many ways to draw your kite. The choice is yours as the designer. Here are two possibilities.

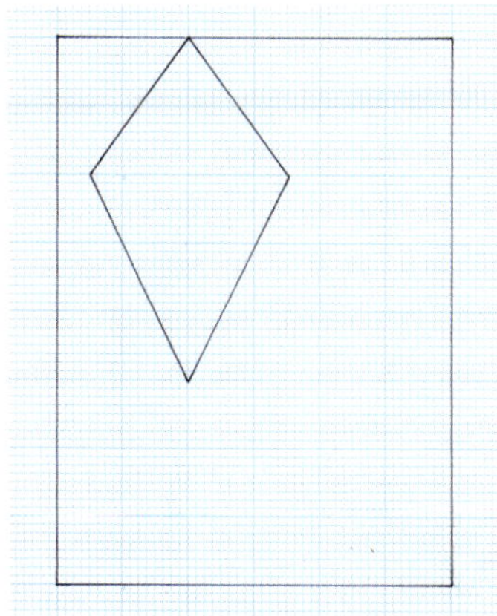

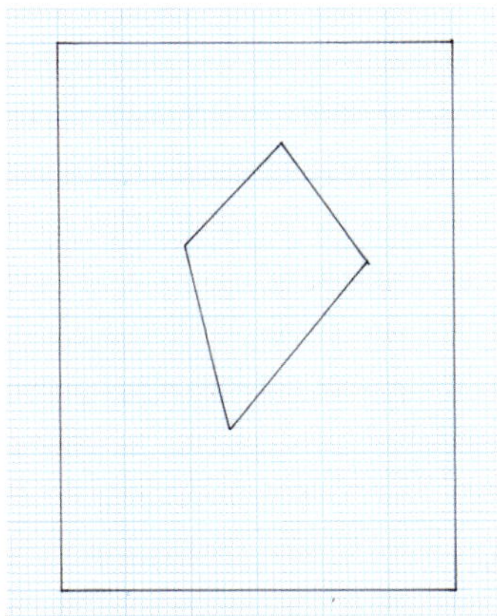

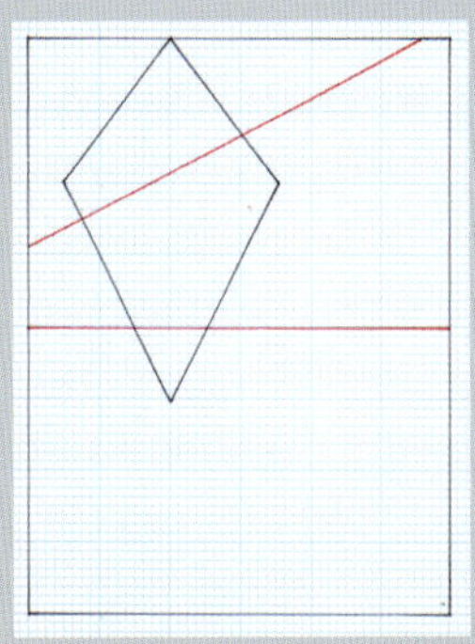

▲ The two red lines are random lines.

AVOID RANDOM LINES

Don't draw lines that aren't in the outline of your kite. I call such lines "random lines" because they have no relationship to your design. Random lines lead to extra work when you piece your quilt and can result in random seams that detract from your design.

When you've drawn your kite, it's time for you to turn the rectangle into a mini kite quilt that can be foundation paper pieced. The background of the rectangle becomes the background of this quilt. Draw lines as needed so you can piece the kite into this background.

The first line you draw should be do two things:

- Be an extension of an existing line. You have the four lines that outline the kite to work with.
- Run from one perimeter to another. These can be perimeters that are opposite each other or adjacent to each other. Just be sure your line goes from edge to edge.

In the chapter 3 subsection "The Paper Police Are Back," page 76, we'll learn additional Paper Police rules that explain more fully why your first line needs to meet these requirements. For now, trust that these rules are key to succeeding in this exercise. Once you've drawn your first line, you're ready to frame in the remainder of your quilt. To do so, extend existing lines.

When you draw your second line, draw it between two perimeters or one perimeter and your first line. If you need to draw a third line, draw it between two perimeters, between a perimeter and your first or second line, or between your first and second lines. Continue drawing as many lines as needed to create a quilt that can be foundation paper pieced.

Number your pieces to determine how many foundations you need. There are many right ways to do this. There are ways that won't work and ways that create more foundations than needed, and thus, more piecing than necessary.

Here are two examples of efficient, easy-to-piece designs that avoid random lines and create as few foundations as possible.

My first kite touches the top perimeter of the quilt. For my first line, I extended the top left line of the kite outline from where it touches the top perimeter to the left-side perimeter.

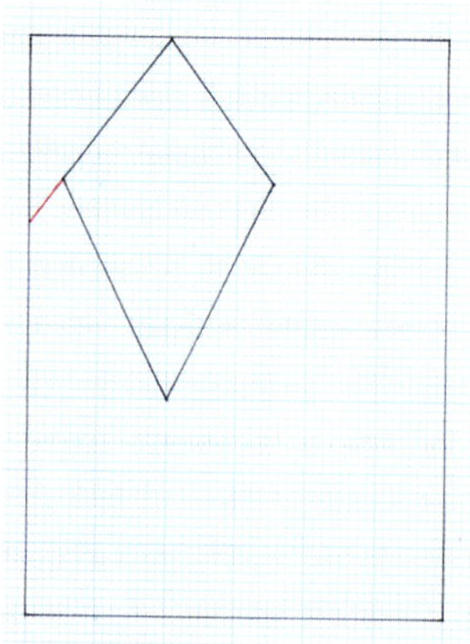

I then extended the bottom right side of the kite from the top perimeter to bottom perimeter.

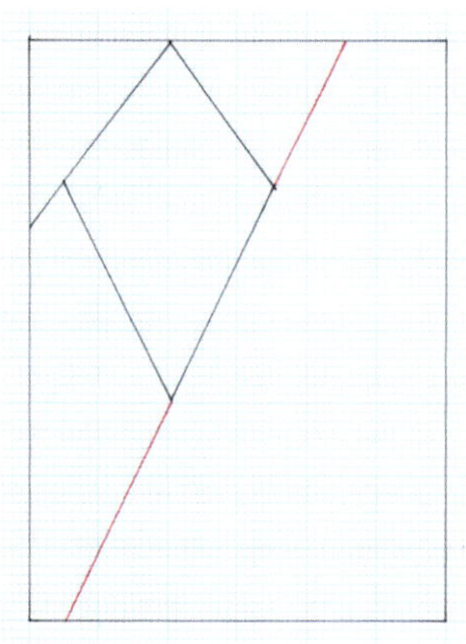

With just two lines, I created a one-foundation mini kite quilt pattern. I finished it by drawing it in permanent marker, numbering the pieces for piecing order, and adding ¼" seam allowances on all sides of the foundation.

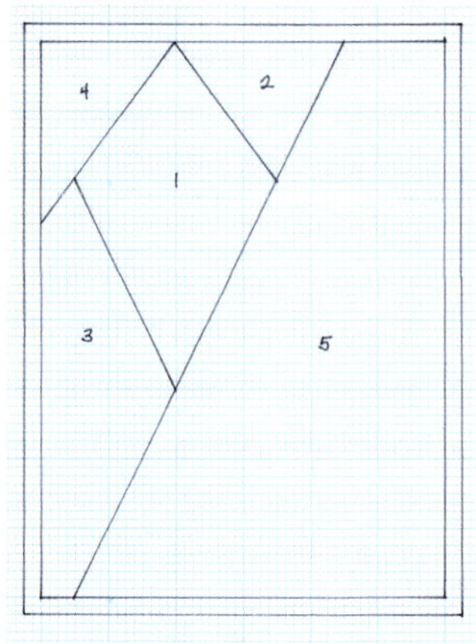

This kite looks firmly planted in the sky, undisturbed by the wind.

For my second kite, I wanted a different look; I wanted to suggest motion. I drew my first line along the right side of the kite from the top perimeter to the right-side perimeter. I could have extended any of the other three sides of the kite from edge to edge of the background rectangle.

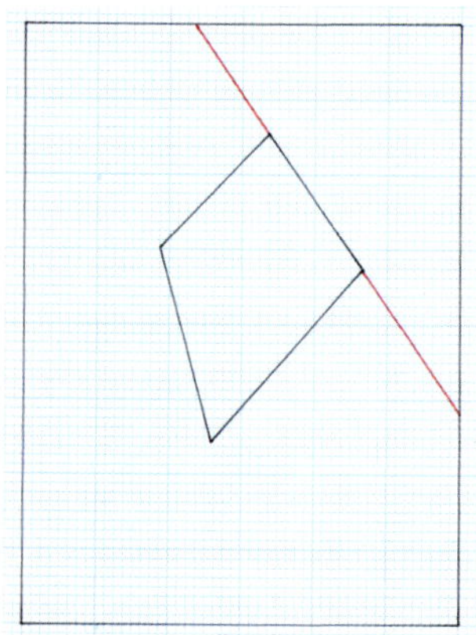

For my second line, I extended the top left side of the kite from my first line to the left-side perimeter. Notice the sense of motion that is emerging.

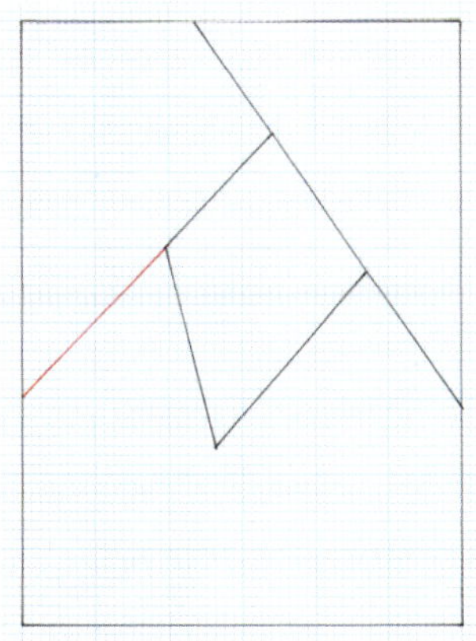

My third and final line ran from my second line to the bottom perimeter, adding to the illusion that the kite was spinning in the wind.

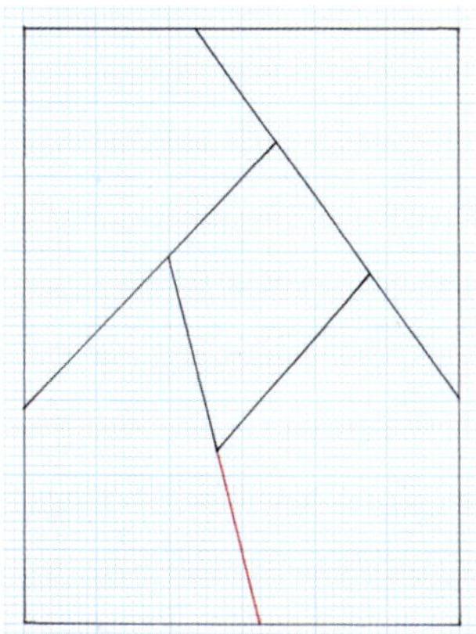

I completed my pattern by drawing all the lines with a permanent marker and numbering the piecing order of each foundation.

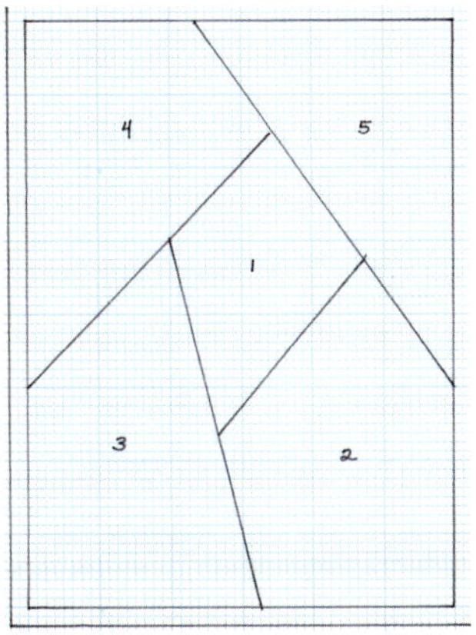

The lines I drew by working my way around the kite created a sense of movement in my finished quilt top.

As you develop as an FPP designer, you will want to consider how the placement of lines—seams—can enhance your designs. In this exercise, do you want your kite to look firmly planted in the sky? Go for symmetrical balance and lines that fix it in the sky. Do you want your kite to look like it could dip and spin to the ground at any moment? Go for asymmetrical balance by drawing lines that create the motion of your kite in a strong wind.

Add Color, Add Detail

On another sheet of paper, draw another 6" × 8" rectangle with your straightedge and a fine-point permanent marker. Switch to your pencil and draw a kite the same as you did before. Draw a straight line horizontally across your kite, then draw a straight line vertically from the top to the bottom of your kite.

You're ready to design a pattern for a mini four-color kite quilt. As before, work only with the lines of the kite. These include the four lines that outline the kite plus the two lines you just drew inside the kite. Where the lines cross in the center of the kite will require nesting seams, so this is a chance to practice using arrows to indicate the directions the seams will press. Remember, the paper dictates that you will always press the seams toward the last piece added. To be able to nest the seams, they need to go in opposite directions.

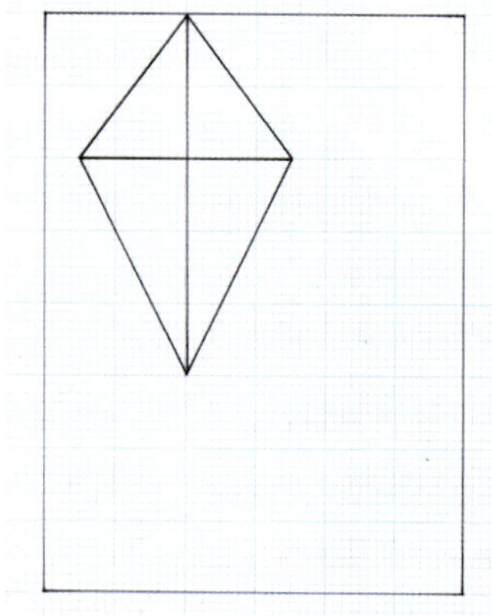

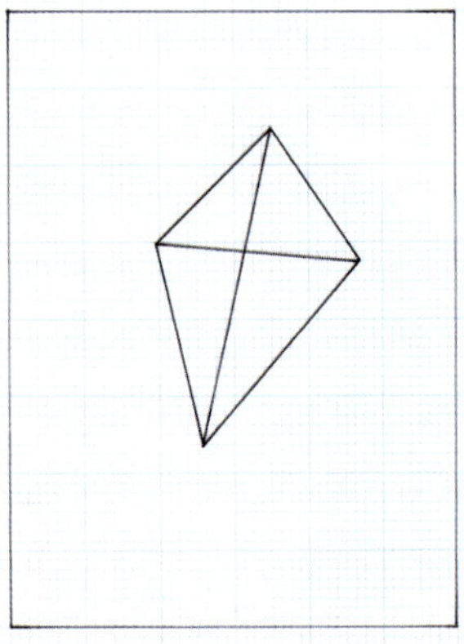

Draw your first line. Be sure it runs from one perimeter of your rectangle to another perimeter. This line should divide your quilt into two parts. I didn't say halves because these two parts needn't be—and likely won't be—equal in size.

This first line should be an extension of a line of the kite. You can extend any one for the four lines that outline the kite or the horizontal or vertical line you drew through the kite. For this exercise, find a design that requires just two foundations. The easiest way to get to two foundations is to extend either the horizontal line or the vertical line rather than any of the lines that outline the quilt.

ERASE AS NEEDED

Keep your eraser handy. It is your best friend. Erase as often as needed to get the design you want.

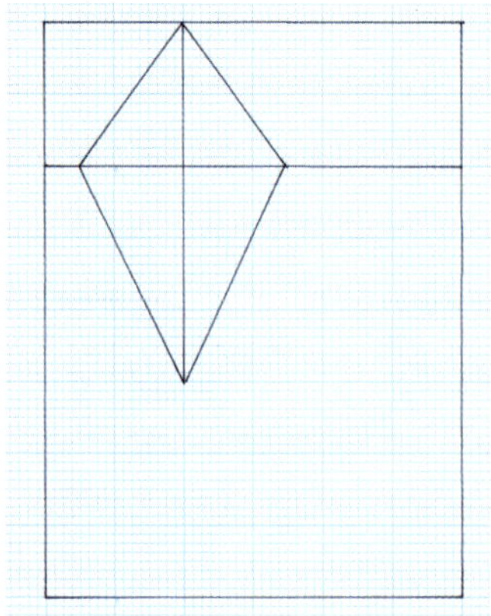

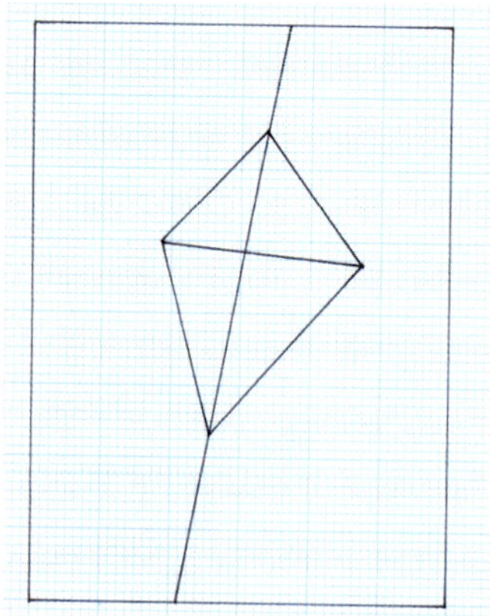

Do not draw a line that is not in the kite. Such random lines have no relationship to your image and require more piecing, which can result in seams in awkward places that distract from your image.

When you draw the first line from perimeter to perimeter, you are doing what I call "anchoring" the line. This concept will be discussed in detail in the chapter 3 subsections "The First Line Must Run Edge to Edge" and "Anchor Every Line," page 76, but let me introduce it briefly here.

When you begin a design, the only anchored lines are the lines that create the perimeter of the quilt, so your first line must go from one perimeter to another. When it does, it becomes a fifth anchored line. As you draw new lines, be sure they are drawn between anchored lines. If they are, they become anchors for your next lines.

One way to think about anchored lines is to see them as lines that divide your quilt into distinct parts. For example, when you draw a line from one edge of your quilt to another edge, you have divided it into two sections. If you were to cut along this line, you would cut your quilt into two pieces that could be sewn back together.

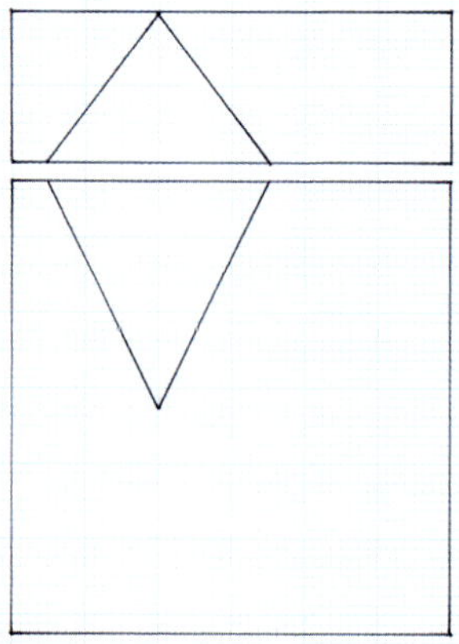

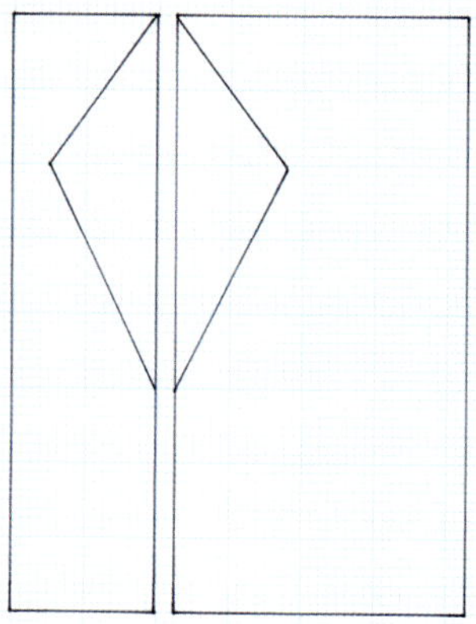

Unanchored lines float in space. If you cut along unanchored lines, you don't get two pieces that can be sewn together; you get slits in the middle of your quilt.

Let's see how this works for my kite that touches the top perimeter. I drew my first line from the left-side perimeter to the right-side perimeter, extending the horizontal line I'd drawn through the kite. My line is anchored because it runs between two perimeter lines, which are by definition anchored lines. My line is not random because it is an extension of a line that is in my image.

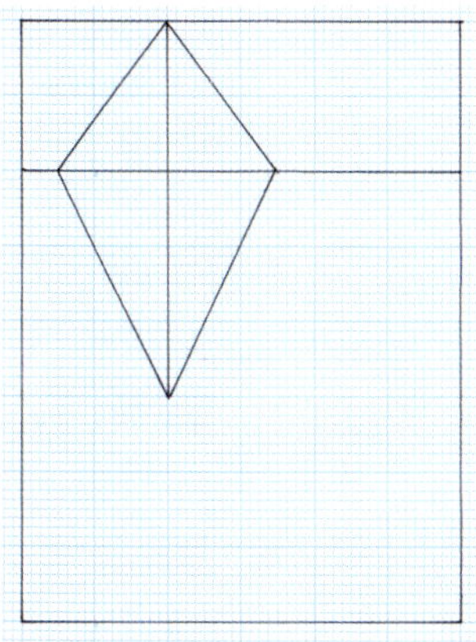

With the first line in place, it was time to design the rest of the mini four-color quilt as follows:

- I selected a side of my first line to focus on, ignoring the other side of the line for now. I turned my attention to the portion of the kite above my first line, ignoring the bottom portion for the moment. I numbered the pieces 1–4, and I had my first foundation completed.

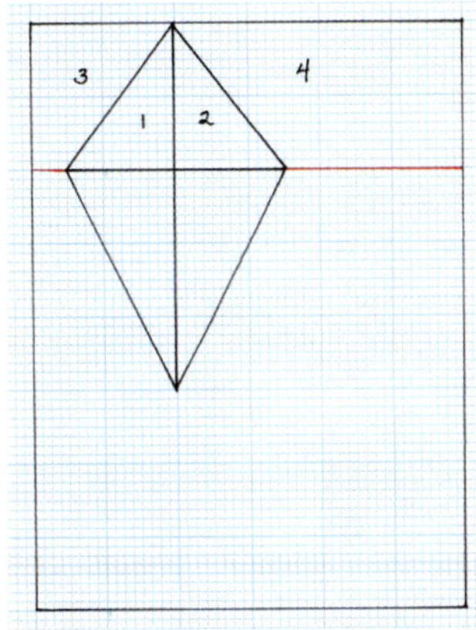

- With the area above the horizontal line fully designed, it was time to work on the portion of the quilt below the horizontal line. My first inclination was to extend the vertical line I drew through the quilt to the lower perimeter. This isn't wrong, but it would have created the need for three foundations, and my goal was two foundations.

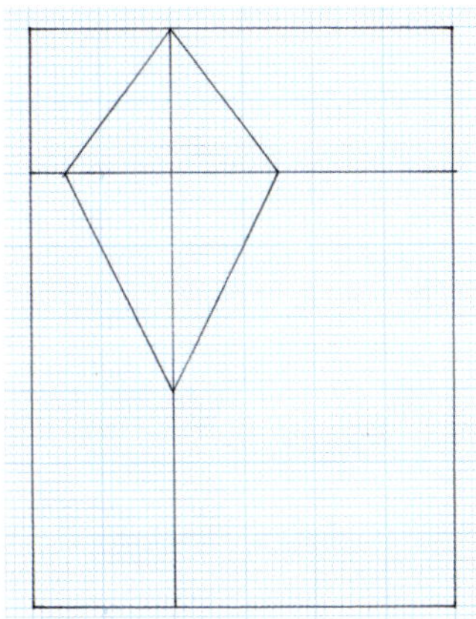

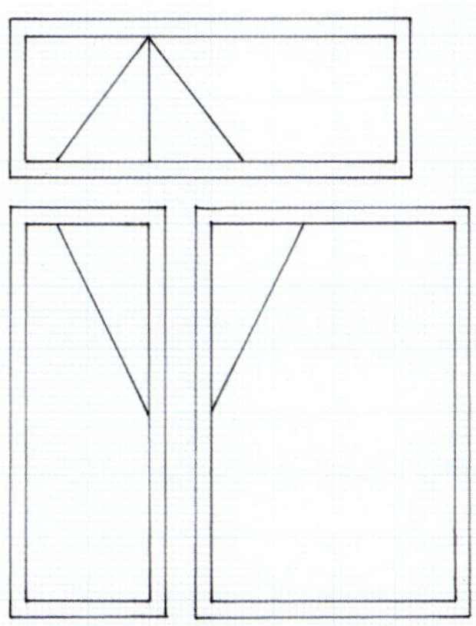

- By extending the bottom right diagonal line of the kite to the bottom perimeter, the lower portion of my quilt became one foundation that I numbered 1–4. My design was complete.

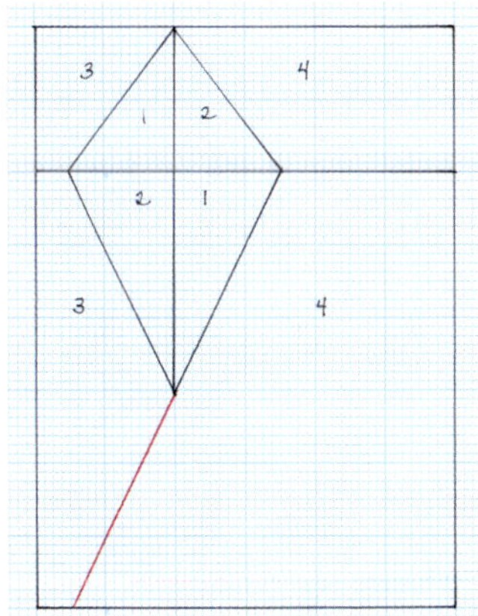

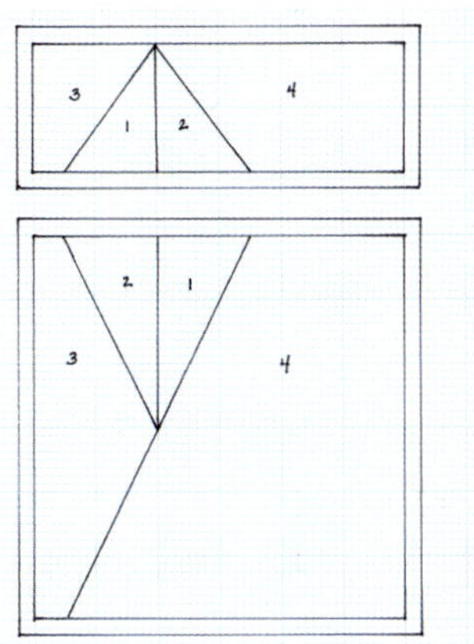

A frequent mistake I see students make is that they draw both the horizontal and vertical lines to perimeters. Doing this requires you to cross one or more interior anchored lines. This creates unnecessary piecing and often adds to the number of foundations needed. Extending lines across anchored lines creates corners, and as we've learned, the paper doesn't let us turn corners. Corners force us to break our designs into additional foundations. The added lines mean unnecessary seams that distract from the main image.

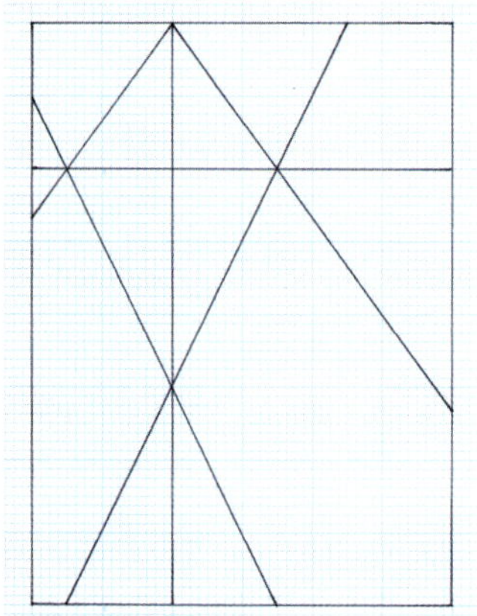

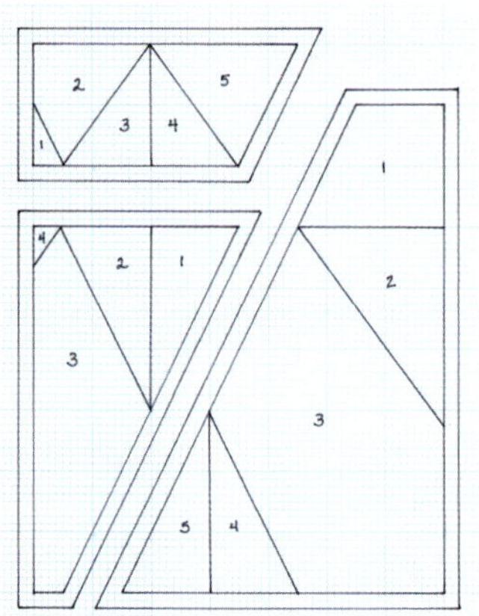

You can avoid this problem. Once you've drawn an anchored line inside the perimeter of your quilt, you can use it in place of a perimeter line on one end of your next line. Once you have two or more interior anchored lines, you can draw future lines between these lines instead of drawing to perimeters. If you find yourself crossing a nonperimeter anchored line to get to a perimeter, don't. Stop at the nonperimeter anchored line.

Turning to my floating kite, here's what I did:

- I extended the vertical line I'd drawn through the kite to the top and bottom perimeters.

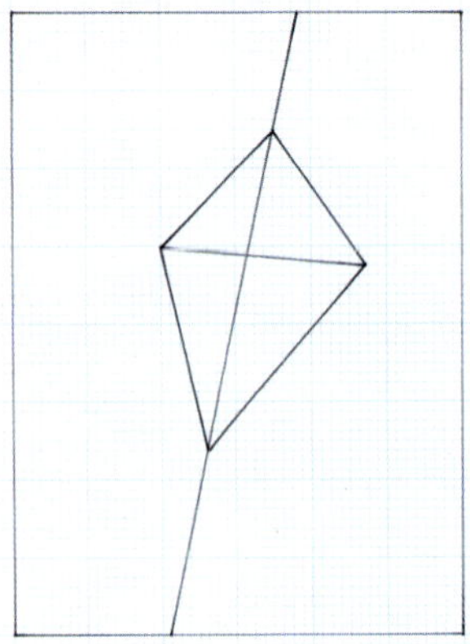

- I decided to work the left side of this line next with the goal of creating a two-foundation pattern. By extending the top left diagonal line of the kite to the left-side perimeter, I was able to create one foundation on the left side. This diagonal line added to the sense of motion.

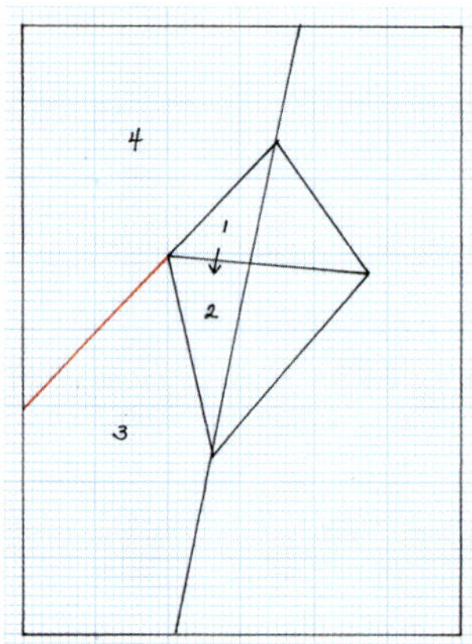

- On the right side, I could have gotten to one foundation by extending either the top right diagonal or the bottom right diagonal. I went with the top right—a designer's choice. I reversed the numbering of pieces 1 and 2 from where they are on the left side so I could nest the seams in the middle of the kite.

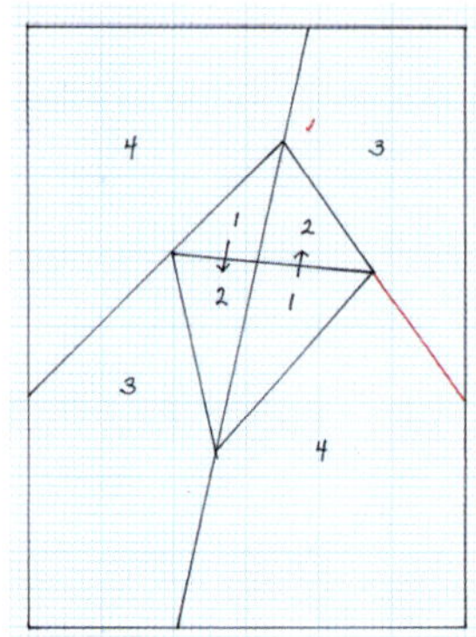

With my design complete, I was ready to reverse the foundations, then divide the foundations and add ¼" seam allowances around the perimeter of each foundation. These seam allowances are needed to join foundations or are needed at the edges of the quilt. This process will be explained in detail in the chapter 4 subsection "Seam Allowances: Their Time Has Come," page 98.

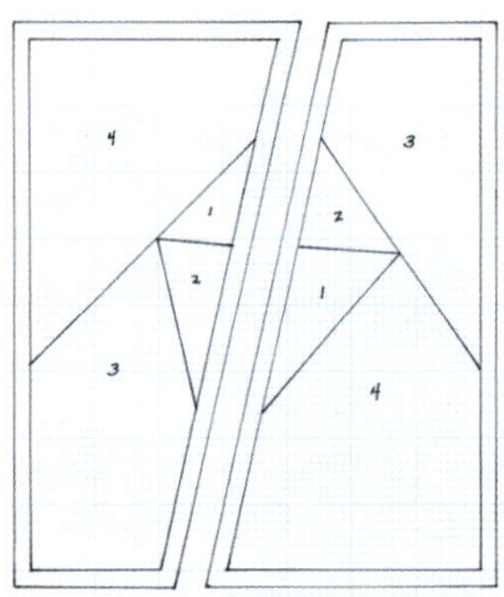

FEATHER YOUR NEST

Did you remember to number your pieces so they can nest when you join foundations? In my design, I numbered the top half of the kite with piece 1 on the left and piece 2 on the right. I reversed these positions for pieces 1 and 2 on the bottom half of the kite. Drawing arrows toward the directions the seams will press will help you plan for nesting seams. Remember, the paper requires you to press toward the last piece added.

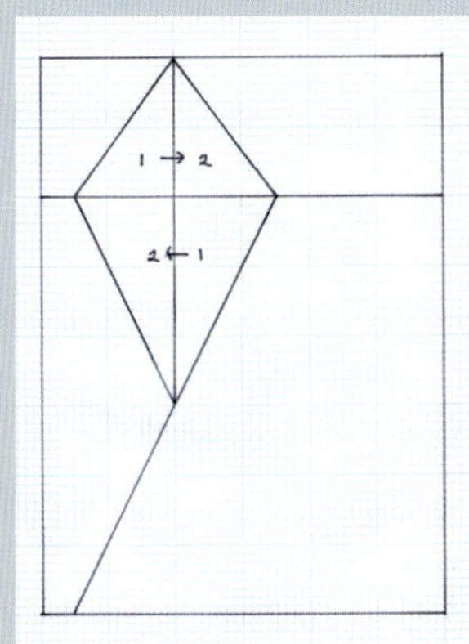

Place a Rainbow in the Sky

I thought it would be fun to create a rainbow-colored kite, so I divided my kite into eighths. This wows folks, but here's the secret: Adding these extra lines doesn't add foundations. It adds pieces within the foundations, but the number of foundations doesn't change.

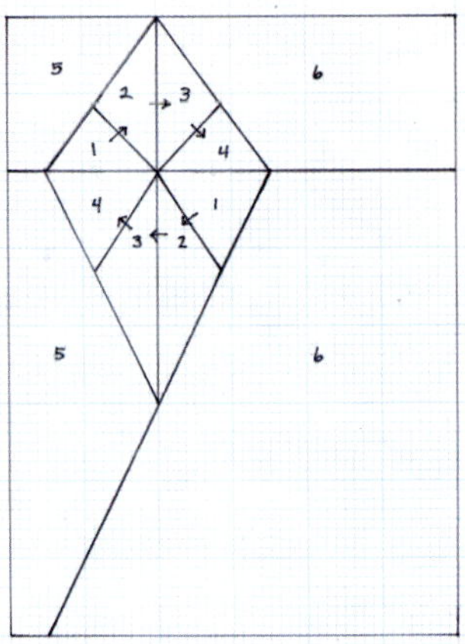

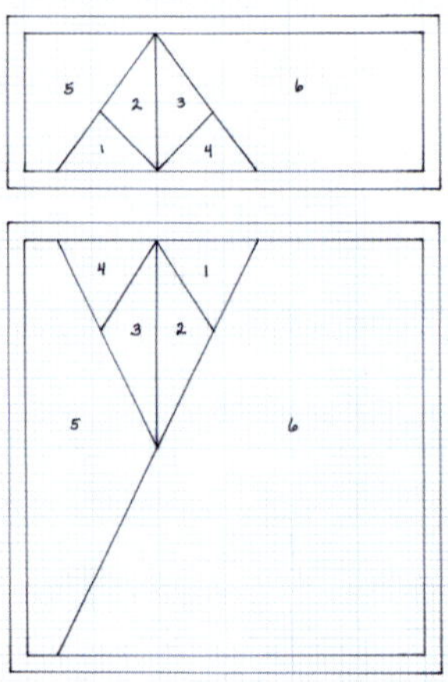

▲ Rainbow in the Sky block, designed and pieced by Dana E. Jones

Expanding to eight pieces within the kite raises a concern for the FPP designer. While it's easy to draw lines that cross, there is a limit to how many lines can cross at the same point when stitching. Too many lines crossing at the same point leads to lumps, something that will cause problems when it's time to quilt your quilt. I limit the number of seams meeting at one point to five or six, but this isn't a hard-and-fast rule. For larger pieces, you may be able to push this number a bit higher. For smaller pieces, you will want to reduce this number.

Ready, Set, Go: Design Your First Block

It's time for you to design a block. You will need your pencil, eraser, straightedge, a fine-point permanent marker, and a sheet of gridded vellum paper.

When I'm creating blocks for FPP, I focus on the strengths of foundation paper piecing. Think about what FPP does best: strong angles, sharp points, small pieces, narrow strips, and precision. I especially like designing with narrow ¼" or ⅛" wide strips.

Using diagonal lines within square or rectangular blocks can create the impression of blocks set on point without the hassle of calculating those tricky setting triangles at the edges and corners of your quilt.

The size and shape of your block is up to you. Your first step is to draw the perimeter of your block with a fine-point permanent marker. These lines are your first anchored lines. You will draw them with a permanent marker so you won't accidentally erase them as you work. Once you've drawn the perimeter, switch to a pencil. Draw all your lines with your straightedge, and don't be afraid to erase often.

You do not have to work in a square. Rectangles or other shapes are fine. As you work, keep the Paper Police rules in mind. Think about such things as these:

- piecing order to enable pressing away from light fabrics and toward dark fabrics when possible
- piecing order to enable nesting of seams
- avoiding too many seams crossing at the same point
- designing with as few foundations as needed for the look you want. Try various numbering orders to help you reach this goal.

When you've completed your design, I recommend you make your block. This will help you perfect your design.

You will want to see how your block will look in a quilt. Toward this end, you can "tile" your block. Tiling means joining multiple copies of a block, much like putting floor tiles together. There are various computer programs you can use to do this, or you can do this by hand by making multiple small photocopies of your block that you can cut apart and arrange and rearrange.

▲ When Overpass block, 8" x 6," is tiled, the diagonal lines in the block create the look of blocks set on point despite being straight set. Designed and pieced by Dana E. Jones

You can position all the blocks identically, or you can rotate them 90 degrees, 180 degrees, and 270 degrees, then combine all these versions for a variety of patterns. Try setting your block on point.

I am often delighted by the secondary patterns that emerge when I twist and turn my blocks.

If you've included diagonal lines in your block design, you may find the blocks appear to be set on point in a quilt layout despite the fact they are straight set.

You may surprise yourself when you find you've fallen in love with block quilts again or for the first time. I experience this often when I design blocks and when I tile blocks designed by my students. Have fun with your new skill with blocks.

▲ This block, designed and pieced by Dana E. Jones, is just 6" × 6", a testament to how foundation paper piecing allows you to work with narrow and small pieces.

▲ Rotating blocks and setting them on point can create high-energy patterns over the surface of a quilt.

▲ Avs & Orange block, 6" x 6," designed and pieced by Dana E. Jones, includes narrow strips and diagonal lines.

CHAPTER 3

DESIGNING PICTURES *for* FOUNDATION PAPER PIECING

▲ Caohagan Island, Philippines. *Photo by Dana E. Jones*

NOW THAT YOU'VE DESIGNED ONE OR more blocks, you have a handle on the Paper Police rules and what does and doesn't work when designing for foundation paper piecing. The first steps in designing an FPP pictorial quilt are selecting a photo to work from and getting to know it. We'll look at how to do that, learn a few more Paper Police rules, learn how to suggest curves with straight lines, and then dive into your first design.

Look Closely: What Do You See?

In 2014, I spent six weeks on Caohagan Island, a tiny 13-acre island in the central Philippines, researching my book, *Pagtinabangay: The Quilts and Quiltmakers of Caohagan Island.* The book tells the story of the island's community of more than 100 quiltmakers. Even as I was learning their story, they were teaching me to see the world in a new way.

Being immersed in a culture and environment so different from my home in the Rocky Mountains was eye-opening. There are no motorized vehicles on Caohagan. You can walk across the island in a minute, from one end to the other in three minutes, and around the island in 10 minutes. Or you can do what the islanders taught me to do. You can slow down. You can contemplate the new bud on a tree you've seen every day of your life. You can pause at water's edge to see new life emerging. You can study the pattern of a spider's web, tracing it in the air with your finger.

Photos by Dana E. Jones

▲ Jovencia "Hoveng" Abaño free-cut the fish, seahorse, seagrass, and starfish motifs for *Under the Sea*, 62" × 85", 2014. *Photo by Mellisa Karlin Mahoney, quilt from the private collection of Dana E. Jones*

When your live on a tiny island, you see—really see—every square inch of it. You know when a new tree is taking root. You know when flowers will bloom. You know when the tide will rise and ebb. Your life depends on these things.

I returned home committed to seeing—really seeing—the two-plus acres on which I live and the surrounding neighborhood.

Because the Caohagan Island quilters know their environment intimately, they are able to pick up scissors and fabric and cut out motifs of the local flora and fauna with no patterns, no drawing, no templates. They simply cut the familiar shapes straight from fabric.

I live in a drive-by world. I get in my car to go places, even to places where I get out to hike. I drive 30 miles to buy groceries. From my home, I see the vastness of Colorado's Front Range, including peaks that top 14,000 feet. It's an impressive vista defined by curves and points, but no detail of what lives and grows there.

It's when I walk around my yard and neighborhood that I see the detail of the mountains: the short bursts of summer wildflower color, the long winters when rocks peak out of the blanket of snow, the lightning streaks of late spring and early summer thunder bursts, and the golden expanses of aspen in the fall. I see up close the veins of the quaking aspen leaves, the curl of the scorpion plant just before it releases its seeds, bear claw marks in a tree trunk, and icy crystals of a summer hailstorm.

▲ Colorado's Front Range as seen from Panoramic Point in Golden Gate Canyon State Park, Gilpin County, Colorado. *Photo by Dana E. Jones*

Photos by Dana E. Jones

Up Close and Personal with a Columbine

Taking a cue from the Caohagan quiltmakers, I decided to study my state flower, the Rocky Mountain blue columbine. This flower intrigues me with its petal spurs and subtle blend of blue and white. These showy flowers are shy, tending to hide in shady areas up against rocks or partially hidden in stands of aspen and lodgepole pine.

Photos by Dana E. Jones

As I studied the columbine, I learned that its flower is a pentagon, or rather, two pentagons, one inside the other. There are five blue petals that are long and pointed. Invariably, one or several of these petals droop forward or backward. Inside the blue petals are five white petals that are shorter and rounder. They're offset between the blue petals. When you get on hands and knees to look under the blooms, you discover the petal spurs are extensions of the white petals.

The crowning glory of the Rocky Mountain blue columbine is the velvety yellow-gold stamens, which beg to be embroidered.

After studying the Rocky Mountain blue columbine, I began looking for ways to incorporate it into my quilts. My first effort was to work Caohagan Island style. I picked up fabric and scissors and began cutting. I was surprised how quickly I was able to cut out the parts of the columbine without drawing them and without a pattern.

I needed to know what the leaves looked like, so it was time for more close seeing. I found looking through my camera lens helped me focus on details of the columbine.

▲ Columbine leaves.
Photo by Dana E. Jones

Once I knew what the leaves looked like, I was ready to try my hand at cutting them directly from fabric.

▲ Caohagan Island-style free-cut columbine by Dana E. Jones

TAKE A PICTURE

Looking through the lens of a camera can help you isolate and focus on details of your surroundings. You can zoom in and out. This is in keeping with the daily routine of the Caohagan Islanders, most of whom have cell phones with cameras.

▲ Caohagan Island youth checks her cell phone during a trip from Caohagan Island to nearby Mactan Island.
Photo by Dana E. Jones

▲ Detail of My Flower, My Choice block, 2022, designed and made by Dana E. Jones

▲ Rocky Mountain blue columbine drawings and quilt motif by Dana E. Jones

When I signed up for a class taught by Jane Sassaman, her first assignment was to select a flower and become familiar with it. Jane had us draw the parts of the flower toward finding features we could exaggerate while maintaining the essence of the flower. I went immediately to the columbine. Drawing it helped me further understand the flower and leaves.

By the time I was ready to design a columbine block for foundation paper piecing, I was familiar with the flower and the leaves. I decided to do an abstract interpretation that focused on the five-sided configuration of the petals. My first challenge was to draw a pentagon. Thank goodness for online sources to refresh my long-dormant understanding of this geometry. With the pentagon mastered, I began designing the flower. I had 15 points meeting in the center. The paper wasn't happy.

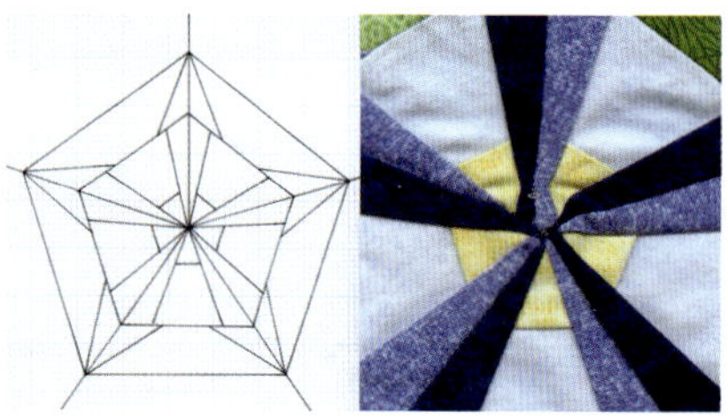

▲ My first FPP columbine design had too many points meeting in the center of the block.

Back to the drawing board. I reduced this to five points. That's still quite a few, but it could be pieced.

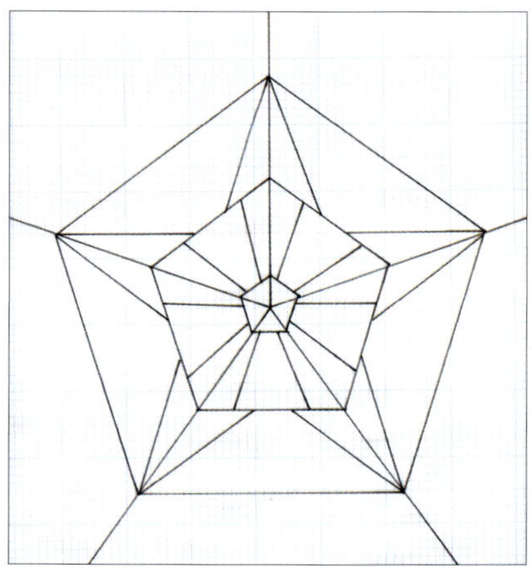

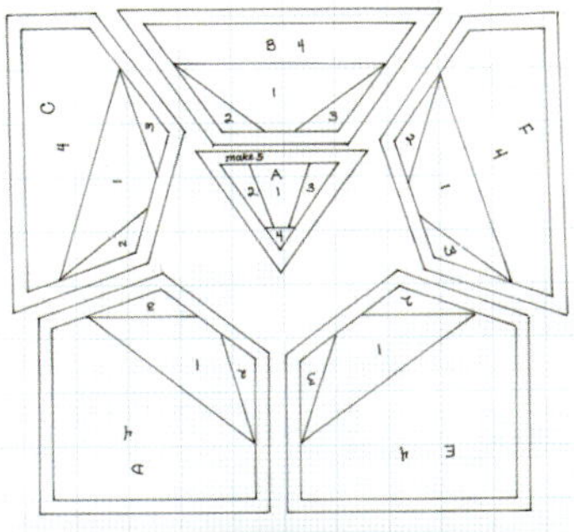

I share all this about the Rocky Mountain blue columbine toward encouraging you to begin designing your FPP pictorial quilt by looking at—really looking at—the image you will work from. If you are a photographer, use a photo you've taken, because in the process of taking the photo, you began studying the object. If you're not a photographer, don't worry; you can study another person's photo. If you draw, you can begin by drawing your object. Sarah Elizabeth Sharp and Kitty Wilkin are among FPP designers who do this.

In selecting an image for your first FPP pictorial pattern, look for a photo of a single object—a solitary bird, animal, flower, building, vehicle, kitchen appliance, household item. Don't use a photo of a person or a beloved pet for your first effort. You will be able to do these before you know it, but they aren't a good starting point, because you are too attached to them and will be disappointed if you don't capture their full likeness.

CHECK OUT BOOKS AND SOCIAL MEDIA

You can find inspiration from quilt books and patterns by longtime and emerging FPP designers. I find these to be among the best sources of trustworthy advice and techniques because they go through extensive editing processes before they get into print. Instagram, Etsy, and other social media can provide inspiration, and I find that checking out websites of quilt shows is a great place to see how folks are using FPP to create new and intriguing quilt designs.

Facebook groups also provide a place to learn what others are doing and to get answers to your questions. Just know that some participants in Facebook groups are learning as they go. They will have good ideas, and they will have suggestions that aren't ready for prime time. As you learn more about FPP and especially FPP design, you'll learn how to find social media posts that are valuable to you, even as you ignore those that aren't.

It's a good idea to take classes with multiple FPP teachers. You'll learn a wider range of techniques toward finding those that are best for you.

Once you've selected your photo, think about why it appeals to you. Answer these questions:

- What is the essence of the image?
- What basic shapes can you identify?
- Will this image work well in fabric? Why or why not?
- What fabric can you use to enhance the image?
- What embellishment—appliqué, embroidery, beading—will enhance your FPP design?
- Do you want to design in a photographic style or more abstractly?

When you've studied your image and answered these questions, it's time to seek inspiration from other designers.

OPT FOR A COLOR PHOTO

It's best to work from a full-color photograph. While you can work from a black-and-white photo, you create a challenge for yourself when you do so, because you don't have color hints to the best places to break your image into foundations and foundations into pieces. While you can design from a drawing or a painting, I recommend you don't do so for your first design. The creators of paintings and drawings have already made designer choices that will limit what you learn from your first design. This is especially true of line drawings.

Let Others Show the Way

You may find it difficult to decide if you want to create a photographic image or an abstract, stylized interpretation of your photo. You may not yet know how detailed you want your pattern to be. Studying the work of others can provide insight into what you like and how you want to design.

Our quilt legacy offers us traditional blocks that are images. Most of these are stylized, not photographic. Consider, for example, blocks that are houses, sailboats, and butterflies.

We know what these are even when they aren't photographic. My *Winter Forest* table runner suggests a midwinter forest through a simple interpretation of pine trees.

Kitty Wilkin, the Night Quilter, provides a more sophisticated image in her Paper Pieced Lupine Pattern. She captures the essence of this flower beautifully, even though she doesn't attempt to suggest curves in the flower petals.

▲ Lupine. *Photo courtesy of Kitty Wilkin*

▲ *Lupine*, 10" × 10", designed by Kitty Wilkin, pieced by Dana E. Jones

Carol Doak, the queen of all things machine paper piecing, has created hundreds of blocks that are familiar objects. With a few lines and just one or two foundations, she captures images from flowers to animals to everyday items such as cowboy boots.

Selecting the right fabric can enhance your design. When I made Carol's Cowboy Boot block, I used fabric that looks like tooled leather. (*300 Paper-Pieced Quilt Blocks*, Martingale, 2004, page 63, block 77)

▲ Cowboy Boot block, 8" x 8", design by Carol Doak, pieced and quilted by Dana E. Jones

Margaret Rolfe is another pro at capturing an image quickly and simply. Her book, *A Quilter's Ark* (Martingale, 2013), features domestic and wild animals, some from her native Australia. Her

▲ *Cat*, 8" × 8", design by Margaret Rolfe, pieced and quilted by Dana E. Jones

▲ *Winter Forest*, 54" × 19", 2025, designed and pieced by Dana E. Jones

Cat offers inspiration for embellishing FPP designs. The cat is sitting on a table that is covered with a checked tablecloth. I can just imagine the cat's three-dimensional tail swishing back and forth. An embroidered face brings a contented look.

▲ *Peacock*, 30" × 35", design by Juliet van den Heijden, pieced by Dana E. Jones. The bird's crest is a good example of straight-line piecing that creates the illusion of curves.

Juliet van der Heijden's book *Animal Quilts: 12 Paper Piecing Patterns for Stunning Animal Quilt Designs* (F&W Media International, 2017) offers more detailed designs. When we look at her *Peacock*, we see that the bird's crest is created with octagons, a hexagon, and a heptagon, all of which read as circles. We see curves in the bird's head, beak, neck, and chest despite the fact that they are created entirely with straight lines.

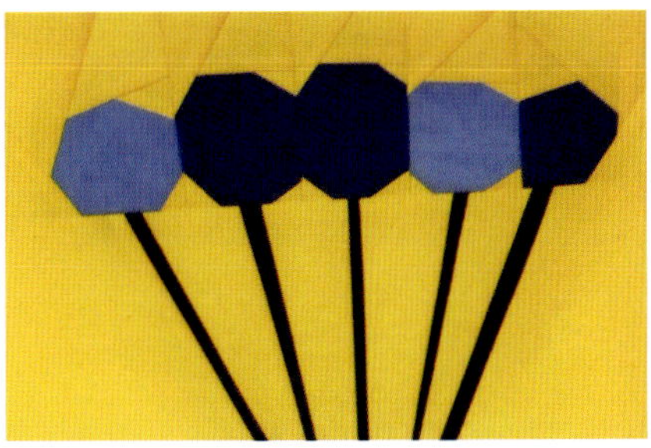

Creating curves and the illusion of curves will be explained in depth later in this chapter.

Lesly-Claire Greenberg's *Vegetable Soup*, featured in *Foundation Pieced Nature Quilts* (Zippy Designs, 2002), shows FPP at its best. Check out the thin purple wedges pieced into the carrots.

▲ Detail of *Vegetable Soup*, 18" × 22", design by Lesly-Claire Greenberg, pieced by Dana E. Jones

If you removed these wedges, the carrots wouldn't look as much like carrots. Think about piecing those wedges into the carrots by other piecing methods. Not so easy, but with FPP, it's a snap. Ditto for the sprouts on the corn, the carrots, and the turnips. Following Lesly-Claire's lead, I searched for fabrics that could read as kernels on the ears of corn. It can be fun to search for the right fabrics to enhance your designs.

In *Adventures in Paper Piecing & Design* (C&T Publishing, Inc., 2018), Sarah Elizabeth Sharp provides insight into her FPP design process. She says to mark the main sections of your design first. This is another way of saying you should outline your subject with anchored lines.

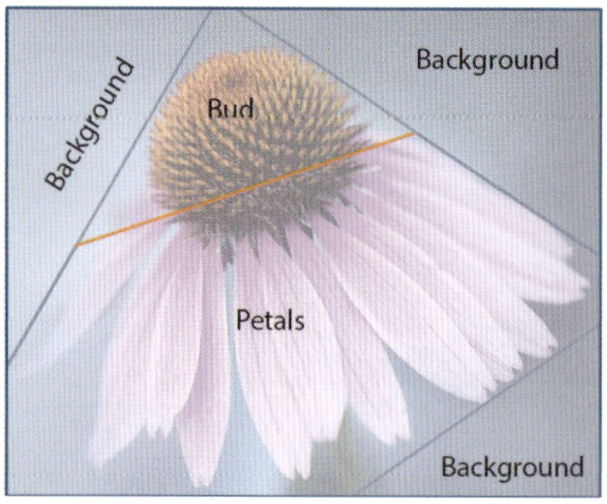

▲ Sarah Elizabeth Sharp's first steps in designing her Electric Echinacea block for her *Plant Lady* quilt were to outline her main subject. Then she drew the line between the flower bud and petals. *Photo by Mai Yong Vang from the book* Adventures in Paper Piecing & Design *by Sarah Elizabeth Sharp (C&T Publishing Inc.), © 2018*

▲ Electric Echinacea block, pieced by Dana E. Jones. Pattern available in *Adventures in Paper Piecing & Design.*

▲ Folding Up the Leftovers, 8" × 18½", designed by Ruth B. McDowell, *photo by David Caras from the book* When Quilters Gather: 20 Patterns of Piecers at Play *by Ruth B. McDowell (C&T Publishing, Inc.), © 2003*

Sarah Elizabeth says to consider which design details you want to keep and which ones you're willing to let go of. The larger you work, the more details you can include. In designing her Electric Echinacea block, Sarah Elizabeth sized it to work with other blocks in her *Plant Lady* quilt. That meant the flower head could be no wider than 3½", so she reduced the number of spikes and petals.

Even though Ruth B. McDowell wasn't a foundation paper piecer, her design work provides insights for FPP design, from how to select fabric for greatest impact to why you should pay attention to the direction the seams will press. The diagram of Folding Up the Leftovers in her book, *When Quilters Gather: 20 Patterns of Piecers at Play* (C&T Publishing, Inc., 2003), shows how she used arrows to indicate the directions she wanted to press pieces. When you do this, you may find you need to add foundations to allow you to press seams in the directions you want.

Ruth's work shows that one piecing method doesn't fit all designs, and more than one method may be needed

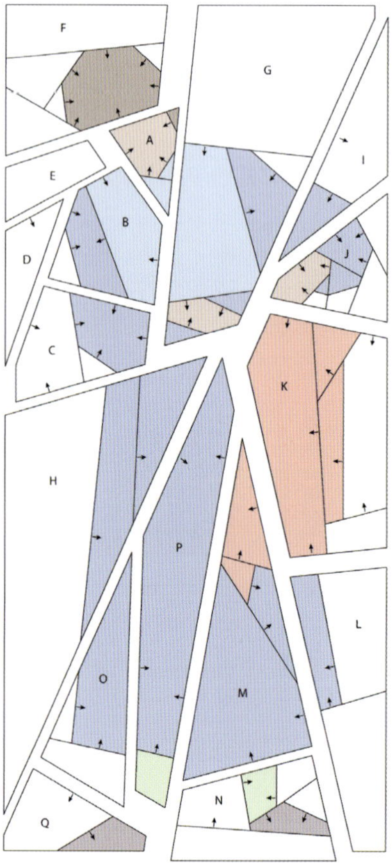

► Piecing diagram for Folding Up the Leftovers, *illustration by Kate Reed from the book* When Quilters Gather: 20 Patterns of Piecers at Play *by Ruth B. McDowell (C&T Publishing, Inc.), © 2003*

▲ *Will It Go Round in Circles*, 45½" × 75½", designed and pieced by Dana E. Jones, quilted by ZJ Humbach

▲ *Tranquil Lake*, 17" × 19", 2011, designed and made by Cynthia England. *Photo courtesy of Cynthia England, used with permission*

▲ *Succulents*, 14½" × 32½", designed and made by Cynthia England. *Photo courtesy of Cynthia England, used with permission*

in a quilt. If you want true curves in a piece, you will want to combine foundation paper piecing with curved piecing or appliqué. Don't be afraid to combine piecing methods in your work.

My *Will It Go Round in Circles* quilt is an example of such a quilt. I foundation paper pieced the background as one large foundation, then turned to Cheryl Phillips's method for insetting circles using her Cut A Round ruler.

I've found design inspiration in three-time International Quilt Festival Best of Show artist Cynthia England's book, *Picture Piecing: Creating Dramatic Pictorial Quilts* (England Design, 2002).

Cynthia is not a foundation paper piecer. She is a "picture piecer," a term she coined. If you haven't taken a class with Cynthia, I encourage you to do so. Her design process has parallels to designing for FPP, and seeing how she works from photographs will inform your FPP design process. Her construction process is different, and her numbering system is not adaptable to FPP. You will especially like her design methods if you want to create detailed, photographic images.

MJ Kinman, author of *Gemstone Quilts: Creating Fire & Brilliance, Step by Step* (C&T, 2020) and *Crack the Color Code: Add Drama to Your Designs Using the Secrets of Color Interaction* (MJ Kinman, Textile Artist, 2025), constructs her quilts with a process she calls traditional piecing with freezer paper. She was inspired by Cynthia England's piecing method. While her construction is not foundation paper piecing, her design process can inform FPP designers. She builds her quilts block by block and says, "The only difference between my quilts and a typical traditional quilt is that my blocks are wonky shapes." That's a helpful idea for FPP designers to consider. You are creating irregularly shaped "blocks" that you will join.

▲ *Devil's Due*, 78" × 53", 2016, designed and made by MJ Kinman. *Photo courtesy of MJ Kinman, used with permission*

▲ *Between River & Sky*, 71" × 69", 2018, designed and made by MJ Kinman. *Photo courtesy of MJ Kinman, used with permission*

MJ's design process is similar to mine in several respects. She studies her subject—gemstones—before she begins designing. She avoids Y-seams by slightly altering lines in her design from the lines in her inspiration image, and she offsets lines to avoid too many seams meeting in one place. When making these changes, she makes sure she keeps the integrity of the image.

Make It to Learn It

Beyond studying other quilters' design techniques and practices, making their patterns is a good way to learn what works and what you like in terms of design styles. The Modern Quilt Guild movement has brought a wealth of FPP patterns by new designers. These designs are often pieced in solid-color fabrics. Among these designers is Mike O'Dell, pattern designer and founder of Legit Kits. Mike sometimes uses color palettes from nature and his surroundings and sometimes creates more fanciful palettes. Each of his quilts suggests a story. He compares his designs to single frames of comic strips. His images often bleed off one or more edges of the quilt, letting viewers complete them in their imaginations as they develop the stories. As you design, think about Mike's approach to composition. Consider various ways to crop your images.

BACKGROUND GRID OR NOT?

Some FPP designers begin their design process by drawing a grid over their inspiration image. Then they design within each square or rectangle of the grid. Sewing these foundations together can be easier than joining irregularly shaped foundations. Grids can be sized so that foundations can be printed on 8½" × 11" paper. This eliminates the cost and need to print foundations on larger paper, and it eliminates the need to tape portions of foundations together when they've been printed on paper smaller than the foundations.

If you choose to work this way, you will have to add seams where they wouldn't be needed if you worked with irregularly shaped foundations. These seams can distract from your image, especially if you are working with fabrics that show every seam line. Matching seam lines between the foundations can become challenging, because exact matches are more often necessary than when you work with irregularly shaped foundations. It may be difficult to hide the grid, especially when you are working with light-colored or solid-colored fabric. Other times, you'll find that the grid makes piecing faster and easier. Over time, you will find when working with an underlying grid is best and when it's not optimal.

▲ From left to right, *Deep Dive*, 2022; *Statue of Liberty*, 2023; and *The Kraken*, 2023, all 60" × 80", designed by Mike O'Dell for Legit Kits. *Photos courtesy of Legit Kits, used with permission*

If you get discouraged making your first FPP pattern, Mike's story can inspire you. It took him 18 months to create his first pattern, which he did full size—60" × 80"—on his dining-room floor.

Sarah Pitcher of Pitcher's Boutique, LLC, is another designer to check out. She has the patience and skill needed to create detailed images that have curves on top of curves, all made with straight lines. Sarah began designing for FPP in 2016. She wanted to make a Halloween door hanging, but the patterns she found were simpler than the image she imagined, so she drew her first design.

Sarah has turned what she describes as her inclination to overcomplicate everyday things into a blessing in her quilt designs.

"I can overcomplicate designs, and they turn out looking very realistic," Sarah says. "The biggest challenge is knowing where to divide each section and where to not add another seam because it will become too bulky. That can take trial and error. The more you sew FPP patterns, the more you realize what you can and cannot do."

Sarah began designing with paper and pencil but soon realized that correcting mistakes was time consuming, so she looked for a faster way to design. She now works with multiple design programs. Though learning to work digitally was a huge learning curve, she finds working this way easier and faster.

Sarah initially worked from images she found online, and she used photos she took. Over time, she began to draw her own images, in part because there are things she imagines in her mind that are not in this world. She learned to draw on her tablet, using various drawing programs and apps. She says that drawing on her tablet has helped her improve her drawing skills.

If you want to learn to design for FPP, Sarah recommends you commit time to work and rework your designs until they are what you envision.

"If I was going to give someone advice on how to perfect the details of a pattern, it would be to design it, try sewing it, and then design more, sew it again, and just keep doing that over and over," Sarah says. "What you can accomplish or create might not happen today or tomorrow, but if you keep putting in the effort, love, and joy, you soon will have the next quilt, pattern, or design that will inspire so many more."

▲ From the top, *Hair HIGH-land Coo*, 25" × 25", 2024; and *Mother Earth*, 45" × 60", 2025. *Photos courtesy of Sarah Pitcher of Pitcher's Boutique, used with permission*

Sarah has created a Facebook community of foundation paper piecers, aptly named Foundation Paper Piecing Group. It's a good place to see her newest designs plus connect with other foundation paper piecers.

Once you've taken the time to study what other FPP designers are doing and have made several of their quilts, you'll likely be anxious to start designing your own patterns. First, a few more Paper Police rules.

The Paper Police Are Back

In chapter 2 of this book, I mentioned several additional Paper Police rules you'll need to perfect as you create more intricate designs. Let's look at these.

Lines to Nowhere Go—Nowhere

There is no way to create foundations using lines that go nowhere. These are lines that float in space. They may be related to lines in your image, but the ends of these lines don't connect to anything. Following the next Paper Police rule will help you avoid lines to nowhere.

The First Line Must Run Edge to Edge

The first line you draw must go from one edge of your quilt to another edge—perimeter to perimeter. You can draw your first line horizontally to connect the sides of your quilt, vertically to connect top and bottom, or diagonally to connect adjacent sides. The key is going edge to edge. When you follow this Paper Police rule, you'll draw an anchored line and be off to a good start.

Anchor Every Line

Every line you draw must be anchored to lines that are anchored. You will begin your design by drawing the perimeter of your quilt. The four lines that define the edges of your quilt are your first four anchored lines.

When you draw your first line between two perimeters, this line becomes an anchored line. Now you have five anchored lines to work with.

Your next line can anchor to this line and a perimeter line or to two perimeter lines.

As you work, be sure each line you draw is anchored. Even one unanchored line will throw off your design because there is no way to piece it. When you draw lines between unanchored lines, they aren't anchored. Your design becomes a house of cards, ready to collapse for lack of a solid base.

Avoid Random Lines

Random lines are lines that don't relate to lines in your photo. Such lines break your image in illogical places. They increase the number of pieces you'll have to stitch, and they result in seams that can distract from your main image.

Instead, draw lines suggested by your image. As you work, find a line in your image that you can extend to the perimeters of your quilt or to other anchored lines. I chose to draw a line suggested by the top of the eagle's head. Because this line is suggested by the image, it's not random.

Every Line Becomes a Seam

Every line you draw becomes a seam, and every seam provides an opportunity for a fabric change. You want to draw lines that enhance your design, and you want to avoid lines that cut through your image at awkward points. For example, I could draw a line through the eye of the eagle, but that seam will distract from my finished image because it's not a logical place for a seam. It would also be difficult to align the top and bottom of the eagle's eye when joining the two foundations that would be required.

BALD EAGLE TOP PICK

The eagle photo used here is a good choice for a first pictorial FPP design. Because the eagle is silhouetted against the sky and photographed alone with an uncluttered background, the designer can focus on a single image: the bird.

Stay Sane: Work Section by Section

Work section by section of your image to avoid going crazy. When you draw your first line, it will divide your photo into two parts. Select one side of the line to design first, ignoring the other side. As you draw each line, pick a side of the line and work only on that side until it is fully designed, then tackle the other side of the line. Work from larger sections to smaller sections, adding detail as you go.

This may seem tedious, but discipline yourself to work this way. Jumping around to various parts of your photo leads to unanchored lines and the need to rework portions of your design or even the need to start over.

KEEPING THE CURVE

If you're designing a small quilt, you may be able to suggest a curve with a few lines. If you enlarge your design, the points where the lines meet the curve will appear sharper, and you can lose the appearance of the curve. Adding lines can solve this.

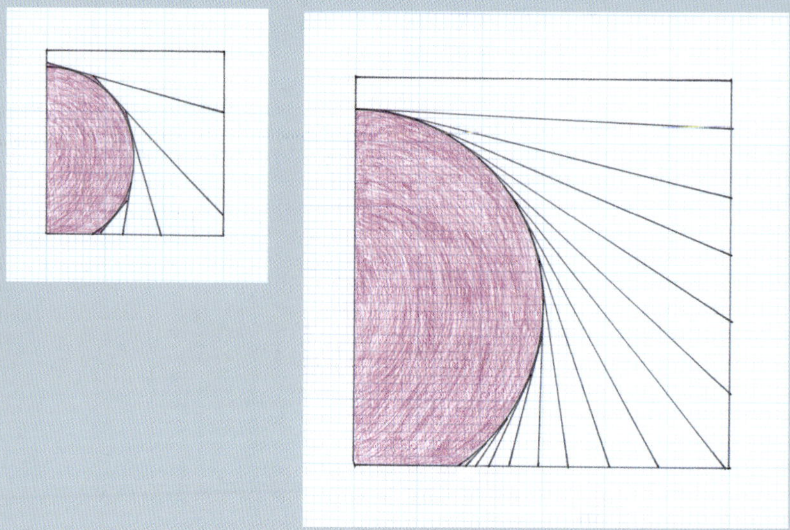

HUG YOUR RULER

Work with a straightedge. Always. When you get ready to stitch your design, you need your lines to be straight, perfectly straight. You will be tempted to quickly sketch short lines or to draw over a line to tweak it, thus creating a slight double line. These will throw you off when you're piecing, so grab your ruler and never let it go.

Your Eraser is Your New BFF

Work in pencil and erase as often as you need to. Drawing a line in a certain place will seem like a good choice until you try to draw the next line. Keep your eraser handy.

Don't Be Too Literal

You don't have to draw every line in your inspiration photo. You want to capture the essence of your subject—the basic shapes, colors, textures—but you don't need to capture every detail. There will be lines suggested by your image that require gymnastics to piece and may lead you to believe you have to allow Y-seams here and there. When this happens, step away from your design for a few minutes. When you return to your design, you'll see you can make a subtle change in the angle or positioning of a line that removes the Y-seam.

I created such a problem for myself when I designed *Peace Cranes Over Hiroshima*. I was so wedded to the exact slant of the crane's head that my design included a slight bend, which required a Y-seam. Altering the angle of one line removed the bend. No more Y-seam.

The larger your quilt, the more detail you will want to include. I often work smaller than my final design, so when I enlarge it, I add detail by adding more lines.

Shine Bright: Lessons from a Star

Just like a kite teaches us about FPP design, so does a five-pointed star. Study the star, then draw, trace, or copy it.

Follow the steps below to create a mini quilt with a star in its center. Use your straightedge.

- Draw a box around the star in permanent marker. Don't let the box touch any of the points of the star. This box is the perimeter of your star quilt. The lines that form the box are your first four anchored lines.

- Set your marker aside and work with a pencil for the rest of this exercise.
- Divide the quilt into two parts by drawing a line edge to edge. Avoid drawing a random line by extending an existing line of the star. You will have to draw this line through the star. There are multiple places you can do this. Two possibilities are shown here.

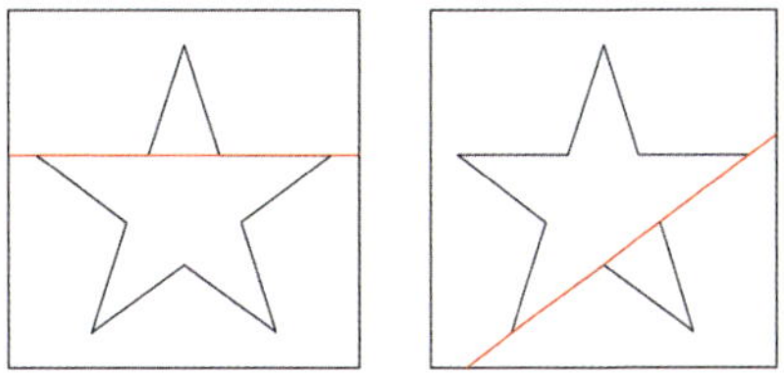

- Select one side of the line you just drew. Divide this side into one or more foundations, then number the foundations for piecing order.

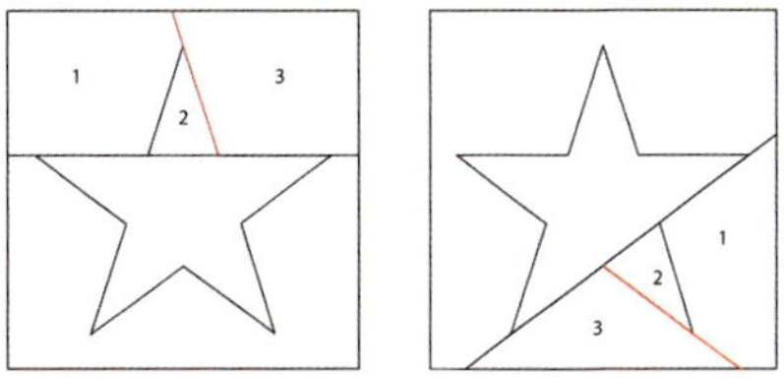

- Divide the other side of the line into foundations and number the foundations for piecing order.

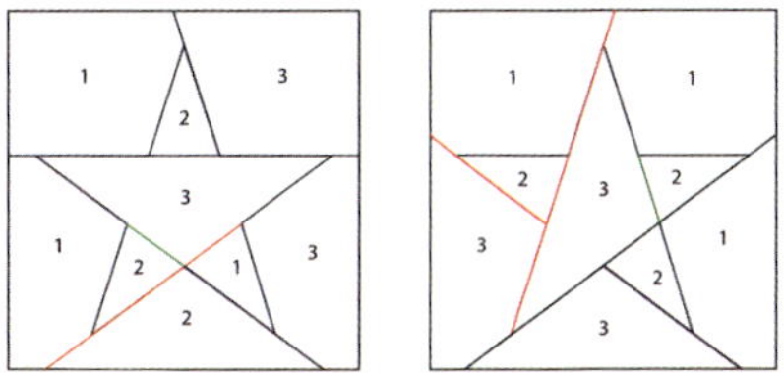

- Using your straightedge and a different color highlighter for each foundation, outline your foundations.

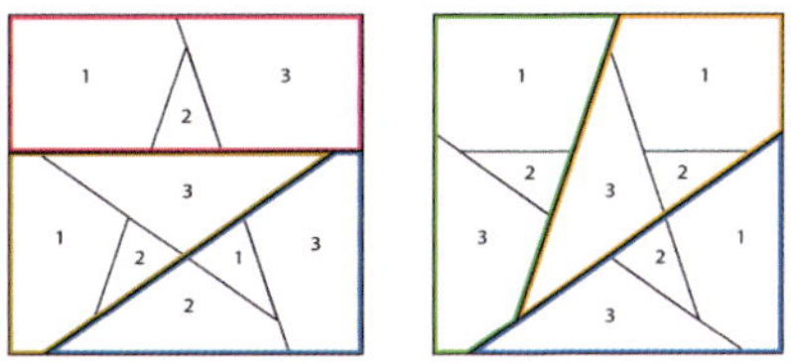

- Remember, you'll design as you want your finished piece to look. When you complete your design, you'll reverse the foundations because FPP designs are stitched in mirror mode. To reverse your foundations, simply turn over your design and trace it on the back or reverse it in a copy machine. Be sure the copy machine copies at 100 percent of the size of your original.

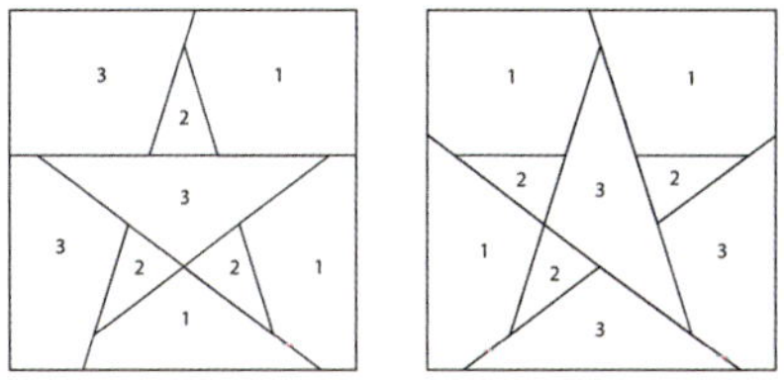

- Label each foundation with a capital letter.

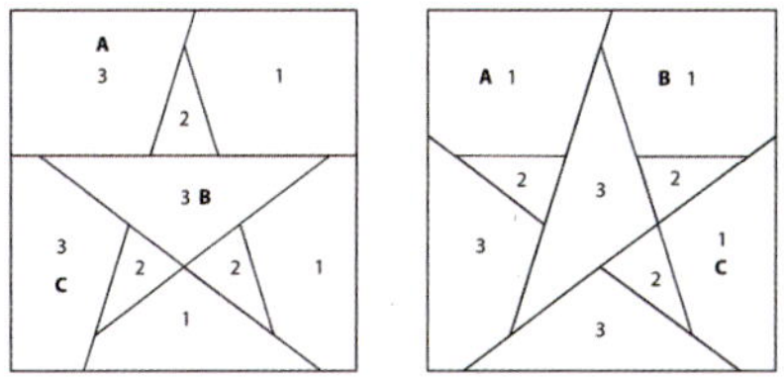

- Mark the foundations to show how to piece them together. There are many ways to do this. My favorite is using hash marks in a variety of colors. Use permanent markers to avoid color bleeding or ironing onto your fabric.

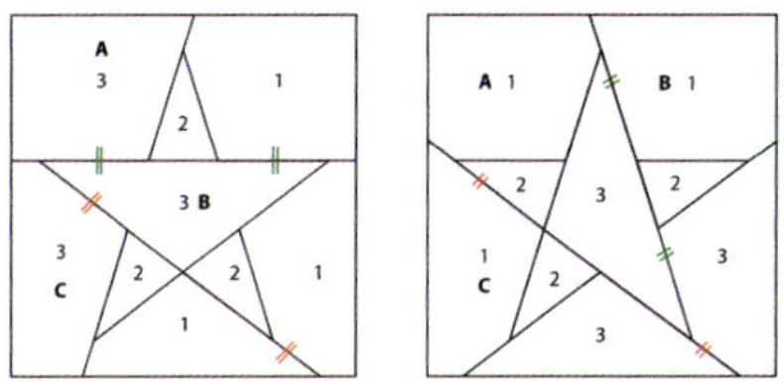

- Cut the foundations apart.

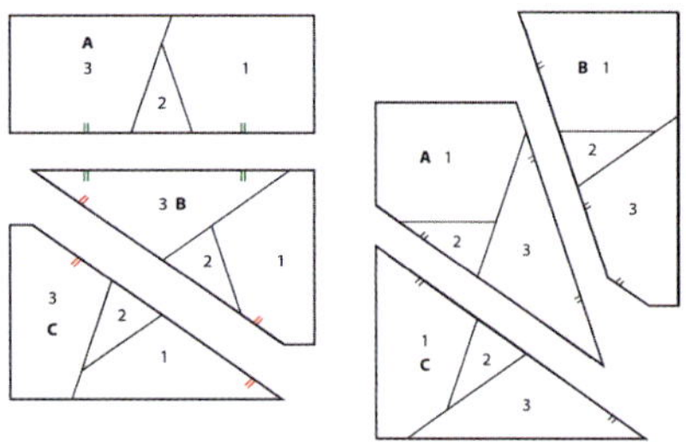

- Add ¼" seam allowances around the outside edges of every foundation.

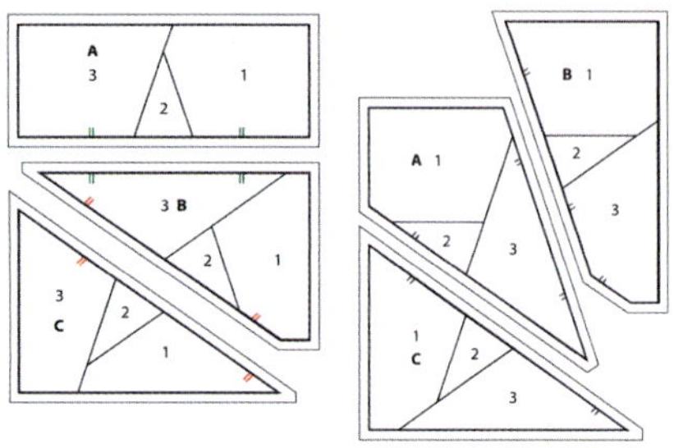

- Transfer your foundations to the foundation paper you like to work with. You can do this by hand or on a copy machine. If you use a copy machine, be sure the copy is 100 percent of the size of your original.

Labeling foundations, adding seam allowances around foundations, and other finishing touches will be explained in detail in chapter 4, "Polishing Your Foundations," page 94.

There are many ways to divide this star. I've shown two.

FOCUS ON THE CENTER OF THE STAR

If you want to fussy cut the center of the star so you can put an image or motif in the pentagon that is in the center, you will need four foundations, because you'll need more seams to allow for the fabric change in the center of the star.

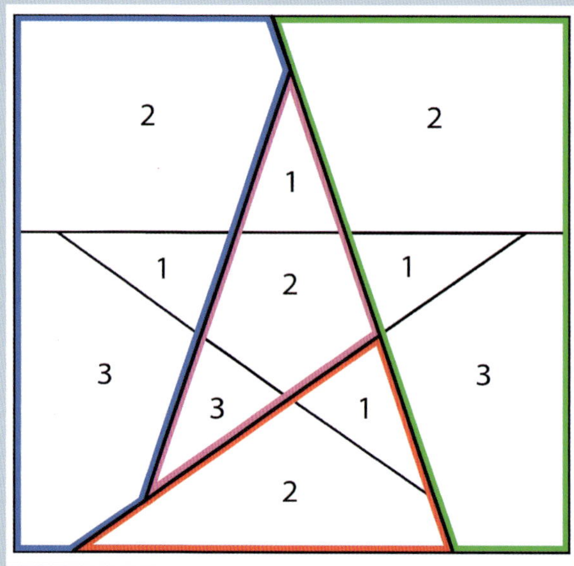

▲ *Bird on a Branch*, 20" × 15½", designed and pieced by Dana E. Jones, quilted by Rita Meyerhoff

Out on a Limb: Lessons from a Bird

I created *Bird on a Branch* to illustrate best practices in applying the Paper Police rules. Let's walk through my design process.

I began by selecting a photo. I made sure there were no copyright restrictions on it. You never know when you will want to enter your quilt in a show, use it to teach others, or sell it, so it's best to use a copyright-free image or get written permission from the photographer. I used a royalty-free photo from Pixabay, being sure to follow their regulations for use. The photo of a European robin is by German photographer Lars Nissen.

I decided to focus on the bird, ignoring the background except for the branch on which the bird is sitting. I cropped the image to enhance the bird as the focal point and kept the asymmetry of bird on the right side of the photo.

▲ European robin. *Photo by Lars Nissen from Pixabay*

I enlarged the cropped photo to fit on an 8½" × 11" sheet of paper. For your first design, I recommend you don't work smaller than 8½" × 11" or larger than 11" × 17".

I taped my photo to my work surface. I chose a cutting mat to work on, so I could carry my drawing around and leave my photo in place between work sessions. I sometimes work on a light box.

I hinged a sheet of translucent vellum over my photo. You can find reasonably priced vellum at office-supply stores and online. I taped the vellum down on one side only, so periodically I could lift it up to insert a sheet of copy paper between the vellum and the photo. This helped me better see the lines I'd drawn and to be sure I'd anchored them. It can be difficult to see pencil lines on the vellum when it is right on top of a photo.

I'm right-handed, so I hinged the vellum on the left side. If you're left-handed, you may want to hinge it on the right side. Across the top also works. To create the hinge, I ran a piece of 1" wide masking tape along the edge I'd selected, then I added horizontal strips of tape along the top and bottom, so the ends of the vertical piece of tape wouldn't work loose as I drew.

Next, I drew the perimeter of my quilt, using a straightedge and a fine-point permanent marker. I used a permanent marker so I wouldn't accidentally erase these important first anchored lines as I worked. Once I'd drawn the perimeter, I put the permanent marker away and used a pencil for the rest of my design.

I studied my photo to find a place to divide my image into two parts by drawing an edge-to-edge line. This is where my voice as a designer kicked in. I tried vertical, horizontal, and diagonal lines.

I opted for the horizontal line because the branch was a natural dividing line. Your first line can run between opposite edges of your quilt or adjacent edges. It can divide your image evenly or unevenly. The line just has to be anchored to perimeter lines on each end.

I recommend designing the focal point of your image first. In my piece, that is the bird. Because the bird is above the horizontal line, I worked above the line first. I came back to the area below the first line only after I'd designed everything above the line.

I began framing in the bird with my second line. To avoid random lines—lines that have no relationship to the image—I studied the edges of the bird then drew a line suggested by the left side of the bird's breast. I anchored this line to my first line and to the top perimeter of my quilt, so it became an anchored line.

Since the bird is to the right of this line, I next designed the area to the right of my second line. My third line continued framing in the bird.

After drawing each line, I chose a side of the line to work as I continued around the bird.

I made a decision early on to use the bird's beak as a defining line. Because the beak was small, I wanted to be sure it would be pieced as one piece. That meant using it to suggest placement of other lines. The first such line was the line that framed the bird's body on the right side. This line touched the end of the bird's beak.

I drew a line along the left side of the bird and across the top of the branch, and the bird was framed in.

ANCHOR CHECK

This was a good time to slide a sheet of copy paper between the photo and the vellum to check to ensure that all my lines were anchored.

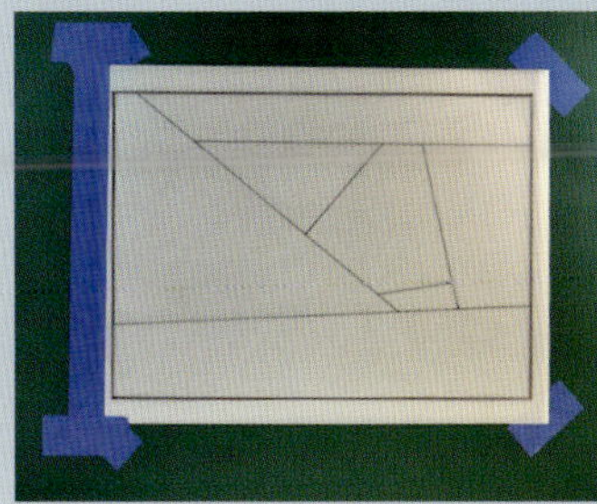

Next, I drew the lines needed to capture the curves along the outline of the bird's body. The more lines I drew, the more curved my design appeared. At 8½" × 11", a few lines sufficed.

STAY THE COURSE

When you get to this level of detail, it's easy to start jumping around from one area of your design to another. Avoid that temptation. Force yourself to draw anchored lines and to work one side of each line fully before moving on. You will find you are working from larger to smaller sections. For example, I designed the area around the bird's eye in full detail before I designed the rest of its head.

With all but the bird's head, neck, and beak outlined, I was ready to design the interior of the bird's body. I used the lines of the beak to draw my first lines inside the bird.

With these lines in place, I could finish outlining the bird's head, neck, and beak. This required tiny pieces. I don't mind having these when they enhance my design.

Color was key to placement of my next lines. Because every line becomes a seam and every seam allows for a fabric change, color is a good guide as to where to break areas into multiple foundations and foundations into pieces. I wanted to hang on to the subtle color variations in the grays and browns as well as the bolder oranges.

I next finished the interior of the bird. Color remained my guide for drawing foundations and pieces within the foundations for the bird's breast and wings.

As I worked, I decided to redraw my first horizontal line so the bird's tail was entirely below the line. Don't make a decision like this lightly. Every line in your design is based on your first line being anchored. Making such a change means extending or shortening every line that is anchored to your original line to the new line if you are to avoid having your design collapse in on itself.

The area above my first line—the line I drew horizontally along the branch—was almost complete. All that was left to design were the portions of the limb that were above my first line. I could have made this easy by straightening out the branch, but branches aren't straight. I wanted to keep the curves. That meant some sliver piecing. In this case, the seams didn't distract from the image. Branches aren't smooth, so the seams actually enhanced the appearance, suggesting the grain of the wood.

With the upper portion of my quilt designed, I turned to the area below my first horizontal line. I wanted to keep the small notch in the bird's tail, which meant a few more pieces but no extra foundations. I was able to design the entire lower portion of the quilt as one foundation.

JUST ASK

I often work from my own photos, but getting permission to use a photo can be as simple as asking the photographer to grant it. Be sure to get the photographer's permission in writing.

My design complete, I enlarged it from 8½" × 11" to 20" x 15½". Originally, I'd planned to embroider the bird's eye. At the larger size, I decided to piece the eye. That meant adding six small pieces around a black center to ensure the eye looked round. At 8½" × 11", this would have been difficult to piece, but at the larger size, it worked well.

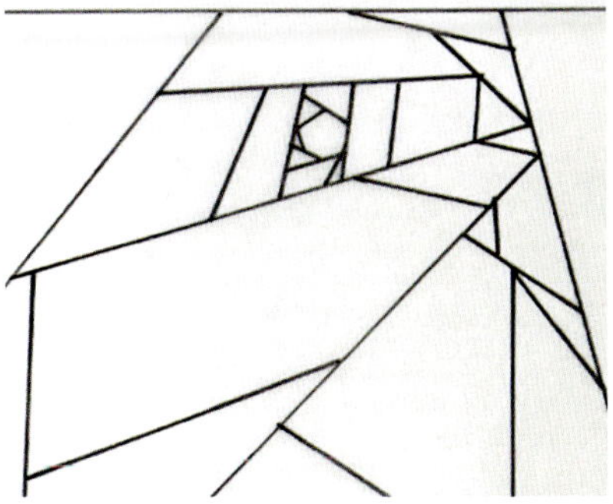

I drew my completed design in permanent marker. Doing so helps you catch lines that aren't anchored and lines that you drew without your straightedge. Fix these lines now. When your full design is in permanent marker, go over it with your eraser to remove any traces of pencil lines and smudges.

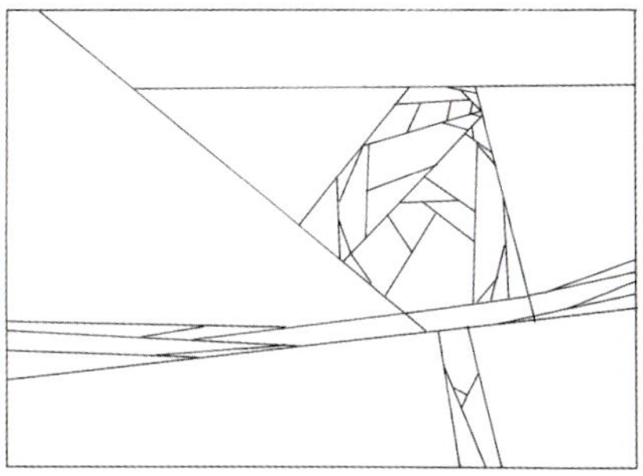

I copied my design in reverse, making sure it was 100 percent of my original.

GO FOR THE FINE LINE

When you enlarge your design on a copy machine, your lines will get bolder and irregular in width. These lines will be difficult to sew along. I recommend you trace your enlarged copy with a fine-point permanent marker. This removes the irregularities and gives you fine lines to sew along.

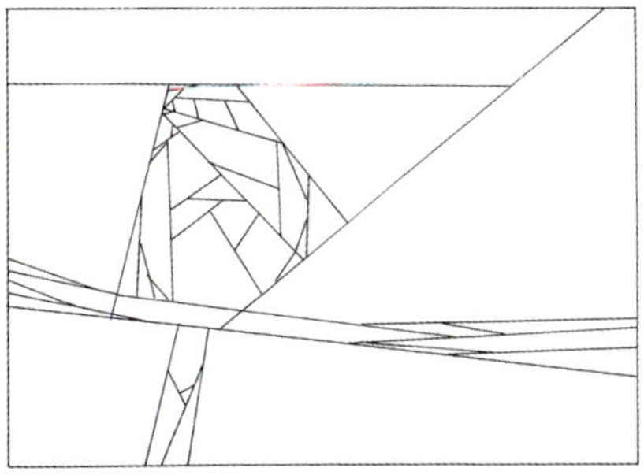

Next, I labeled the foundations. There isn't a standard labeling system for FPP patterns. I use capital letters to name the foundations and numbers for the piecing order. Labeling foundations will be discussed in detail in the chapter 4 subsection "Know Your ABCs and 1, 2, 3s: Label Your Foundations," page 94.

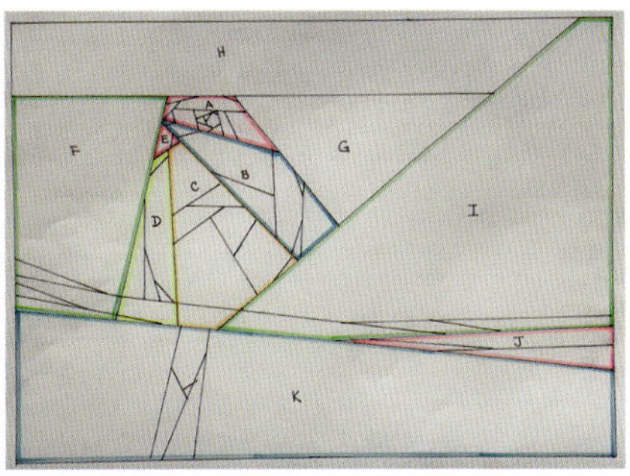

When numbering pieces, remember that each foundation starts with 1.

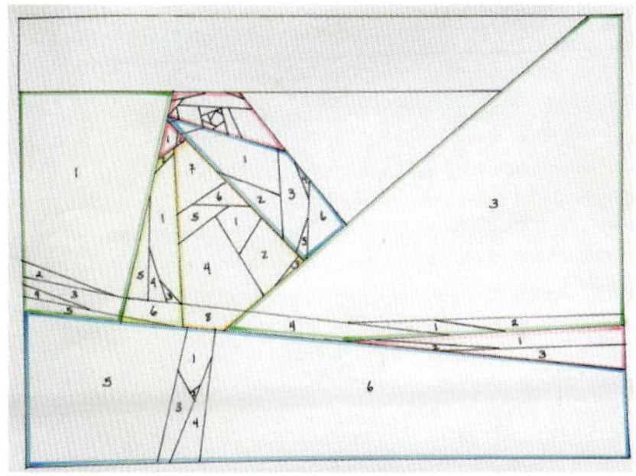

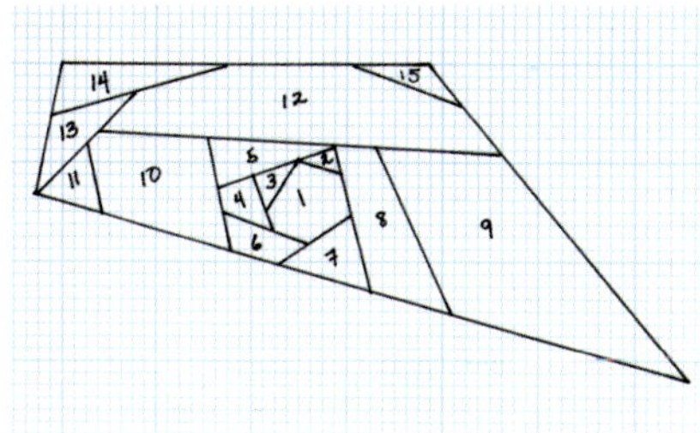

I color my patterns. This helps me select fabrics and lets me know I'm using the right fabrics in the right places when piecing. Making color copies can be expensive, so I usually color in one of the black-and-white copies I've made and use it as a guide in fabric placement. I use Prismacolor pencils because they don't hide my design lines.

Before I cut my foundations apart, I drew hash marks between them with a range of colors of fine-point permanent markers. These become the guides for joining foundations once they've been pieced. These go only between foundations, not between pieces, because there is no purpose for them between pieces. This will be explained in detail in the chapter 4 subsection "Draw Rainbow Hash Marks," page 97.

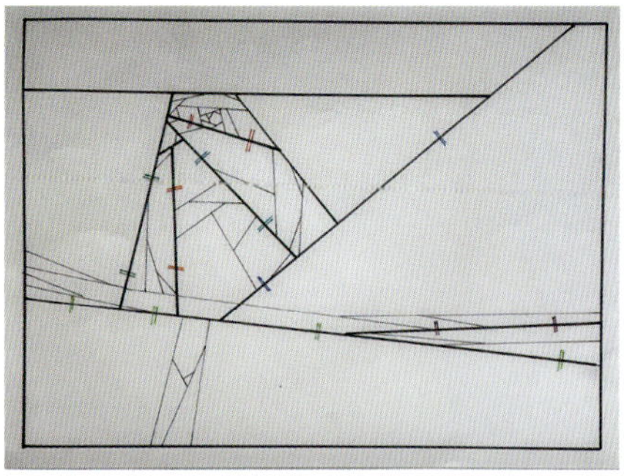

I cut the foundations apart and added ¼" seam allowances around all the edges of all the foundations.

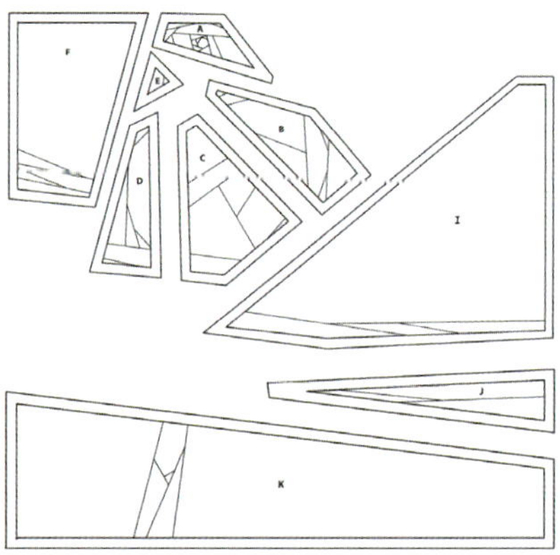

I made two copies of my foundations: one on foundation paper to use to piece my quilt and one on copy paper for my files. If you make a mistake in piecing, you'll be glad to have a master copy of your foundations. You may want to make the quilt more than once. Having a copy of the foundations will make that easier. If you've designed digitally, save a digital copy.

GOING DIGITAL

I recommend you do your first pictorial design by hand for the reasons I explained earlier in this book. When you've completed your first design, it's a good time to begin to work digitally if that's your preference. Drawing on your computer or tablet will give you precise stitching lines. When you work digitally and have a design with repeating foundations, getting multiple copies of foundations is as simple as printing them out. Most programs will let you reverse your design for the mirror image with one click.

As you become more familiar with the FPP design process, you may decide to design digitally from beginning to end. Many software programs work for this. I suggest you select one you know and like to work with. If you have a technical background, you may know a CAD program. Use it. If you are a graphic designer, you may be fluent in the Adobe Suite of programs such as Illustrator and Photoshop. Use them. If you haven't worked with a drawing program, check out free apps or see if you have software that can be used to design. One student told me she designs in PowerPoint. I'm not sure how, but if a program works for you, use it.

If you're starting from scratch in terms of drawing digitally, check out Electric Quilt (EQ8), which is designed for quilters. It has a function that will break your designs into foundations. This is a nice feature, but plan to study those foundations carefully. Is your image divided into foundations the way you want it to be? You will be able to stitch the EQ8 FPP patterns without concern about Y-seams, but in more complicated designs, there may be lines, which equal seams, where you don't want them. Pieces may be numbered in a different piecing order than suits you. That's where your knowledge of FPP design comes in. You can move the lines to position them as you want them, and you can renumber pieces. You'll be able to try a variety of color and fabric choices quickly.

▲ *Bird on a Branch* pattern drawn digitally then colored in, also digitally

Fabric selection was next. I focused first on the bird. I searched my stash for fabrics in the right colors and for fabrics that suggested feathers. There is no replacement for auditioning fabrics, so that's what I did until I had selections that worked.

Next, I chose fabric for the branch. Every once in a while, you have just what you need in your stash. You know it and can go right to it. Such was the case for the branch fabric.

Selecting fabric for the sky proved more difficult. When I stumbled on a long-forgotten cut of ombre blue in my stash, I knew it was perfect. Thus began the challenge of positioning the light and dark portions and stretching a somewhat small cut to fill the space.

The beauty of fabric selection is that it remains a subjective process decided only by the designer's sense of what works and what doesn't. Enjoy that freedom.

MAKE COPIES OF YOUR DESIGN

Make multiple copies of your design. Be sure they are 100 percent of your original. I can't tell you how many to make. I always have extras, but I find that spending a few extra pennies is worth the assurance I won't have to redraw my design if I make a mistake.

SWATCH CARDS

If you're designing a quilt where the same fabric will be used in multiple places, I recommend you create a fabric swatch card. While my ***Bird on a Branch*** didn't require one, it was a lifesaver when I made my ***Peace Cranes Over Hiroshima*** quilt. You can assign each fabric a name or number that you can write on the foundations. This will be explained in detail in the chapter 4 subsection "Get the Right Fabric in the Right Place," page 95.

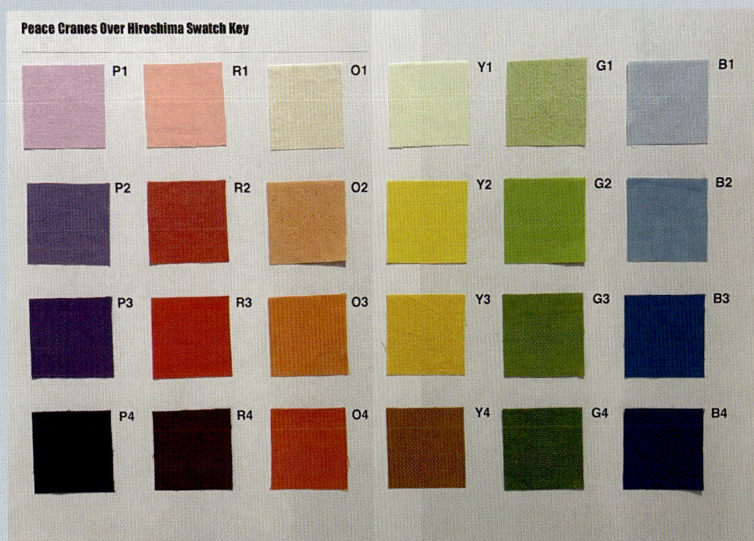

▲ My swatch card for *Peace Cranes Over Hiroshima* proved invaluable in being sure I placed the right value of the colors in the right places.

Curves Ahead: Creating an Illusion

The first rule of foundation paper piecing—you must use straight lines—provides a challenge when you want curves. How can you create the appearance of curves with straight lines?

When I began designing for FPP, my designs were stylized. I replaced curved lines with straight lines. This is one approach, an approach that leads to interesting images.

This approach doesn't work if you're seeking a photographic image.

The illusion of curves is possible with FPP. There are several routes to get there. The concept behind each method is to draw lines that touch the curve at one point along the curve. The more points along the curve you touch with lines, the rounder your curve will appear. This may sound cumbersome, but we are assisted by the fact that our eyes see curves where we expect to see them. We know a tire is round, so we see it as round. We know an elephant has a curved trunk, so we see it as curved.

◀ *Poinsettia* and *Sunflower*, both 6" × 6", designed, pieced, and quilted by Dana E. Jones

Boxed Curves

One way to draw curves is to box them in. This method works well for full circles. To try this method, draw a 6" × 6" square. Draw a circle inside this square, making sure the circle doesn't touch the edges of the square.

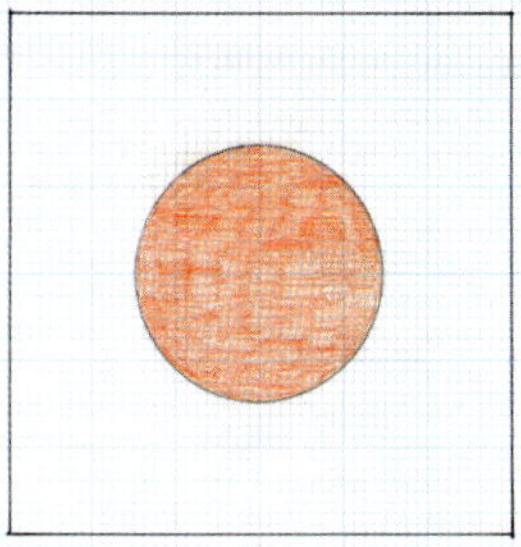

Select a point on the circle and draw a horizontal line that touches this point and runs from edge to edge of your square.

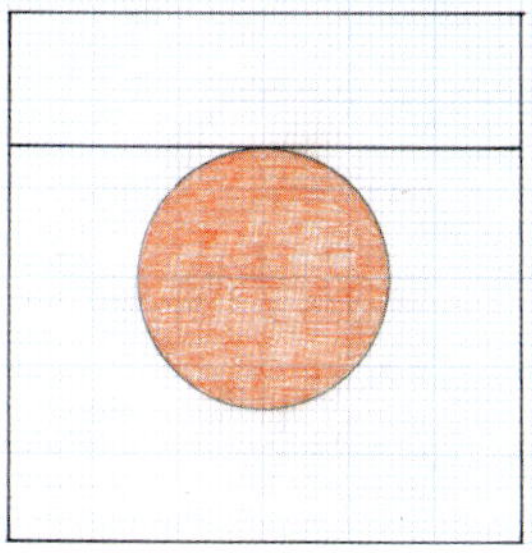

Draw a second parallel horizontal line across the bottom of your circle.

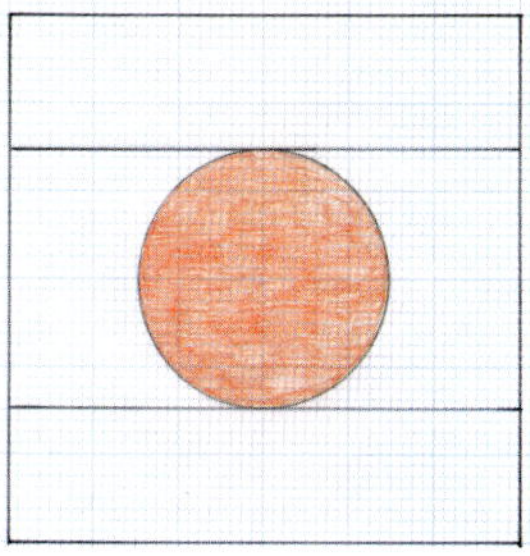

Both of these lines are anchored to two perimeter lines of your square, so both become anchored lines you can use when drawing your next lines.

Draw vertical lines on each side of your circle that touch the circle at midpoint.

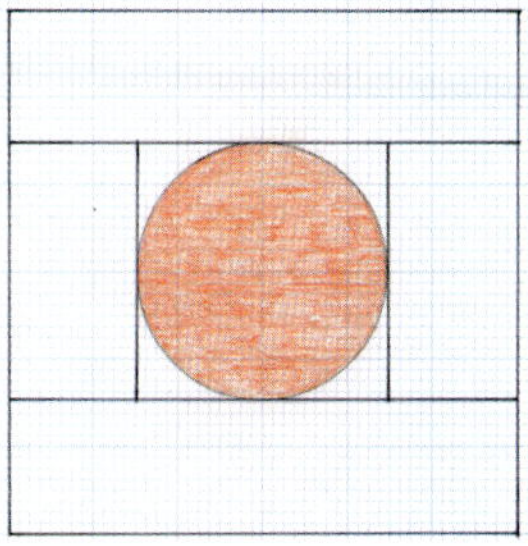

Note that these lines are drawn between your horizontal lines. They do not extend to the perimeter of your square. This is because the horizontal lines are anchored lines. Extending the vertical lines to the perimeters would add unnecessary piecing and seams that would distract from your image.

Your next step is to remove the square corners by drawing diagonal lines.

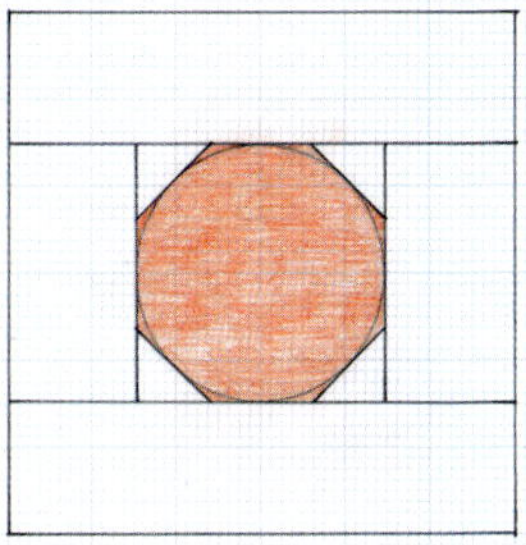

These four lines may be all you need to convey the sense of a circle, especially if you are working small. If you are working larger, continue to draw diagonal lines. The more lines you draw, the rounder your image will appear. Just be sure you can piece what you draw.

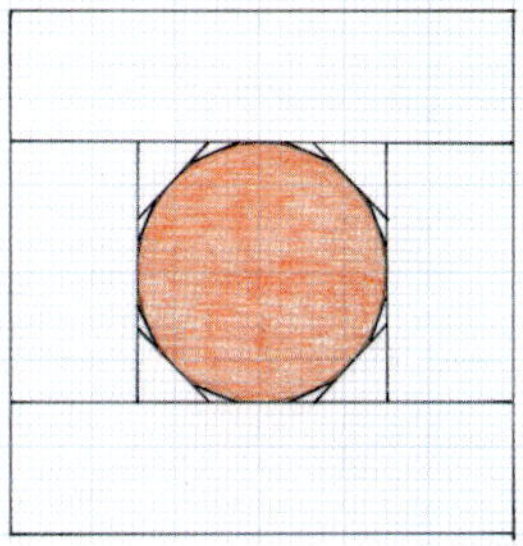

One impact of boxing in a circle or a curve is to create a sense of stability. Maaike Bakker's plate on a shelf in her book *Cups and Saucers: Paper-Pieced Kitchen Designs* is an example of this. The symmetry of the foundation gives the plate an appearance of stability that suggests it can be propped upright on a shelf and will not roll off.

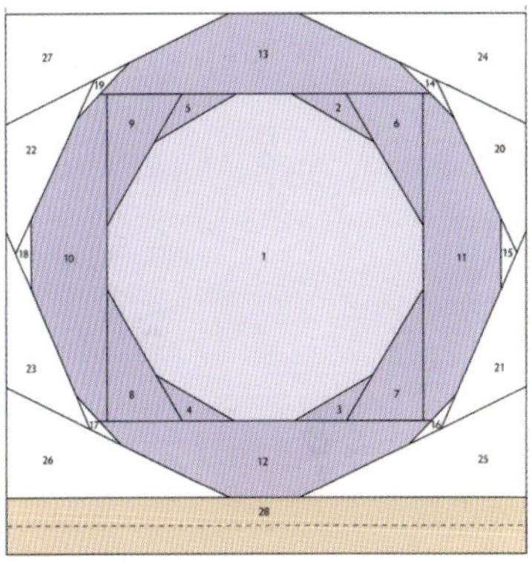

▲ Foundation for Plate block, 6" × 6", from *Cups and Saucers: Paper-Pieced Kitchen Designs,* designed by Maaike Bakker. *Used with permission, pattern available from www.ateliermaaikebakker.nl*

▲ *Colorful Cupboard*, 59½" × 63½", 2013, designed by Maaike Bakker, pieced by Annette Aardema-Lenstra, Jetty Bakker, Maaike Bakker, Toos van der Leeden, Françoise Maarse, and Martine Zandberg. *Photo courtesy of Maaike Bakker, used with permission, pattern available from www.ateliermaaikebakker.nl*

Radiating Curves

If you want a sense of movement, the next method for creating the appearance of curves gives you that. Lines radiate out from the perimeter of the circle in a pattern that creates a circular motion. This is a good way to suggest a car rolling along or a ball flying through the air.

Begin as you did before by drawing a 6" × 6" square with a circle inside it. Draw a diagonal line that touches the circle at one point and runs from edge to edge of your square. This anchored line is necessary so you can anchor the rest of the lines you draw.

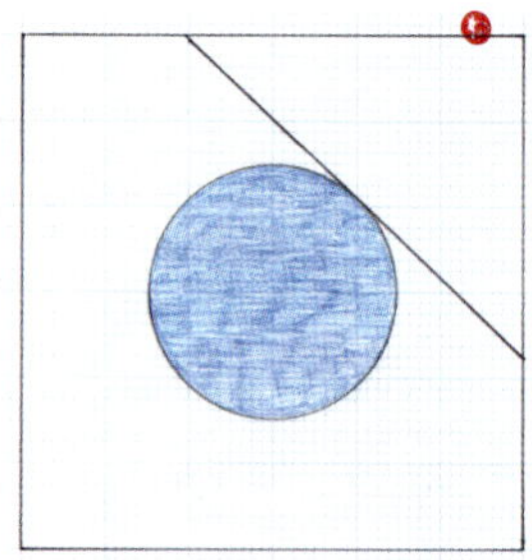

▲ *3 Plates on a Shelf*, pieced by Dana E. Jones using Maaike Bakker's foundation

Select a second point along the circle that is close to the first point. Draw a diagonal line from your first diagonal line to the perimeter of your square from this point.

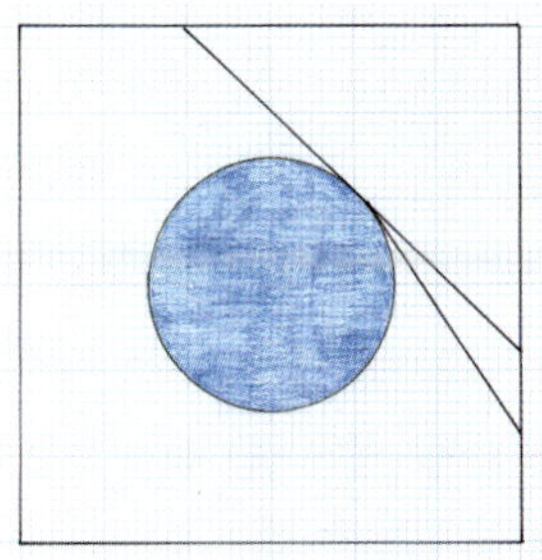

Continue moving along your circle, drawing diagonal lines from points along the circle to a perimeter of your square. The closer your points are along the circle, the rounder your circle will look.

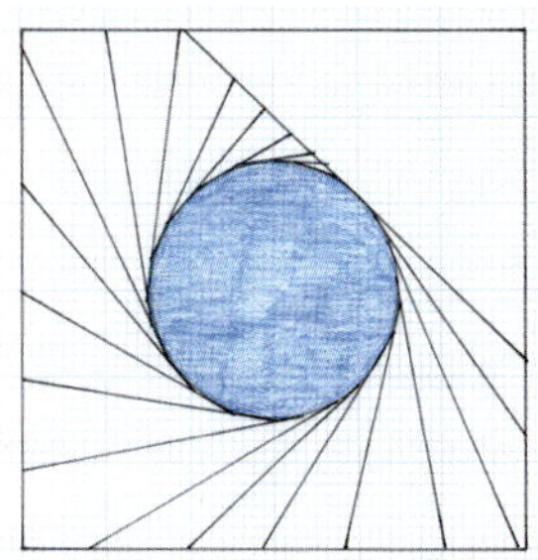

As with the boxing method, the number of lines needed varies by your image and the size of your work. Your goal is to create the illusion of a circle or curve, which can take a few lines or many lines.

Radiating Boxed Curves

I've shown how to create curves using full circles. You will sometimes include full circles in your designs. More often, you will have curves that are not full circles. Don't worry. The same techniques work. You will find yourself combining boxing and radiating methods.

To see how this works, draw a 6" × 6" square with a circle inside it. Begin as you did for the radiating method by drawing a diagonal line between adjacent perimeters and through a point on the circle.

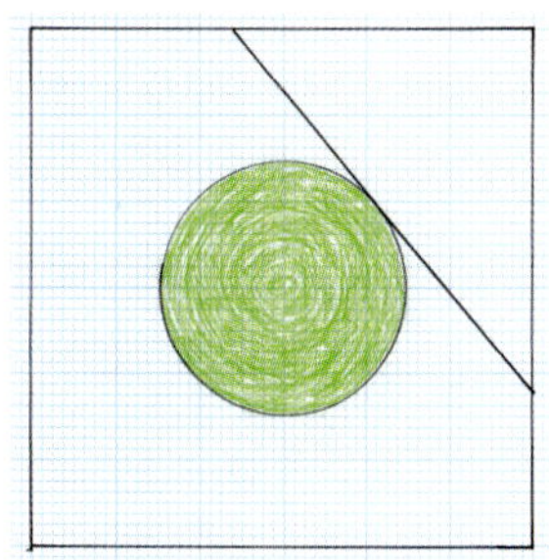

Switch methods. Draw a vertical line from the diagonal line near the point on the circle to the bottom perimeter.

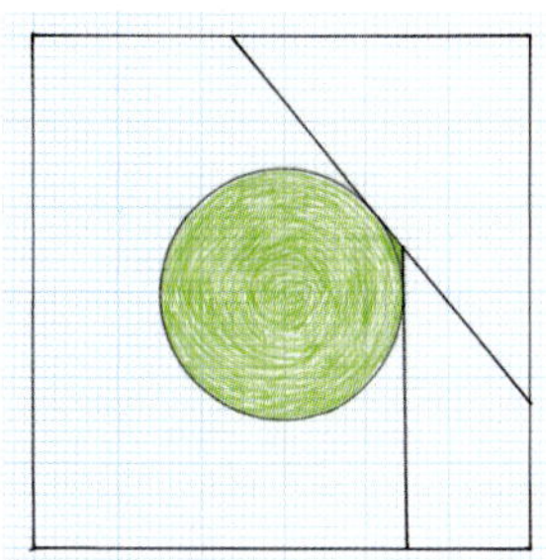

For your next line, go into radiating mode. Draw a diagonal line from the vertical line you just drew to a perimeter, touching the circle at one point.

Your next line will be a horizontal line followed by a diagonal line followed by a vertical line. You will continue alternating lines this way until you have enclosed the circle. As in the first two methods, the closer your reference points on the circle are from line to line, the rounder your image will appear.

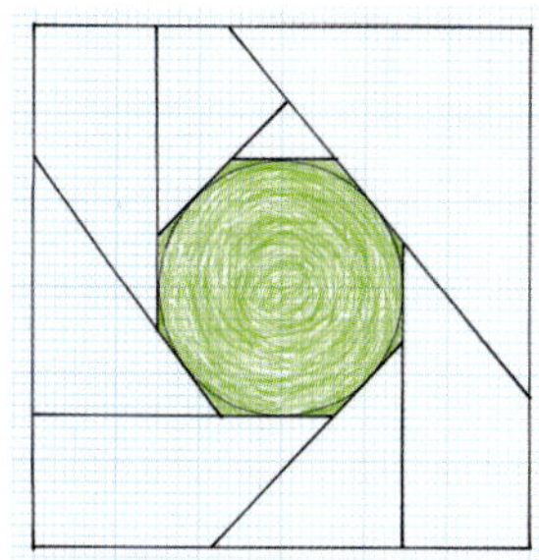

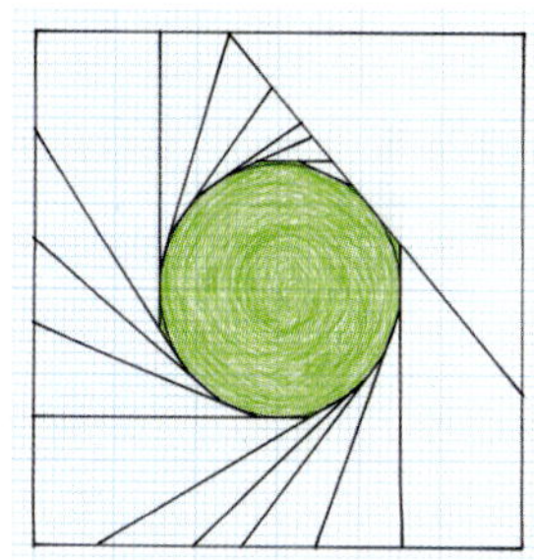

In practice, you will find you will use variations on these methods, mixing and matching them as works on each curve you draw.

Ready, Set, Go: Design a Picture to Foundation Paper Piece

You're ready to create your first FPP pictorial pattern. Select a photo. Keep it simple for your first design. Go for a single object and make it an object you aren't too attached to. Your favorite cat or dog is for later when you have more experience and can better capture all that you love in your pet. Ditto in terms of photos of your favorite people. For that matter, don't do people yet. They can be difficult to capture. They will be good future projects.

Study your photo. Answer the following questions:

- Why do you like this photo?
- What stands out in this photo?
- Does the photo have a range of color values? If you're not sure, convert your photo to a black-and-white photo. This will help you see value variations.
- Is there one or more details in this photo you want to include in your design?
- Are there details in the photo you can eliminate?
- Do you want to crop, enlarge, or otherwise manipulate the photo before you begin your design?

CONCAVE CURVE? NO PROBLEM

Your first crisis in drawing curves may come when you encounter your first concave curve. The illustrations here have focused on curving around the convex curves of a circle. Suddenly your main image has a concave curve. Don't panic. For every concave curve, there is an opposing convex curve. When you encounter a concave curve, treat the background where the convex curve is as the shape you are curving around. You're back in familiar territory.

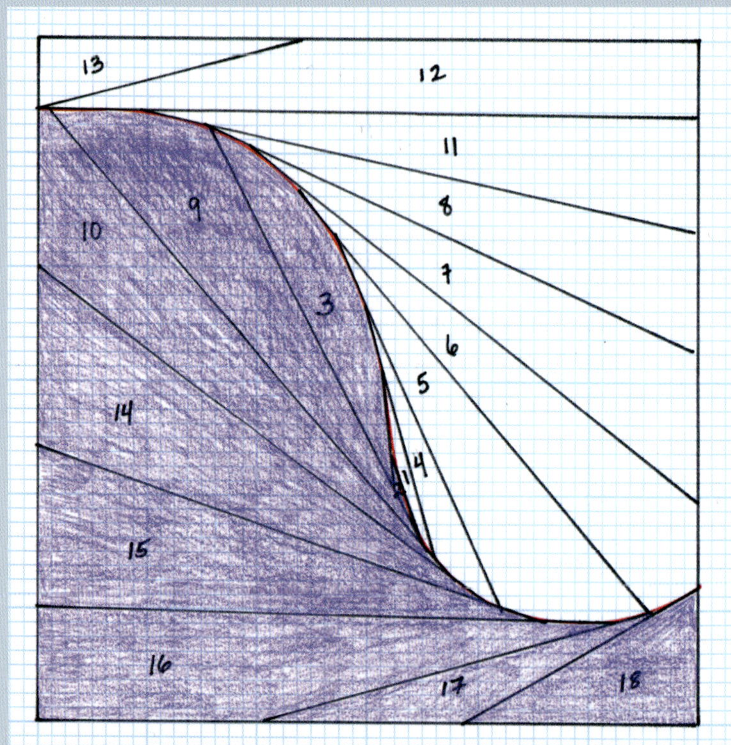

With these questions answered, you're ready to design. Step by step, here's what to do:

- Print your photo the size you want your quilt to be. Your home printer may be limited to printing 8½" × 11" and 8½" × 14". Your local copy shop can enlarge your photo. This doesn't need to be expensive. You don't need a high-quality print.
- Tape your photo to the surface you will work on. I use blue painter's tape because it's easy to remove. I often work on a cutting mat, nongridded side up. Other times, I work on my light box. You will be drawing on vellum, so even when you are using a permanent marker, it won't bleed through, which means you don't have to worry about marking on your work surface.

- Hinge a sheet of translucent vellum over your photo. Don't tape the four corners down. Instead, hinge the vellum on just one side, so you can lift it up to insert a sheet of copy paper between the vellum and the photo. This helps you see where you've drawn lines. It can be difficult to see your pencil lines when the vellum is right on top of your photo.

- Using a fine-point permanent marker, draw the perimeter of your quilt on the vellum, then set the marker aside. You'll design with pencil so you can erase as often and as liberally as needed. I recommend drawing the perimeter in permanent marker because these are your foundational anchor lines. You don't want to accidentally erase them.

- You're ready to draw the first line of your design. It must be anchored to two perimeter lines. You can draw it from side to side, top to bottom, or diagonally between two sides. It will divide your image into two parts.

- Select one side of your line and design everything on that side of the line, following the Paper Police rules. You may be tempted to jump around your image, designing here and there. Don't. The danger is that you will fail to anchor your lines. Once you start down that path, it can be a dead end with no option but to start over on your design. No amount of erasing can help you easily recover this mistake. Be methodical. Every time you draw a line, be sure it is anchored to anchored lines. Work one side of each line you draw, coming back to the other side only after you've finished the side you chose to work on first.

If you get confused or exhausted, take a break. Everything will look better a few minutes, hours, or days later. But don't go weeks or months unless you want to start over. Coming back to a design too long after you start it can be difficult.

Enjoy designing. To finish off your pattern, you'll need to create a system for labeling your foundations, cutting them apart, and adding seam allowances. And you'll create a map of how you'll join the foundations. Chapter 4, "Polishing Your Foundations," page 94, will provide guidance on all of this.

▲ I began designing a bald eagle quilt by having my local copy shop print my photo large—about 36" x 48". I picked up a large sheet of translucent vellum at an art-supply store. Then I taped the photo to my light box, hinged the vellum over it, and began my design. *Photo by Dana E. Jones*

CHAPTER 4

POLISHING *your* FOUNDATIONS

YOU'VE CREATED YOUR FIRST foundation paper-piecing design. It's time to polish your foundations for ease in piecing. We've been designing by hand. I believe this is the best way to learn the FPP design process. Computer design programs require you to draw with a computer pencil or mouse. Drawing by hand prepares you for this.

I'm far from a Luddite. I appreciate the accuracy and speed of computer design programs. A variety of software programs can be used to design for FPP, and now may be the time for you to use your favorite program. Software specific to quilting may have functions that break your designs into foundations. If you use these, note the breaks. They may not be the optimum. Applying what you've learned in this book, you can adjust them for the look you want. Make use of the best of both manual and computer design worlds.

Check the Mirror: Flip It

Up until now, we've ignored the fact that FPP patterns are mirror images of the final quilt. It's time to reverse your design. You can do this by hand, copy machine, or computer. To reverse your pattern by hand, flip it over and draw it on the back. If you designed it on translucent vellum paper, this will be easy because you can see through it. Be sure to use a straightedge and permanent marker. If you can't see through your paper, work on a light box or plate glass window during daylight hours. If you're using a copy machine, set it to make a reverse copy. Another method is to scan your design then reverse it in Photoshop or similar program or app. Whatever method you use, be sure your copy is 100 percent of your original.

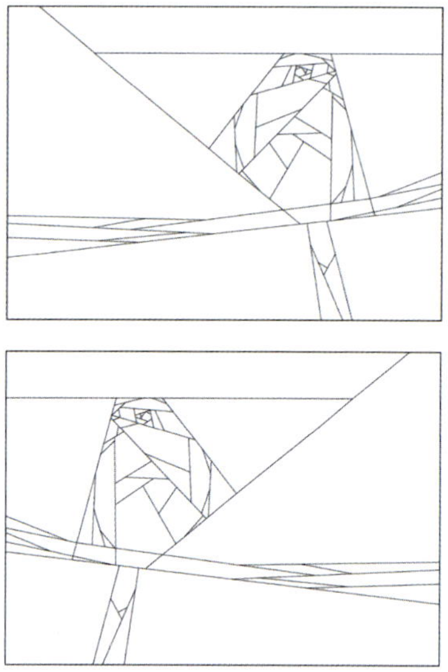

From top, *Bird on a Branch* pattern as drawn and the pattern reversed, designed by Dana E. Jones

Know Your ABCs and 1, 2, 3s: Label Your Foundations

Working with a reversed copy of your design, it's time to label your foundations. There isn't a standard way to do this, but there are four things to include:

- the name of each foundation
- the piecing order for each foundation
- the fabric for each piece
- markings to show where foundations will be joined to each other

Name Your Foundations

Designers employ various methods of naming foundations. I recommend using letters to avoid confusing foundation names with piecing-order numbers. If you have 26 or fewer foundations, use single letters: A, B, C to Z. If you have more than 26 foundations, use double letters: AA, AB, AC to AZ, then BA to BZ, and so forth.

Name your foundations in alphabetical order as they will be pieced together. This will make it easy for you to create a map of how to join them without Y-seams.

NUMBERING'S A TIPOFF

As you number pieces, you may discover that some of your divisions of your pattern into foundations don't work. Don't panic. It's best to discover this before you begin stitching. Reworking the pattern is easier at this point than later. Take time to fix any problems you find.

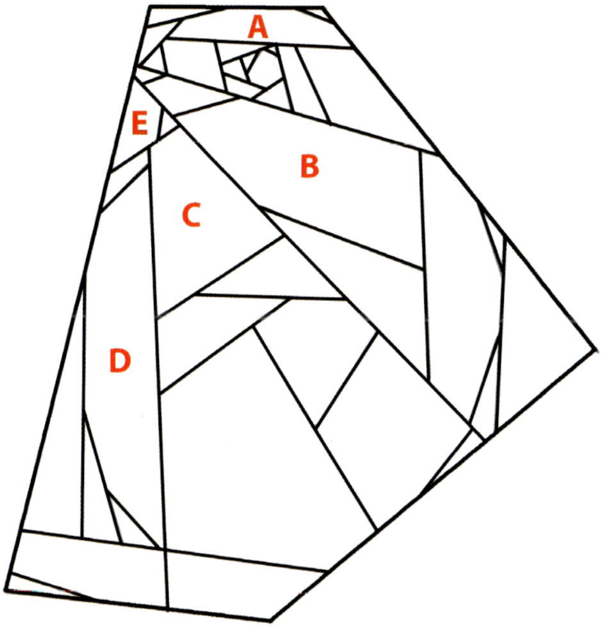

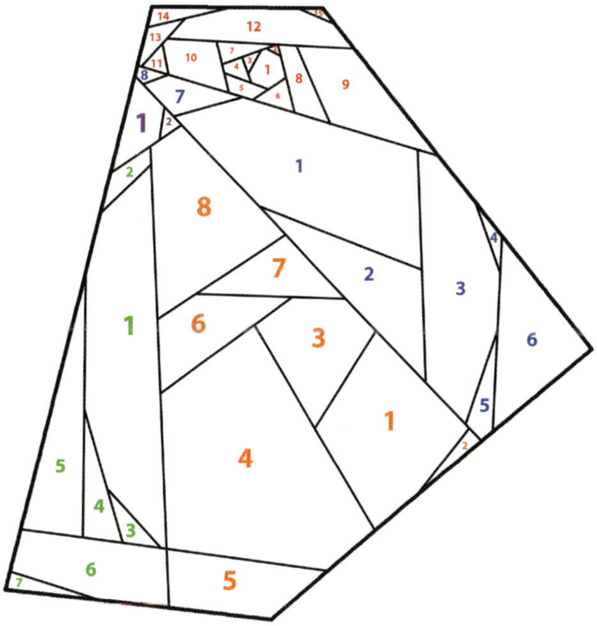

Mark the Piecing Order

Each piece within each foundation needs to be labeled for the order in which it will be pieced in relation to the other pieces in the foundation. Most designers use numbers for this because it's easy for piecers to sew from 1 to 2, 2 to 3, and so on. Begin with No. 1 for every foundation, because foundations are stitched independently of each other, and you will want to start stitching from No. 1 for each foundation.

Get the Right Fabric in the Right Place

When you begin stitching, it is easy to pick up the wrong fabric and not notice your error until you're further into piecing your quilt. By indicating the fabric for each piece on every foundation, you are less likely to make this mistake.

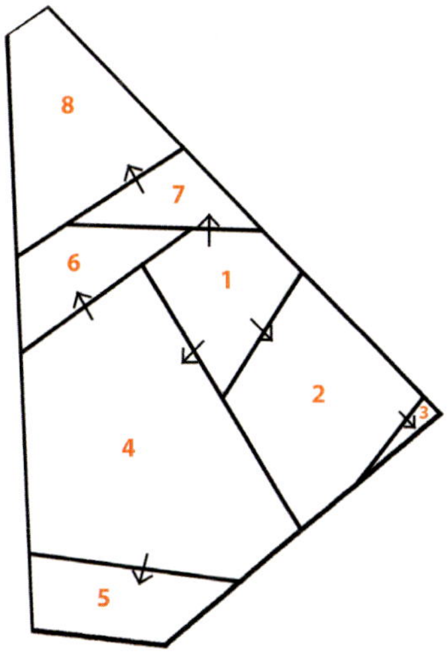

For simple designs, I color my foundations. If working by hand, I use Prismacolor pencils because I can see my stitching lines through them. I don't recommend using markers because they can obscure lines. When working by computer, you can drop colors in digitally.

ADVICE FROM THE SHADOWS

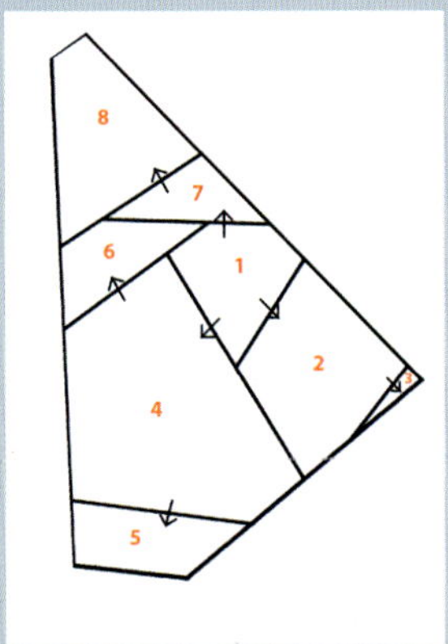

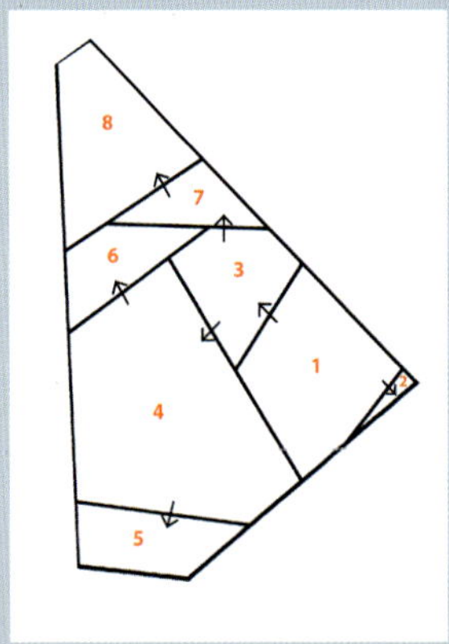

If you haven't considered which directions the seams will press, now is the time to do so. Seams will always press toward the last piece added. For example, when you join pieces 1 and 2, the seam will press toward piece 2. When you add piece 3, the seam will press toward piece 3. You may be able to reverse piecing order to change the directions the seams will press. In foundation C of ***Bird on a Branch***, the diamond-shaped piece in the center of the foundation is white. In the numbering order on the left, this is piece 3. The seam from piece 1, a dark fabric, will create a shadow under the white fabric. By renumbering pieces 1–3, the diamond becomes piece 1, so all the seams can be pressed away from it and there will be no shadows under the white fabric.

If you can't renumber pieces to avoid shadows, consider breaking a foundation into two or more foundations so that you can press seams away from lighter-colored fabrics.

Foundation K of ***Bird on a Branch*** offers a possibility for breaking foundations to avoid shadows. The dark-gray fabric used for the bird's tail might leave a shadow under the lighter-blue pieces that surround it. The longest areas of such seams can be eliminated by breaking foundation K into three pieces.

Breaking the center section that consists of pieces 1–4 into a foundation separate from the pieces on either side would make pieces 5 and 6 stand-alone pieces.

I didn't break foundation K apart because I determined the faint shadows from the darker fabric would not be visible in the final piece. There will be times when you will accept pressing a dark fabric toward a lighter one. That is the nature of FPP.

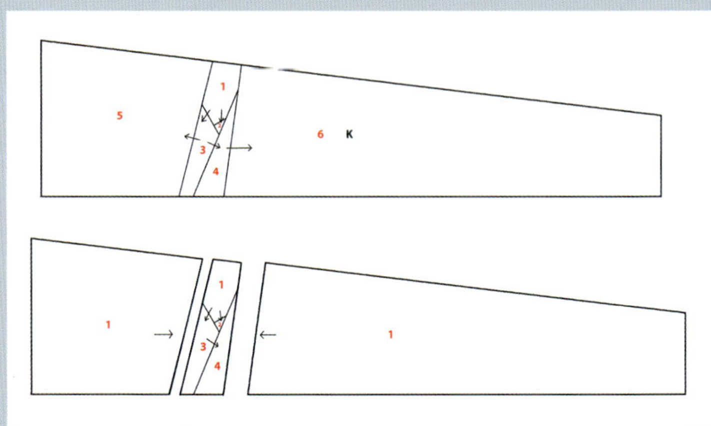

For more detailed patterns, I give each fabric a name and create swatch cards. For *Hot Air Balloon*, a design that is in process as this book goes to press, I plan to use four values of each color, so I named my fabrics with the color and value. I made the lightest value the lowest number, up to the highest number for the darkest value. For example, I had Green 1, Green 2, Green 3, and Green 4, which I shortened to G1, G2, G3, and G4.

As I cut and sew, I compare the labels on my foundations to my swatch card. Like measuring twice and cutting once, I recommend checking that you have the right fabric twice and stitching once.

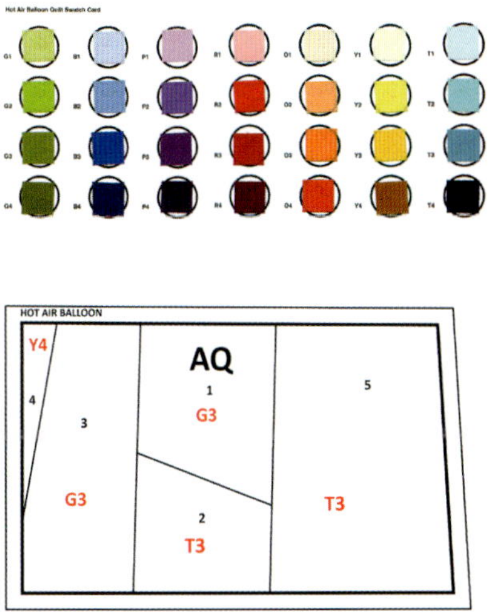

▲ A swatch card will help you place the right fabrics in the right places. This works best when you've labeled each piece on each foundation as to the fabric needed. *Just above, illustration by David Espy*

Draw Rainbow Hash Marks

As your patterns become more sophisticated, you'll be joining foundations with extreme angles and sharp points. It can be difficult to align them accurately. I draw hash marks in a variety of colors along the edges of foundations where they will be joined to other foundations. When working by hand, I use permanent markers. Be sure your hash marks are long enough that they don't get cut off when you separate your foundations. Space allowing, I make them about 1" long, with ½" on each side of the lines that divide the foundations. I find that making double lines is better for precise matching. When working by computer, also make hash marks in a variety of colors.

When alignment is especially challenging and important to the final look of your quilt, I recommend you hand baste seams before machine stitching them. Be sure to baste along the ¼" seam allowance lines so you can check alignment as it will be when you permanently stitch the foundations together. Stitching more or less than a ¼" allowance will not allow you to check for alignment.

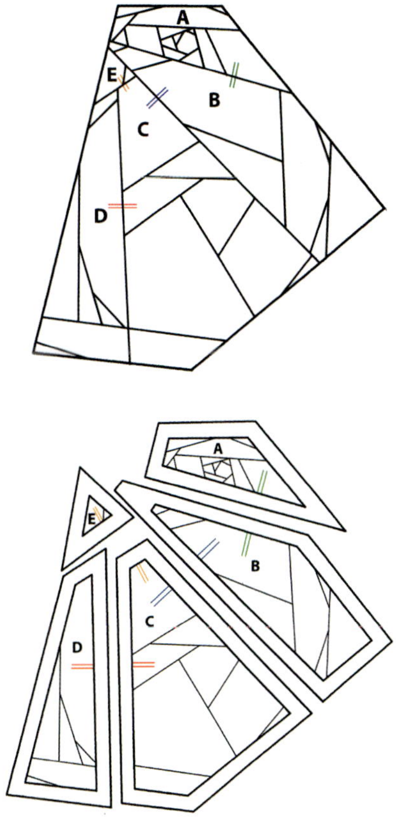

▲ Draw hash marks before separating your foundations.

LABEL 'EM AND BAG 'EM

I label each piece and make a bag for each foundation. As I cut the pieces from the fabric, I label each piece and put it into the bag for its foundation. This takes time upfront, but I'm glad I've done it when I begin sewing.

▲ Getting the right fabric in the right place is facilitated when every piece is labeled by foundation name and piece number. Stitching goes faster when pieces are sorted by foundation.

◀ The pattern for *Peace Cranes Over Hiroshima* has multiple sensitive match points when foundations are joined. I often hand baste these before final stitching.

▲ The finished design for *Bird on a Branch* includes all necessary labeling.

Seam Allowances: Their Time Has Come

Once you've labeled your foundations, it's time to separate them. Before dividing them, be sure you've marked the four necessary things: the name of each foundation, the piecing order for each foundation, the fabric for each piece, and hash marks for joining the foundations.

If working by hand, you can cut the foundations apart or you can trace them, adding space between them so you can add ¼" seam allowances. If you cut them apart, use a rotary cutter and acrylic ruler. If tracing, use a straightedge.

If you're working by computer, how you separate foundations will depend on the software you're using. Quilt-specific software may have a function that does this for you. If you use software to do this, be sure the foundation breaks are what you want. Design software may add seams in places you don't want them. Remember, every line is a seam. In most programs, you can move the lines that are the foundation breaks if they are not where you want them to be. Just be sure to keep them anchored when you move them.

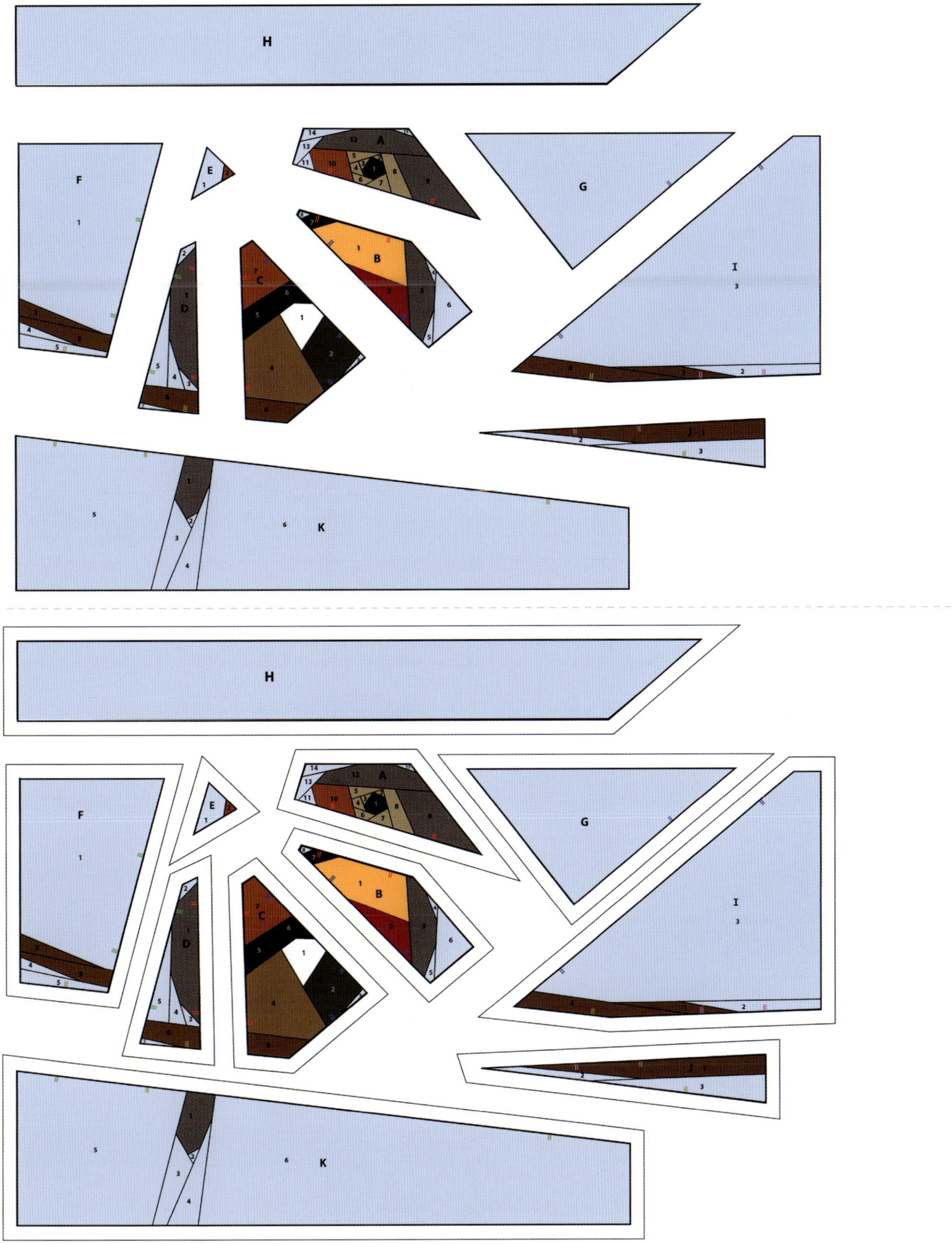

▲ Once all labeling is complete, it's time to separate the foundations and add ¼" seam allowances around all of the outside edges of each foundation.

When you've separated your foundations, add ¼" seam allowances around all the edges.

With ¼" seam allowances added, your foundations are complete.

Map Your Quilt Design

I create a map of my quilt that will be a guide to the order in which I will join the foundations. To make a foundation paper-piecing map, use one of the copies you made of your pattern. Outline the foundations. I use highlighters for this. This map should include foundation names—letters—but not piecing-order numbers, fabric notations, or hash marks.

It will be easiest if foundations can be joined in alphabetical order. For example, foundation A can be joined to foundation B, then foundations A and B can be joined to foundation C. As you draw your map, you may discover that your letter names for your foundations are not in the most logical order. Take time to rename them in the best order for piecing that avoids Y-seams. Before I begin piecing, I post my map in my sewing space so I can refer to it as I piece.

I also create a list of the order in which foundations will be pieced. I use this as a checklist as I stitch. Here's my list for *Bird on a Branch*:

- Join foundations A and B. Set aside.
- Join foundations C and D.
- Join foundation E to foundations C/D.
- Join foundations A/B and C/D/E.
- Join foundation F to A/B/C/D/E.

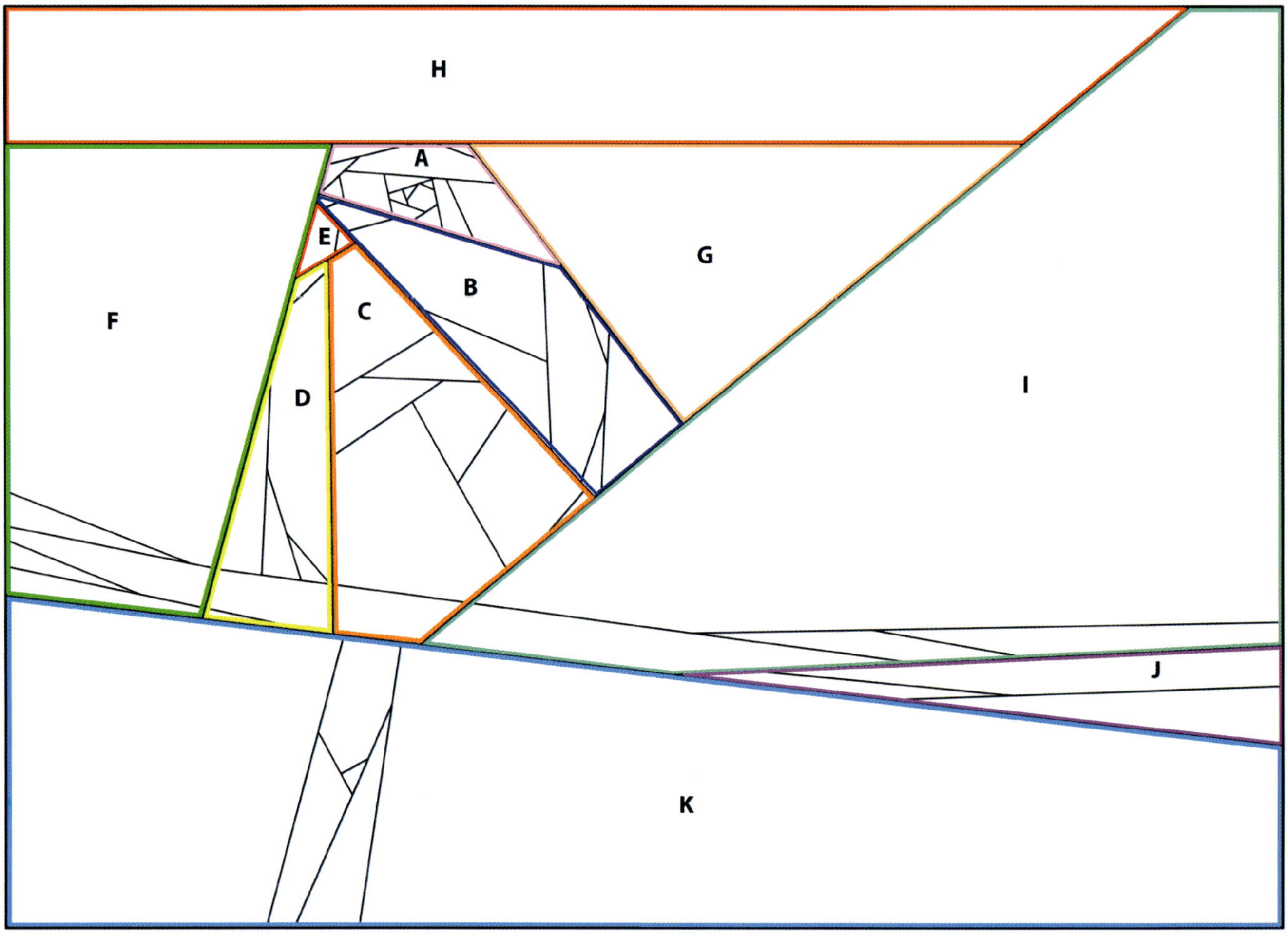

- Join foundation G to A/B/C/D/E/F.
- Join foundation H to A/B/C/D/E/F/G. Set aside.
- Join foundations I and J.
- Join foundations I/J to A/B/C/D/E/F/G/H.
- Join foundation K to A/B/C/D/E/F/G/H/I/J.

I find that the redundancy of the map and the list prevents me from piecing in an order that creates the need for Y-seams. If you find yourself needing to stitch a Y-seam when adding the next foundation, back up and rethink the order. The process you've used to design your pattern ensures you'll never need to stitch Y-seams when joining foundations.

One Final Step

With your foundations labeled and separated, you're almost ready to sew, but first, there's one more step. You need to decide what foundation material you will use. Most foundation paper piecers use paper, but you can use fabric. Options are explained in the chapter 5 subsection "Find the Right FPP Paper for You," page 104.

Don't sew on your original foundations. You'll want these as master copies if you make a mistake when piecing, and if you want to make your quilt again.

Once you've transferred your foundations to paper or other foundation of your choice, you're ready to piece your quilt. As you stitch, you may encounter design flaws here and there. Tweak your design. This is part of learning to design for FPP. Enjoy stitching as you see your first photo-inspired design come to life.

TAKE AN EXTRA QUARTER INCH

When I cut out my foundations, I cut ¼" beyond the seam allowances so I have ½" all around. When I piece my foundations, I extend the fabric to this outer edge or a bit beyond to ensure I don't come up short of the ¼" seam allowances needed to join foundations.

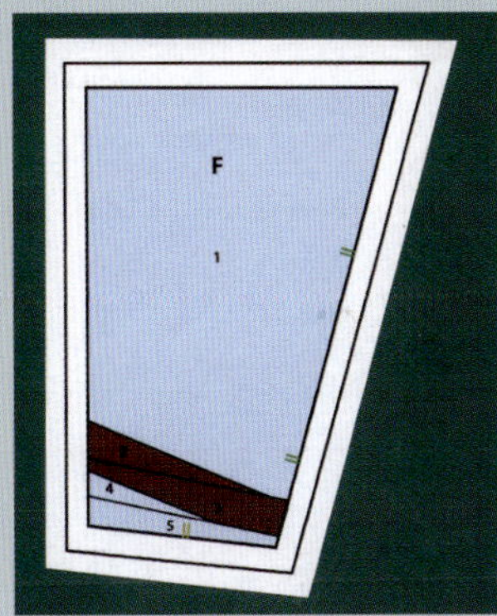

MARKING ALIGNMENT POINTS

In addition to making hash marks, you may want to identify key points to align when joining foundations. I mark these with red dots. When piecing, you can put pins through these dots to guarantee accurate alignment.

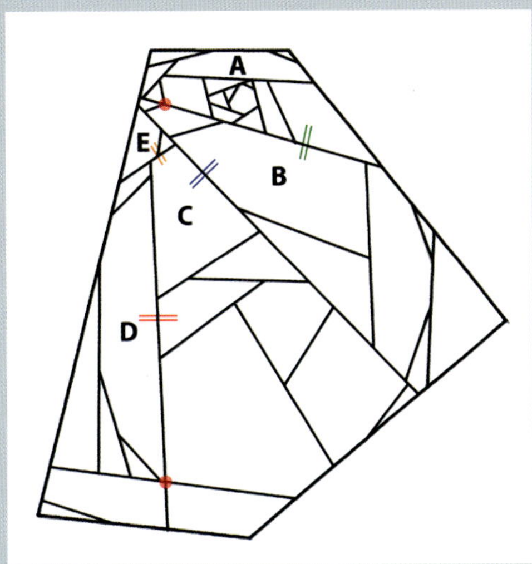

CHAPTER 5

BONUS TIPS *for* SUCCESS

YOUR PATTERN IS COMPLETE; IT'S TIME to make your quilt. Following are ideas to help you with that.

Create Cutting Templates: Efficient Fabric Use, Cutting on Grain

Many quilters have been taught to cut slabs of fabric to use for foundation paper piecing with thought only to being sure that pieces are large enough to cover the space. I prefer more precise cutting when pieces are large or will be joined at extreme angles. For these pieces, I make cutting templates because they do the following:

- facilitate efficient use of fabric,
- result in fabric pieces that are cut the shape needed, which makes aligning them easier, and
- make it possible to cut pieces on grain.

If I need to cut six or fewer pieces with a template, I make the template from freezer paper. My go-to is the kitchen variety, and I find that Reynolds brand adheres to fabric better than other brands, so it can be reused the most times. If I need to cut more than six of the same piece, I use template plastic.

To make a cutting template, follow these steps:

- Tape the foundation to a drawing surface.

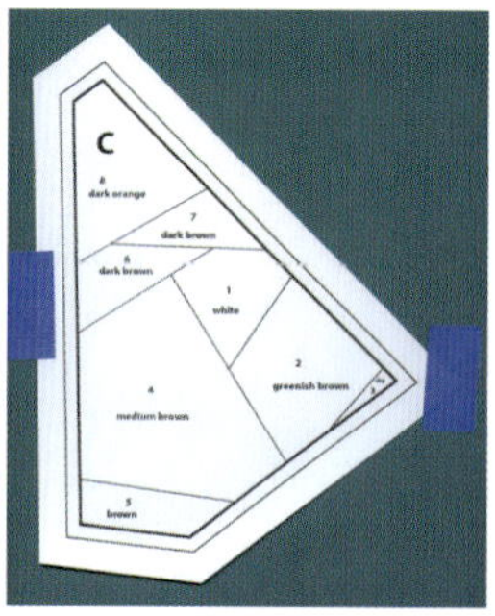

- Tape freezer paper or template plastic over the foundation. If you have a light box, use it.

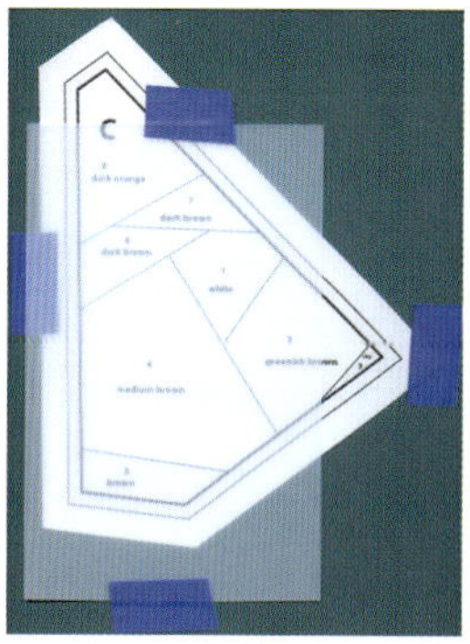

- Using a straightedge and fine-point permanent marker, trace the piece for which you want a cutting template.

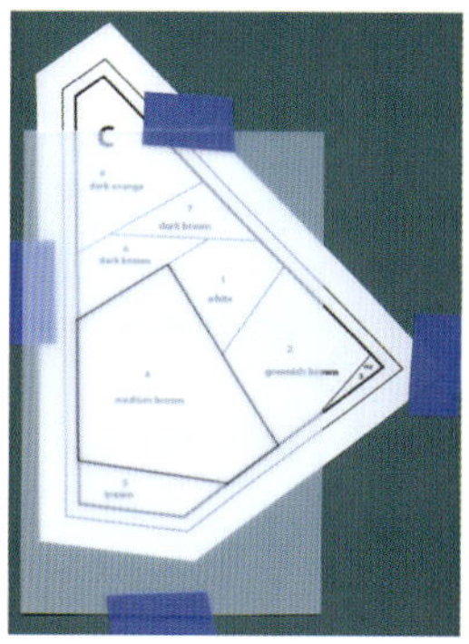

- Add ½" around all sides of the piece. Label your cutting templates with the foundation name, piece number, and fabric.

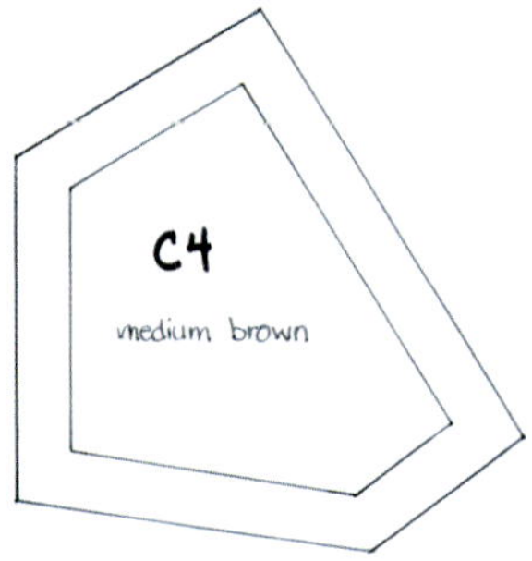

- Blunt extreme points because long points of fabric can get in your way when stitching. This needn't be precise. Remember, cutting for FPP isn't a precise process.

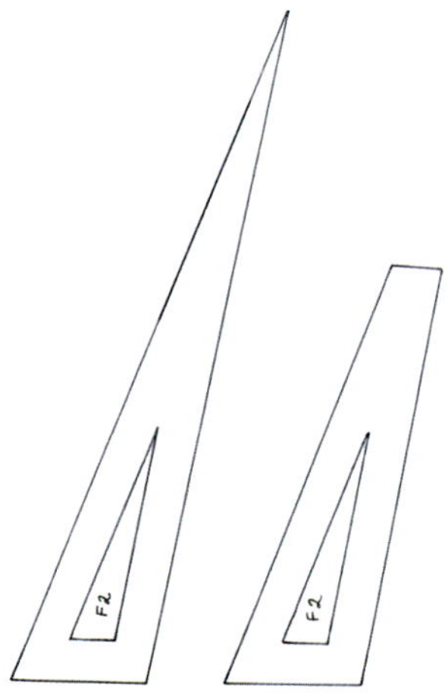

- If you're using template plastic, cut out the template using a rotary cutter fitted with an old blade. For freezer paper templates, leave ½" to 1" of paper beyond the first ½". You'll cut the extra paper off as you cut out the fabric pieces.

GO WIDER

If your pieces will be joined at extreme angles, add ¾" all around for easier alignment of such pieces.

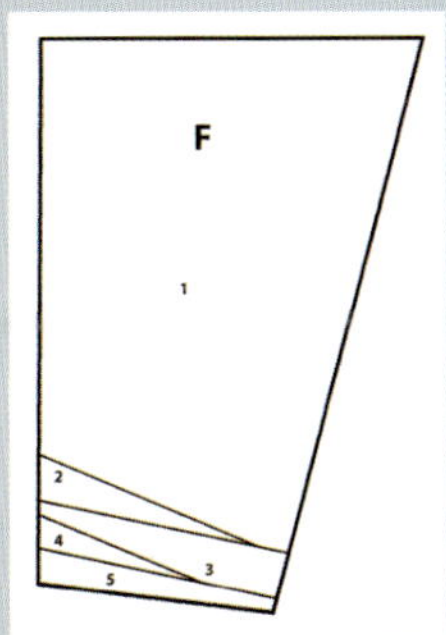

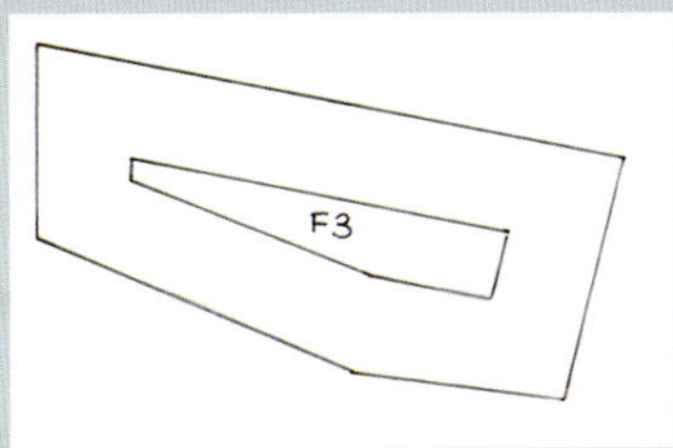

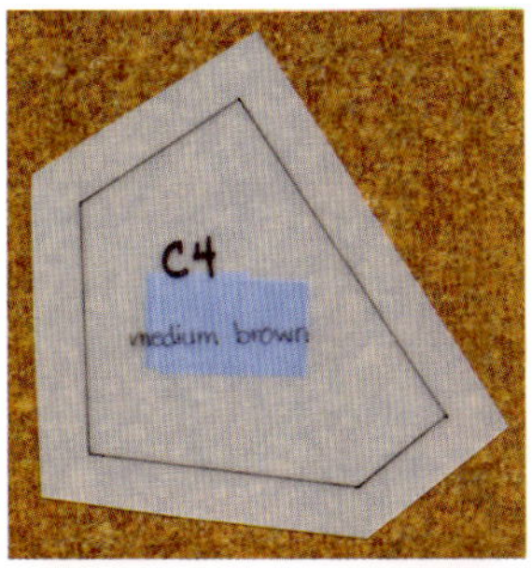

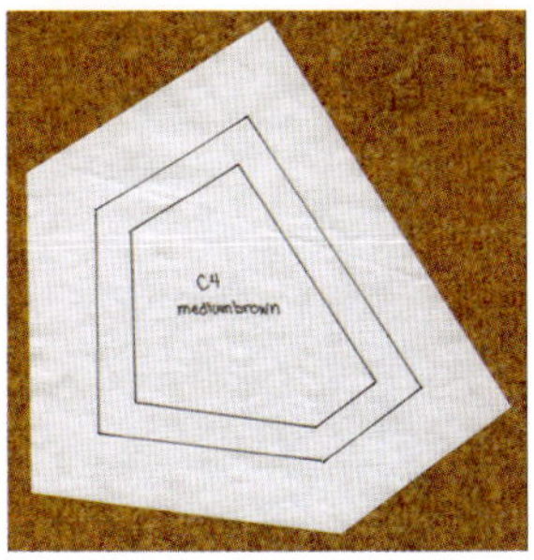

- If you make plastic templates, tape them to your fabric so they won't shift while you're cutting your pieces. Iron freezer-paper templates to your fabric.

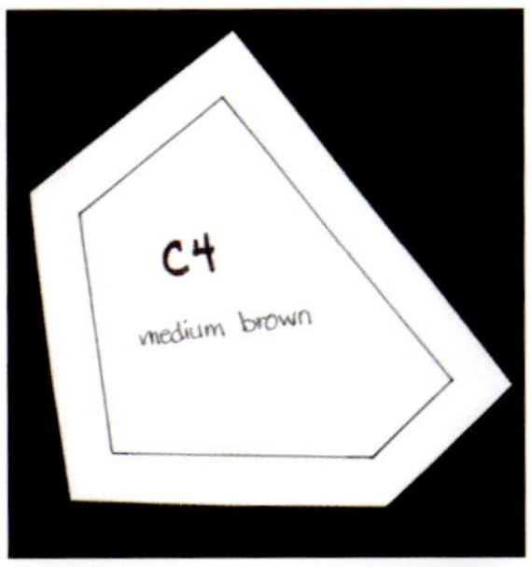

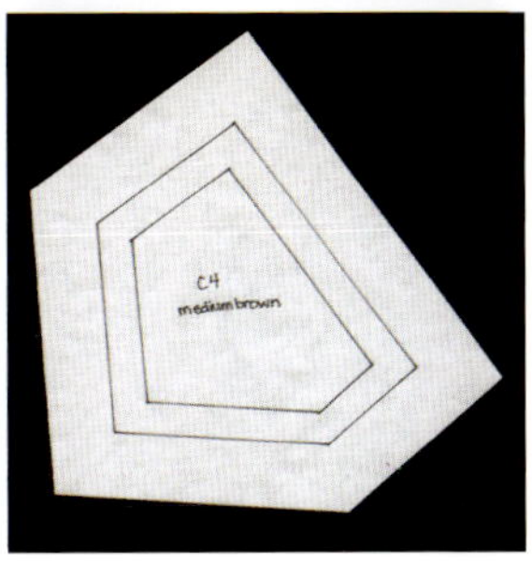

I'm often asked if the templates should be placed on the right side or wrong side of the fabric. I usually make my cutting templates from my foundations, which are the mirror image of my finished piece. This means I place the wrong side of my templates to the wrong side of the fabric.

- Using a rotary cutter and acrylic ruler, cut out your piece. Don't cut along the template plastic without an acrylic ruler. The template plastic isn't thick enough to be a cutting edge, and it's not firm enough to cut along.

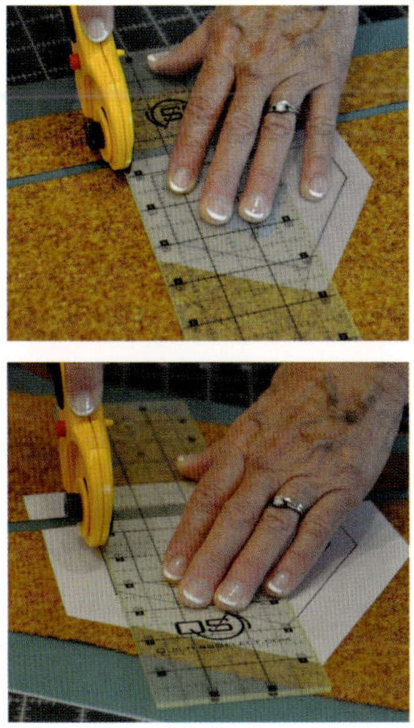

▲ Whether you're cutting out a cutting template made with template plastic (*top*) or made with freezer paper (*bottom*), cut out the fabric with a rotary cutter and acrylic ruler.

- Repeat this process for all pieces for which you want cutting templates.

A benefit of making cutting templates is being able to cut pieces on grain. This will prevent pieces from stretching when you remove the foundations. This is especially helpful for large pieces and for pieces at the edges of foundations. When the paper is removed from the foundation, edge pieces that have been cut on the bias may stretch. Cutting the edges on grain when possible will prevent this stretch.

GETTING FUSSY

Cutting templates come in handy when you want to fussy cut pieces for FPP. Unlike other FPP cutting templates, those made for pieces that will be fussy cut are best made as the piece will appear in the finished quilt rather in the mirror image. This is because this orientation makes it easier to see the image you want to fussy-cut. When using these templates, place the wrong side of the template to the right side of the fabric.

To make fussy cutting templates, draw the finished size of the piece on template plastic or freezer paper, then add ½" all around as you would for other FPP cutting templates. Use the template to isolate the image you want to fussy cut. Be sure the image falls inside the finished size outline and not into the ½" area. That way, none of the image will be lost in the seam allowances. If you plan to cut multiple identical pieces, draw the outline of the fussy-cut image on the template. This facilitates cutting identical pieces.

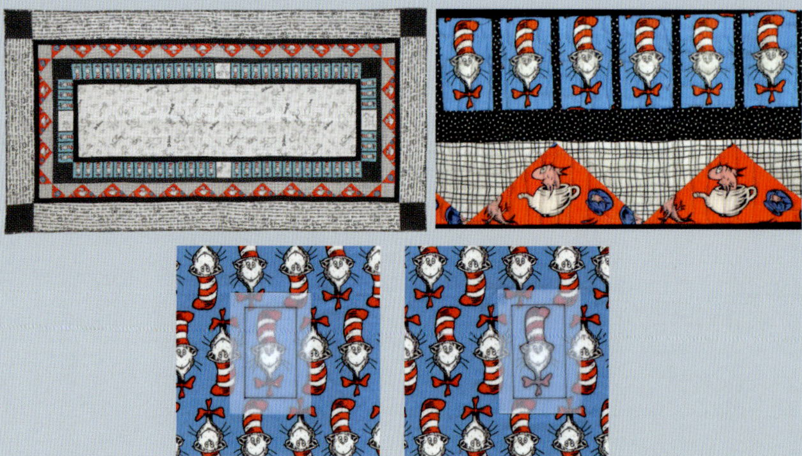

▲ When I designed and made *Black and White and Read All Over*, 41" x 83", 2011, I foundation paper pieced the borders of the Cat in the Hat faces. To get them to line up, I fussy cut each piece using a cutting template on which I drew the outline of the image I wanted in the center of each piece. I did the same for the fish-in-a-bowl triangular pieces. Quilted by ZJ Humbach

Similar stretching can happen over the life of the quilt, especially if it is a wall hanging. This can lead to ripples in your quilt. Cutting edges on grain can reduce stretch, as can tight quilting.

Once you've made your cutting templates, add a grain line. Find the longest outside edge. This is the optimal edge to cut on grain. I draw grain lines as straight lines with crossbars on each end.

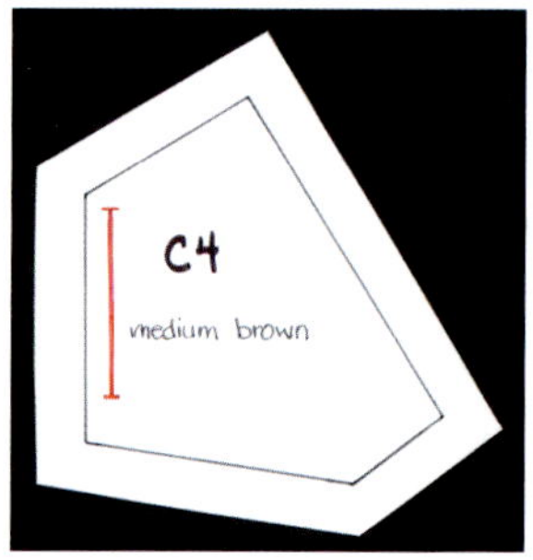

When I cut pieces, I align the grain lines with either the warp or weft grain. The warp grain will stretch a bit less, but either alignment will be preferable to an outside edge cut on a bias.

It's Time to Piece: Tools to Use

I admit I'm a tool junkie. Finding the right tools for foundation paper piecing is a continual journey for me. There are some I can't live without.

Find the Right FPP Paper for You

I often hear quilters say they don't like to foundation paper piece because they don't like tearing off the paper. My first question to these quilters is this: What foundation paper are you using? Their answers vary, but the common denominator is that they are using paper that was never intended to be used for FPP. If you find removing the paper tedious, it may be worth investing in paper that has been created for FPP because these papers have been engineered to make removing the paper easy.

I have favorite papers. At the top of my list is C&T Publishing's Simple Foundations Translucent Vellum paper or other heat-resistant translucent vellum. I like this paper because you can see through it, which makes fabric placement quick and accurate, and it tears off easily and cleanly. Don't confuse this paper with vellum that is heat sensitive. Simple Foundations Translucent Vellum was engineered to withstand the heat of your iron and the heat that is generated in printers and copy machines. It won't melt or pucker from heat. If it curls a bit when ironed, don't worry. When this happens, it doesn't distort your foundation or damage your iron.

Because this paper is translucent, you can trace patterns onto it without a light box. If you prefer to print or copy your foundations, use a laser printer. If you use an inkjet printer, you risk having the ink iron off onto your fabric because the ink sits on the surface of this paper. Vellum papers that are not heat sensitive generally can be used in commercial copy machines. Check the packaging of these papers to determine if they will be safe for copy machine use. Copy your foundations onto this paper with your home printer only if it's a laser printer.

If you copy your foundations at a copy shop, take the paper's packaging with you to share with staff at the shop. Heat-sensitive vellums can melt in copy machines, doing costly damage. You may need to show the staff that this paper is copier safe. This paper is usually 8½" × 11".

My second go-to paper is Carol Doak's Foundation Paper, also produced by C&T Publishing. This newsprint foundation is lightweight and designed for use with inkjet or laser printers and copy machines. Ink from this paper generally won't transfer onto your fabric or iron, but it's always good to test this.

Unlike most other newsprint, this paper won't shrink, curl, or turn brittle. It tears away easily and leaves only a few shards of paper, unlike other newsprint papers, which can leave many shards. You'll need tweezers to remove paper from small pieces only occasionally and only in the tightest corners. If you are copying your foundations onto this paper at a commercial copy shop, take the packaging with you to share with the staff. Newsprint tends to jam in copy machines. This paper won't jam, and the packaging says that. This paper comes in two sizes: 8½" × 11" and 8½" × 14" (legal size).

When I need to make foundations larger than the papers recommended here, I turn to kitchen-variety freezer paper. This paper is getting harder to find, so when you see it, buy it. Working with this paper requires hand drawing your foundations, but the work required to do this is more than compensated for by the ease of stitching large foundations on freezer paper.

A key challenge when stitching large foundations is having large fabric pieces flop back into your stitching lines, a mistake that requires unstitching and restitching. Because freezer paper can be pressed to adhere to your fabric, you don't have to pin pieces in place to prevent the

fabric from folding back into the seam line. When you press the fabric to the glossy side of the freezer paper, the fabric stays in place as you stitch the next piece to your foundation.

Some foundation paper piecers like to use freezer paper for all foundations. Commercial 8½" × 11" sheets of such paper are available. Many of these can be used in printers. I find most of these bulky, but my best quilt bud swears by such paper, and her quilts come out great.

There are wash-away foundation papers and foundation papers and fabric that you can leave in your quilts. These are especially good if you are working with larger pieces—4" × 4" and up.

I recommend you try a variety of papers and other materials to find your favorites. You'll discover that one type of foundation doesn't fit all projects.

Pin for Perfection

While most kinds of pins can be used to hold fabric and foundations together, it's best to use pins that lie flat so they don't distort your fabric. My choice is Iris Superfein pins. These are dressmaker's pins with small heads. If you prefer larger heads, look for pins that have very flat heads and fine shafts. Two possibilities are IBC flat flower-head pins and Clover's flower-head pins for sheer/lightweight fabrics. Avoiding distortion of your fabric from bulky pins is especially important when you are working with small pieces.

Some foundation paper piecers use glue instead of pins. Any washable glue stick will work. Glue sticks made specifically for quilters are smaller, so they give you more control. Check these out if you want to try gluing instead of pinning. Go light with the glue, so it doesn't make removing the paper difficult.

Sharp Needles Last Longer

When you stitch on paper, your machine needles dull faster than when doing traditional piecing, so you'll need to change them more often. My favorite needles are Chrome Professional Microtex needles. They are sharper and stronger than other needles, so they last longer. They cost more than other needles, but since you can use them longer, I find the cost balances out.

Many FPP instructors recommend size 90/14 needles because their thicker shafts make larger holes in the paper, which makes it easier to tear the paper off. These needles also make larger holes in the fabric, so they aren't my choice. I prefer size 70/10, but they don't work well with needle threaders on many sewing machines. A good middle choice is size 80/12. I recommend trying Chrome Professional Microtex in several sizes toward finding your happy place.

Miracle Rulers: Add-A-Quarter and Add-An-Eighth

Carolyn Cullinan McCormick's Add-A-Quarter and Add-An-Eighth rulers are among my most prized quilting tools. I own them in multiple sizes and colors. These ingenious rulers have a lip on one long edge that can be wedged into the seam line ditch when you fold your paper back. Cutting along them gives you a consistent ¼" or ⅛" seam allowance. I find myself using both sizes, but especially the Add-An-Eighth ruler, because I tend to work with small pieces that need seams cut narrower than ¼".

These rulers come in their original design, which has the lip on one long edge, and in a "Plus" version, which has the lip on one long edge and a tapered edge on the other long edge. The tapered edge can be used to fold back your paper before you trim your seams. These rulers are available in many quilt shops and directly from Carolyn's company, CM Designs. The hardest model to find in quilt shops is the 9" Add-An-Eighth ruler. I find I use this ruler more often than its 6" cousin. Ask your local shop if they can get the longer one for you or order it from CM Designs.

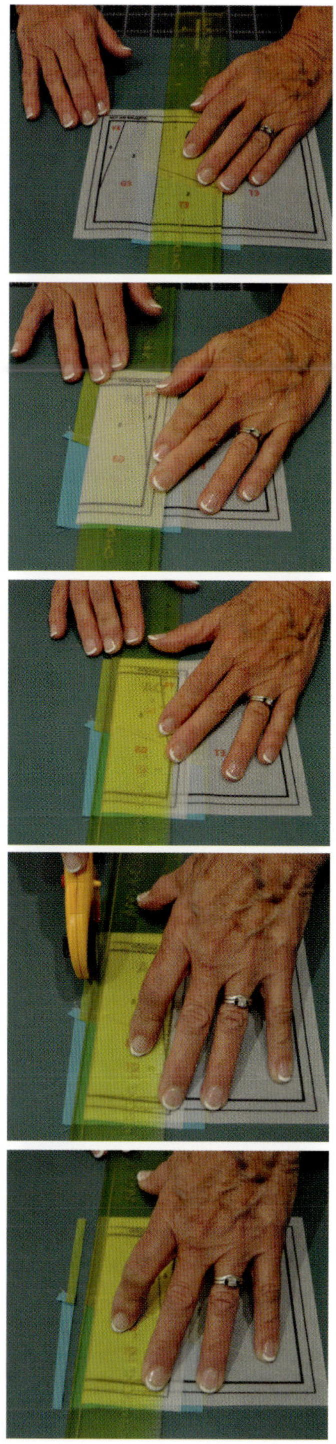

▲ Place the tapered edge of an Add-A-Quarter or Add-An-Eighth ruler in the just-stitched seam line and fold the paper back against it. Then place the lip of an Add-A-Quarter or Add-An-Eighth ruler in the seam ditch to cut an even width seam allowance. Trim the seam.

Thread: So Many Choices

The ever-increasing array of threads can leave your head spinning, but for FPP, don't fret. Whatever thread you use for other piecing will work for foundation paper piecing. A neutral color—beige or gray—is often fine, but take a minute to notice if your thread is showing when you press your seams. When I'm working with dark fabrics, I often opt for a darker thread to ensure I don't see my stitches. While I don't experience this problem with traditional piecing, I do experience it when foundation paper piecing.

When you are joining two pieces of fabric and are concerned the thread will show when you press your seams, choose thread that is the color of the darker of the two fabrics.

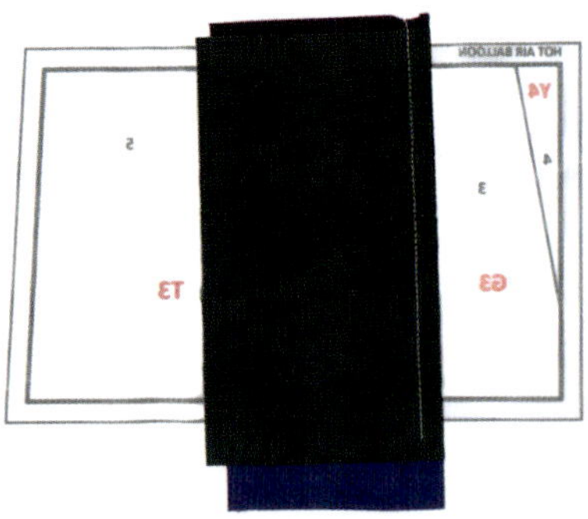

Pressing Matters, Really Matters

When foundation paper piecing, press as you go, piece by piece, after each piece is added. You often don't get a second chance to press a seam because it gets stitched into place when you add the next piece. If you are casual about pressing your pieces out, you risk getting tucks in your seam lines that will get stitched down when you add the next piece. The only way to recover from this is unstitching and restitching. In the long run, you'll save time and frustration if you press as you go.

There are tools that can assist you in this goal. Wool pressing mats have become the rage among quilters for good reason. They pull the heat from your iron away from the fabric. This allows you to lift your iron from the fabric with less concern that your fabric will revert to its unpressed position as it cools.

Use a wooden clapper—a tool borrowed from the tailoring industry—in combination with a wool mat for optimal pressing. The wool absorbs the heat from below your fabric while the wood absorbs the heat from the top of your fabric. In selecting a clapper, consider the comfort of the clapper in your hand and the weight of the clapper. I find that heavy clappers work best but may be difficult for quilters with arthritis to use. Lighter ones will do the job.

When foundation paper piecing, it's important to start with well-pressed fabric because you risk stitching wrinkles into your quilt that cannot be pressed out later. I use one of the several spray products that remove wrinkles from fabric, then I starch my fabric. Using starch is a personal choice. I prewash my fabrics, so I find I piece better when I've starched my fabric.

One last thing on pressing: Don't use steam. Your paper won't like it, and you're likely to stretch your fabric because FPP pieces are often pieced on the bias.

Light Up Your Work

Because I come from a publishing background, I have long used a light box in my work. Using one when quilting comes naturally. When foundation paper piecing, I use a light box for several tasks. The first is when I'm designing. Although working with translucent vellum overlays removes the need to always have a light box under my inspiration photo, I often find it useful to work on one. This is especially true when color gradations in my inspiration photo are subtle or the quality of the photo isn't top-notch. When I need to reverse my designs to create the mirror image, I go to the light box.

I also use my light box when piecing. Except when working with very dark fabrics, I put my foundations and fabrics on my light box to align the next piece. This saves holding my foundations up to the light and squinting to see the seam lines or having to fold back the fabric and trim it to align it with the next piece.

If you don't have a light box or you're working on a piece that is larger than your light box, you can use a plate glass window. This is a daytime activity, but even on overcast days, you'll usually have ample light.

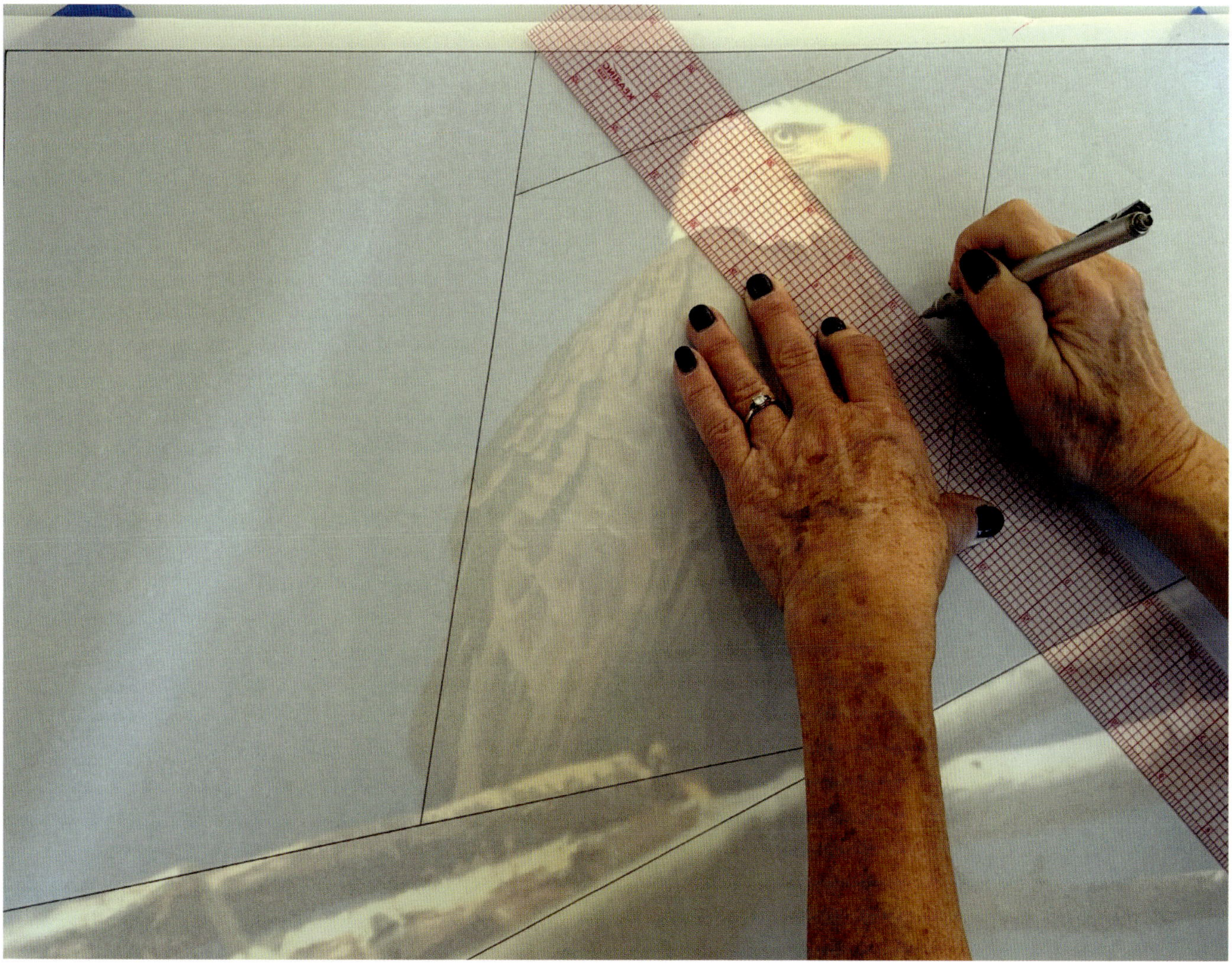

▲ Working on a light box makes it easier to see details in an inspiration photo.

GALLERY *of* AUTHOR'S WORK

When a quilt instructor opened a class by asking us to identify our quilting superpowers, I instantly had my answer: foundation paper piecing. I like the precision FPP facilitates. I like the extreme angles, sharp points, and narrow and small pieces that FPP makes it easy to piece. I especially like the design process, followed by seeing those images come to life in fabric. The next few pages feature a half dozen of the quilts I've designed and pieced. They include block quilts; abstract imagery; and a pictorial image of one of my favorite flowers, an iris, which I photographed in my sister's garden.

My thanks to the talented long-arm quilters who quilted my quilts: Rita Meyerhoff, Crystal Wentz, and Barbara Lloyd. My thanks also to the equally talented crew at Assist Art Services in Littleton, Colorado—including David Chambers, who photographed the quilts; Sean Tracey, who color-corrected and perfected the images; and Jacob Wallace, who coordinated this work.

I hope my creations will inspire you as you design your own unique FPP patterns and quilts.

▲ *Don't Call Me Girl (a.k.a Barbie Quilt)*, 48" x 48", 2023, designed and pieced by Dana E. Jones, quilted by Rita Meyerhoff

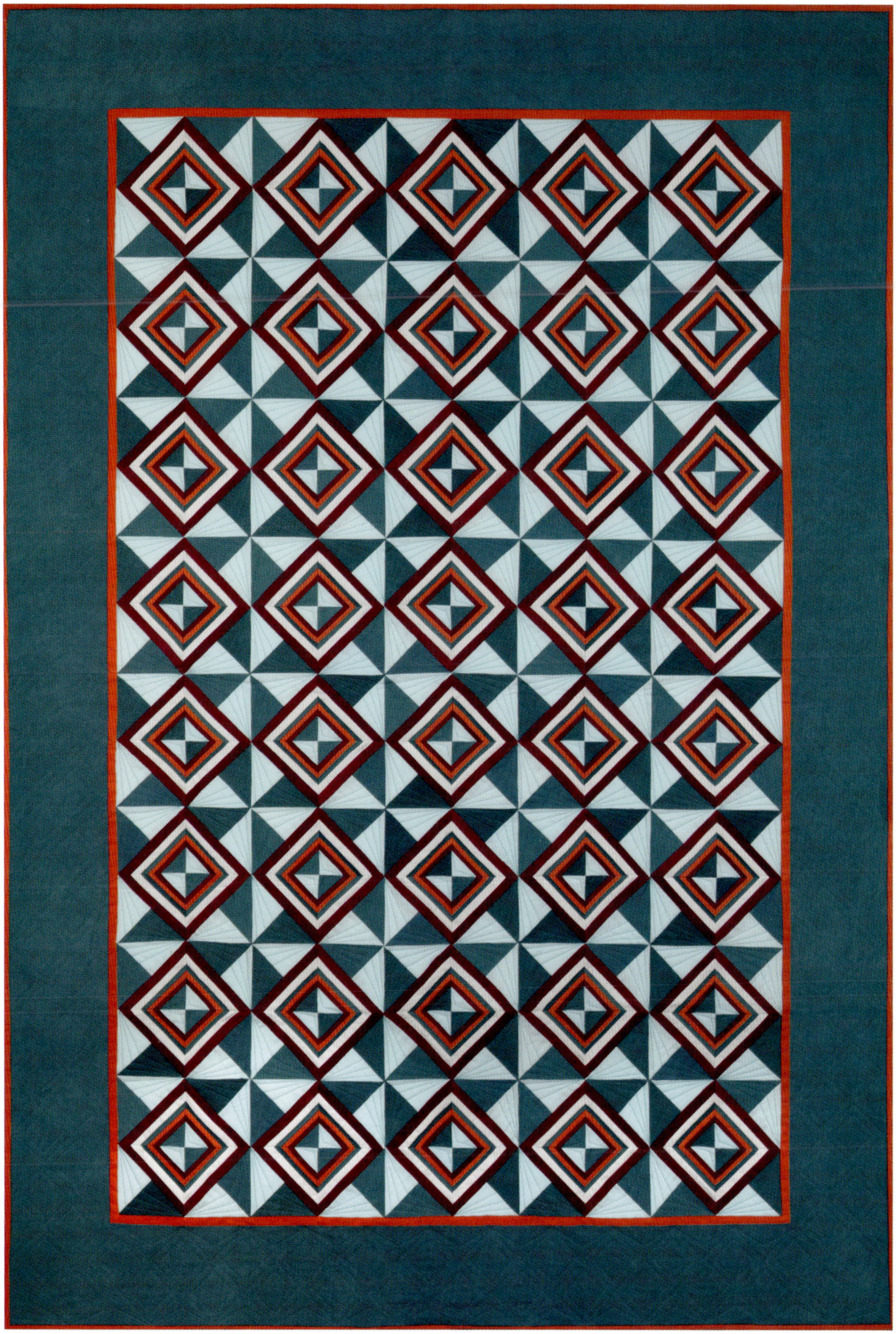

▲ *Avs & Orange*, 53" x 77", 2025, designed and pieced by Dana E. Jones, quilted by Crystal Wentz, Meadow Lane Stitching

▲ *Weave,* 61" x 72," 2025, designed and pieced by Dana E. Jones, quilted by Barbara Lloyd, Dancing Needles Quilting, Severance, Colorado

▲ *Warp Speed*, 62" x 62", 2023, designed and pieced by Dana E. Jones, quilted by Rita Meyerhoff

▲ *Gravitational Pull*, 34" x 52", 2026, designed and pieced by Dana E. Jones, quilted by Rita Meyerhoff

▲ *Purple Lightning*, 38" x 52", 2026, designed and pieced by Dana E. Jones, quilted by Rita Meyerhoff

GALLERY *of* STUDENTS' WORK

IT IS OFTEN SAID THAT WE LEARN BEST WHEN TEACHING OTHERS. This is definitely my experience as I work with those who take my FPP design classes.

Quilt Block Designs

Designing blocks is a great way to learn to design for foundation paper piecing. I'm always amazed at the creative blocks made by those who take my classes on designing for FPP. Here are some examples. *Photos by Assist Art Services, David Chambers photographer, Sean Tracey color correction*

▲ Morning, 5½" × 5½", 2023, by Debbie Legiadre, South Carolina

▲ Stardust, 12½" × 12½", 2022, by Linda Billard, Virgina

▲ Rays of Sunshine, 12" × 12", 2025, by Esther Kleinkauf, Idaho

▲ Anchors Away 1, 8½" × 8½", 2024, by Karen VanWinkle, Texas

▲ Anchors Away 2, 8½" × 8½", 2024, by Karen VanWinkle, Texas

▲ Untitled, 9" × 9", 2023, by Sandra Reinke, Colorado

▲ Spin Cycle, 7½" × 7½", 2024, by Vicki Zerfoss, EB Quilts Company, Virginia

▲ Dressed to the Nines, 12" × 12", 2024, designed by Lynda Tavernini, Alberta, Canada, and pieced by Kristi Stimson, Alberta, Canada

▲ Hootie, 15¼" × 15¼", 2024, by Robin Beattie, Colorado

► Diamond in the Rough, 10" × 8½", 2022, by Sue Ewing, Colorado

▲ Teal Time, 6" × 6", 2024, by Lynda Tavernini, Alberta, Canada

▲ Converging Geese, 10½" × 10½", 2024, by Jana Lipscomb, Oklahoma

▲ Peaks, 6" × 6", 2024, by Gail E. Mickelwait, Virginia

Blocks designed by my students look stunning in their quilts. Joan Duncan's *Untitled* and Linda Billard's *Sagittarius A* are two examples.

▲ *Untitled,* 49" × 49", 2023, by Joan Duncan, Colorado. For the back of her quilt, Joan used skills from class to piece a traditional Palm Leaf design. Joan frequently makes two-sided quilts.

▲ *Sagittarius A*, 31" × 31", 2022, by Linda Billard, shows the incredible overall designs possible when FPP blocks are twisted and turned for impact.

Pictorial Quilts

Once you understand the Paper Police rules for FPP design, you're ready to create a quilt inspired by a photograph. Those who take my Demystifying Design for Foundation Paper Piecing class do beautiful work.

▼ *Iris*, 15" × 19", 2024, by Barbara Skimin, Michigan

▲ *Kingfisher*, 11½" × 17", 2021, by Linda Billard, Virginia

▲ *Calla Lily*, 10½" × 14½", 2022, by Mary Arter, California

▲ *Hill Country Roadrunner*, 21" × 16", 2025, by Betsy McConnell, Texas

► *Spring Blooms*, 23" × 23", 2024, by Vicki Zerfoss, EB Quilts Company, Virginia

▲ *Zebra in Teal*, 16" × 24", 2022, by Debbie Legiadre, South Carolina. Debbie mounted this quilt on stretchers for ease in hanging it on a wall.

◀ *Ye Olde Tree*, 13½" × 18", 2024, by Sandra Reinke, Colorado

▲ *Mr. Skull*, 16" × 16", 2024, by Emily Kaiser, Missouri

◀ *Red Brick House*, 34" × 28½", 2022, by Vicki Zerfoss, EB Quilts Company, Virginia

▲ *Pegasus*, 46½" × 48", 2022, by Peggy Natoli, North Carolina

▲ *One Badass Bird*, 42" × 54", 2023, by Robin Beattie, Colorado. This stellar quilt took first place in art quilts at the 2023 Colorado State Fair.

PATTERNS *for* QUILT BLOCKS

Cool Star Block

Size: 12" × 12"

Designed by Dana E. Jones

The Cool Star block is made with four pieced half-square triangles. It's a good example of how to create extreme points when foundation paper piecing. Set the block on point for a more dramatic look.

Cool Star Block

12" × 12"

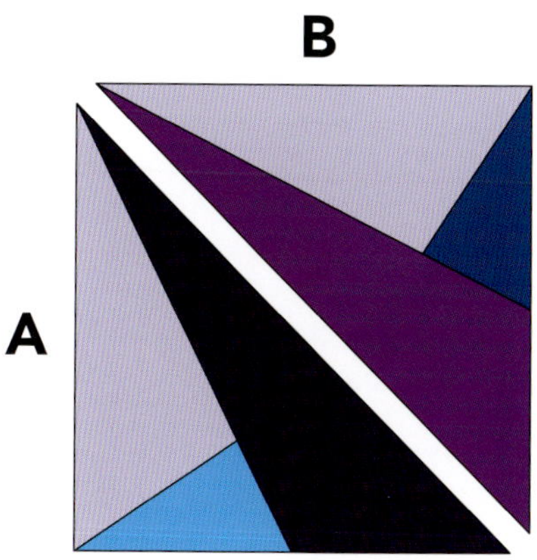

A/B Unit Assembly

Make 4

Press seams open

Cool Star Assembly

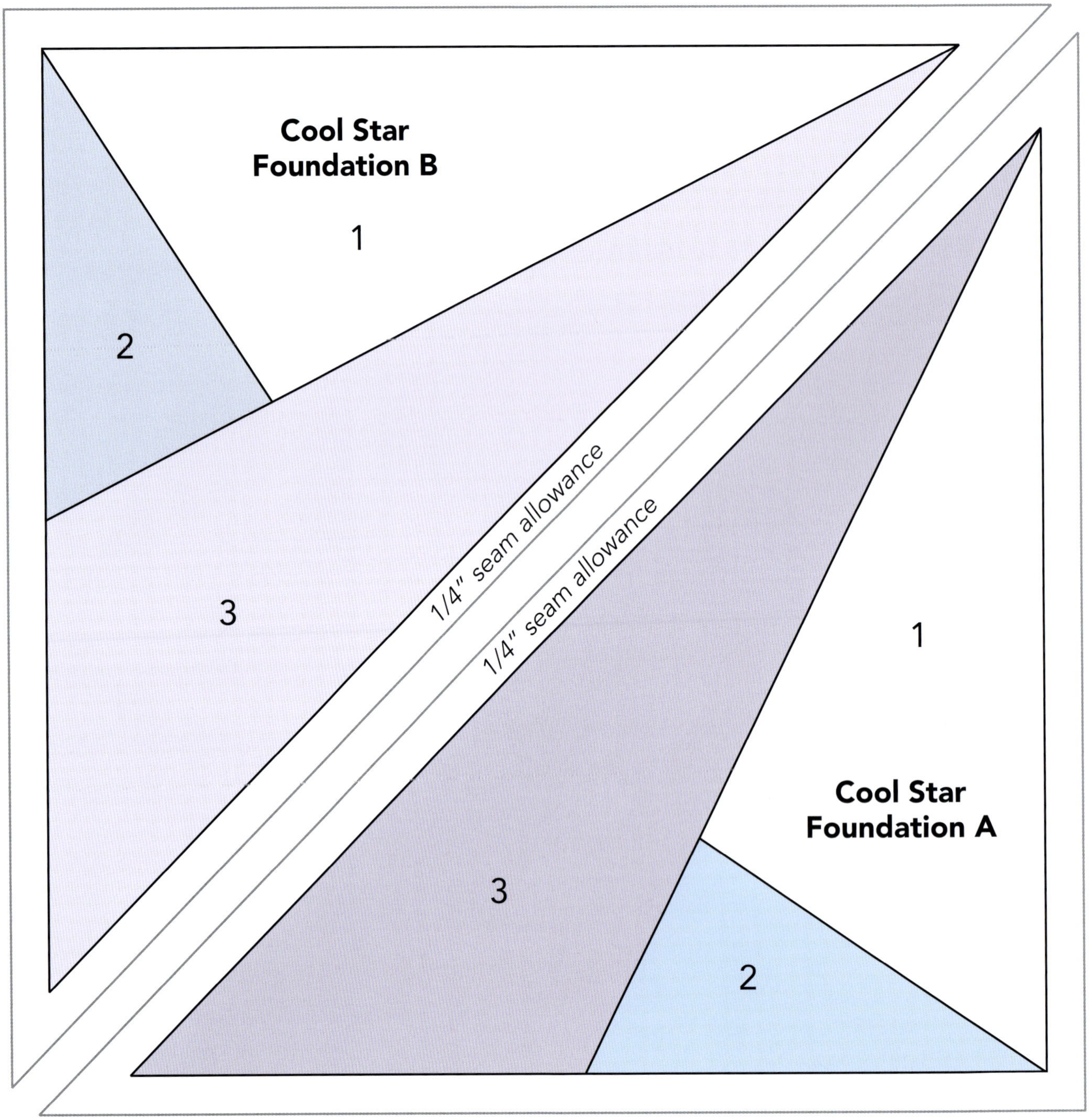

1 inch

Print Check

Foundations must print at 100 percent. When printing, choose none, actual size or 100 percent. Double-check the accuracy of your printout by measuring the 1″ print check with a ruler.

Avs & Orange Block

Size: 8" × 8"

Designed by Dana E. Jones

Like the Cool Star block, the Avs & Orange block is made from four pieced half-square triangles. It shows how easy it is to piece narrow strips with precision when foundation paper piecing. When multiple Avs & Orange blocks are joined in a quilt, the block appears to be set on point even though it is actually straight set. This is because of the use of diagonal lines in the design. Use of light and dark values in the corners creates a sense of motion, making the block appear to be spinning.

After I selected the teal and maroon fabrics for the block, I knew another color was needed. I selected orange, and it brought the block to life. The teal and maroon are team colors for the Colorado Avalanche, my favorite hockey team. The orange is a nod to my alma mater, the University of Illinois.

Avs & Orange Block

8" × 8"

Foundation A

Make 2

Foundations B and C

Make 2

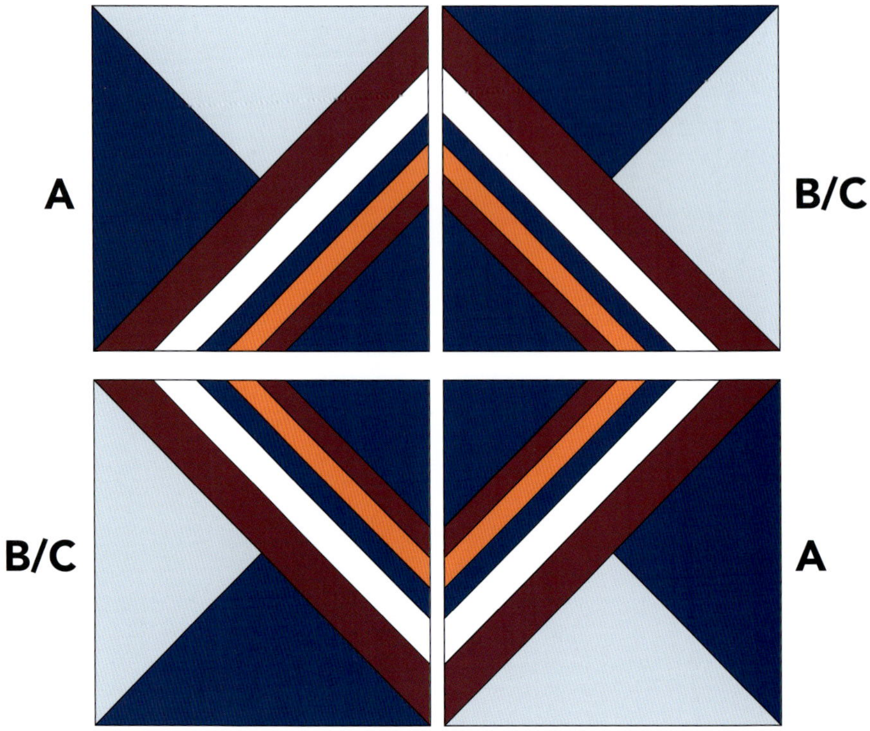

Avs & Orange Assembly

1 inch

Print Check

Foundations must print at 100 percent. When printing, choose none, actual size or 100 percent. Double-check the accuracy of your printout by measuring the 1″ print check with a ruler.

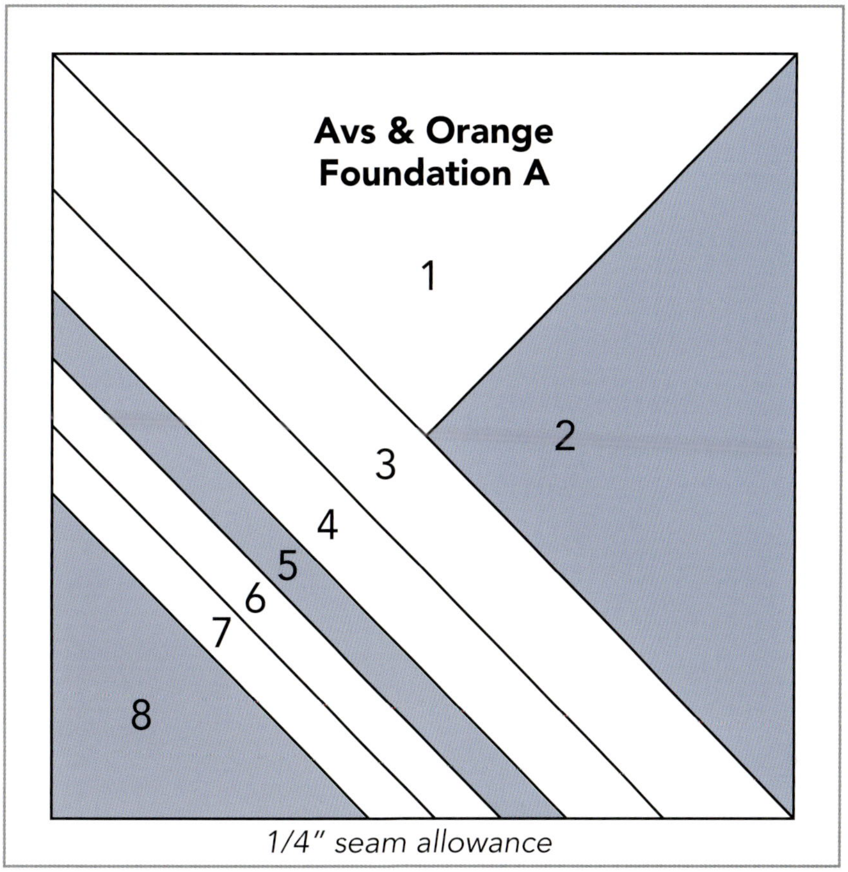

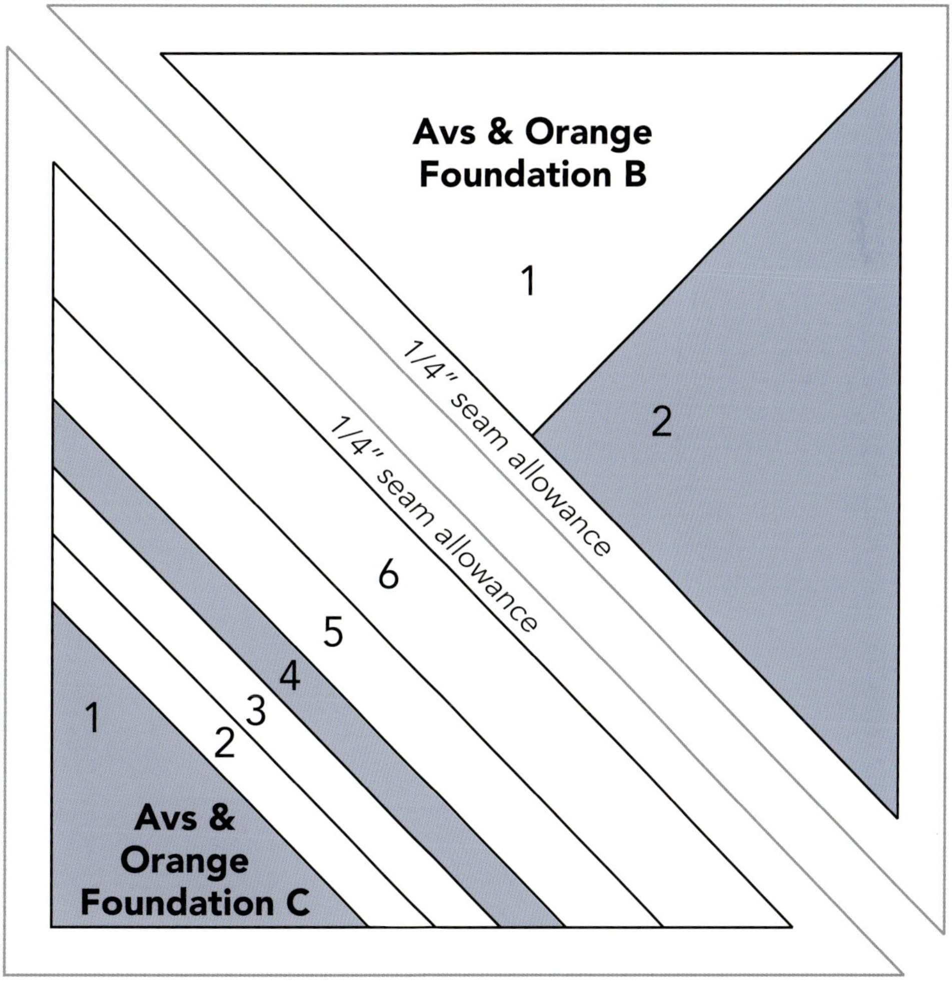

Overpass Block

Size: 8" × 6"

Designed by Dana E. Jones

The Overpass block, like the Avs & Orange block, shows the ease in piecing narrow strips when foundation paper piecing. To make Overpass, you'll piece five foundations, but note that foundation A repeats top and bottom and foundation B repeats side to side. Geometric blocks often have foundations that are used multiple times. When Overpass blocks are joined into a quilt top, strong diagonals are created throughout the quilt.

Overpass Block

8" × 6"

A/B Unit Assembly

Make 2

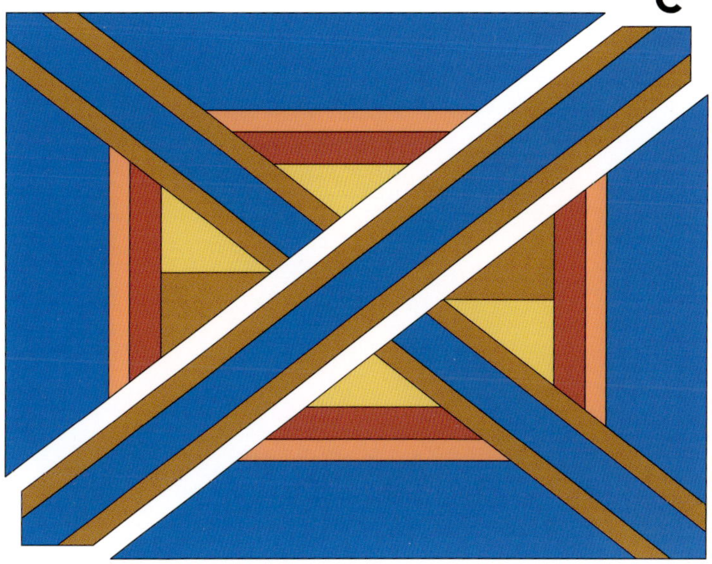

Overpass Assembly

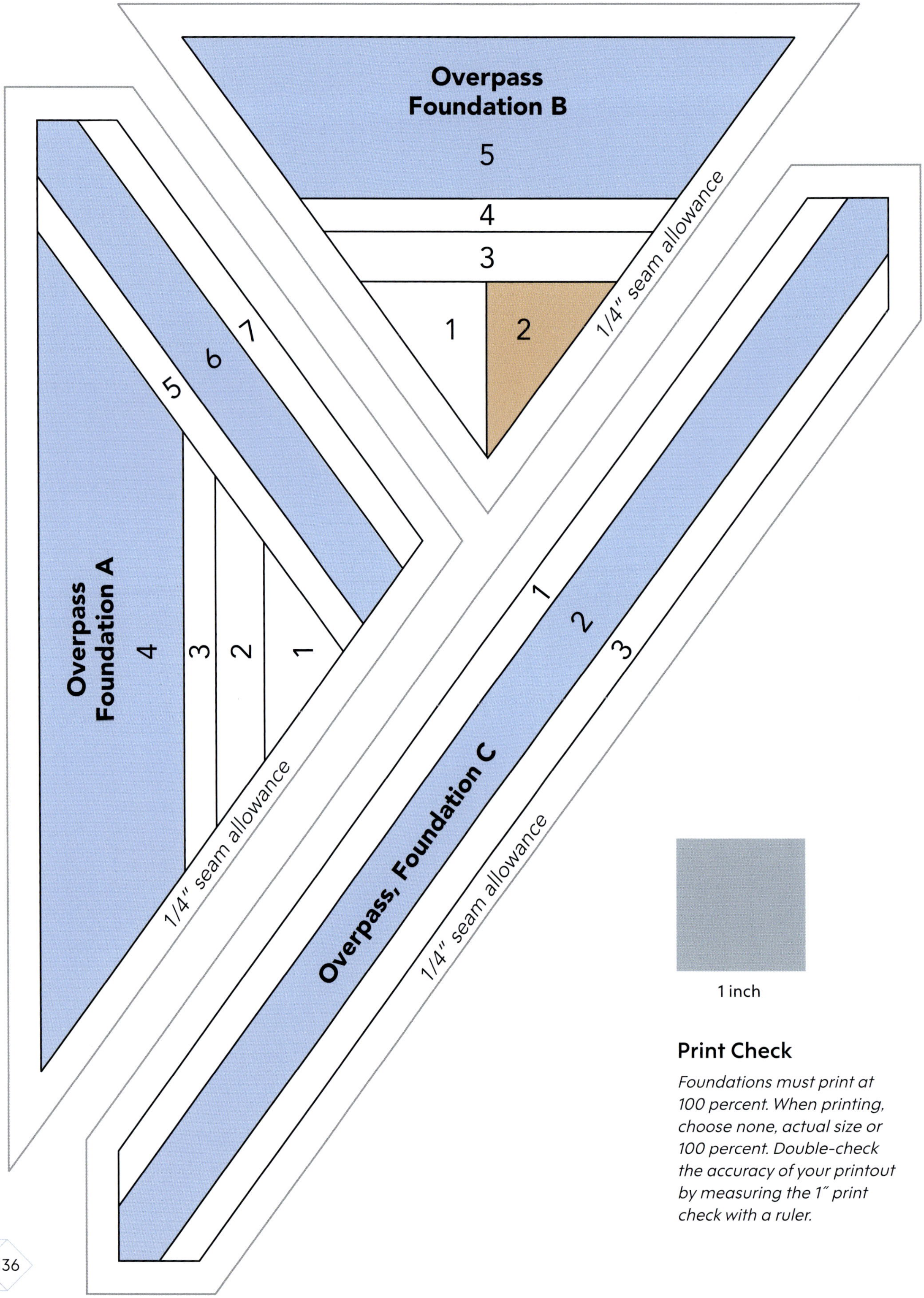

1 inch

Print Check

Foundations must print at 100 percent. When printing, choose none, actual size or 100 percent. Double-check the accuracy of your printout by measuring the 1″ print check with a ruler.

Weave Block

Size: 12" × 12"

Designed by Dana E. Jones

The Weave block requires more foundations than the other blocks patterned in this book, and it requires partial seaming when joining the foundations. This extra step maintains the appearance that the pattern has been woven. Don't confuse partial seaming with Y-seams. The illustrations here show you how to stitch the partial seam, which is easier than stitching a Y-seam. The woven effect continues across the quilt surface when multiple Weave blocks are joined in a quilt top.

Weave Block

12" × 12"

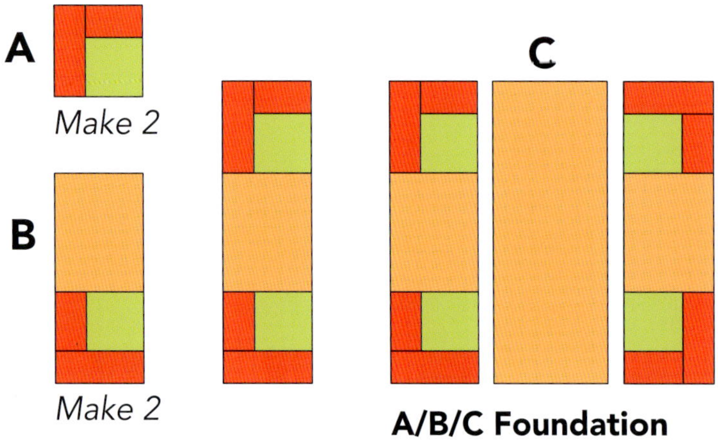

A/B/C Foundation Unit Assembly

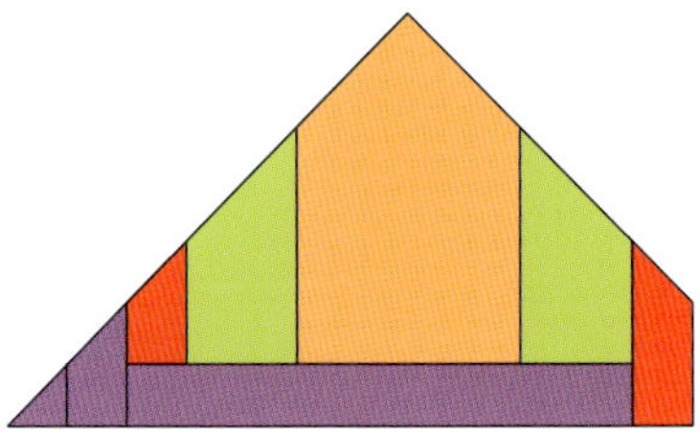

D Foundation

Make 4

Weave Assembly

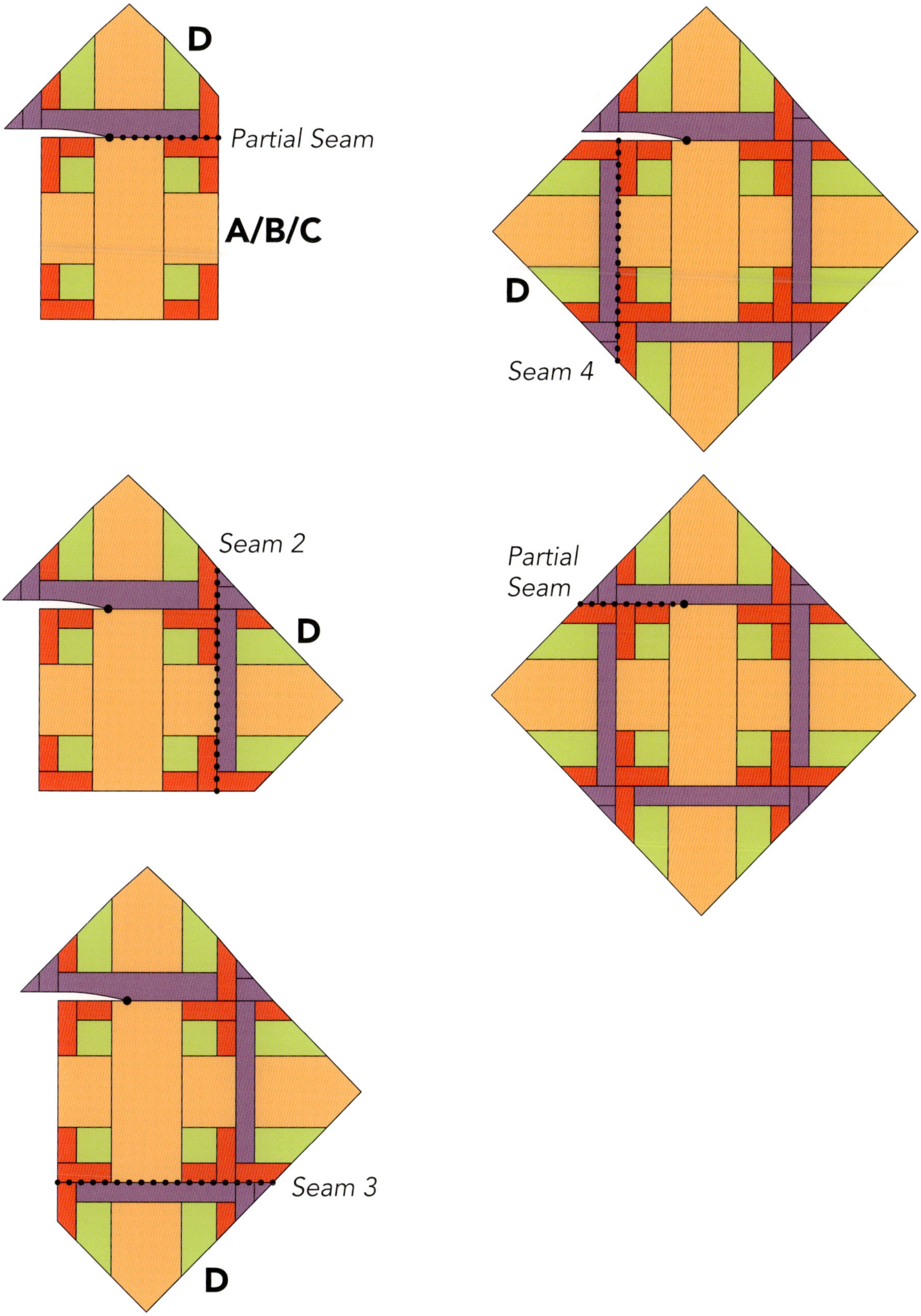

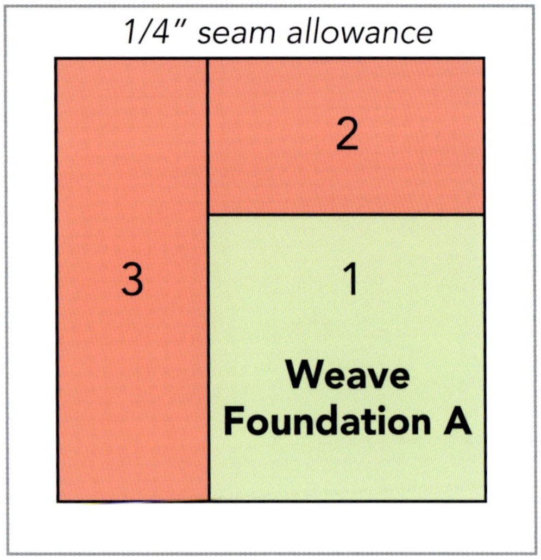

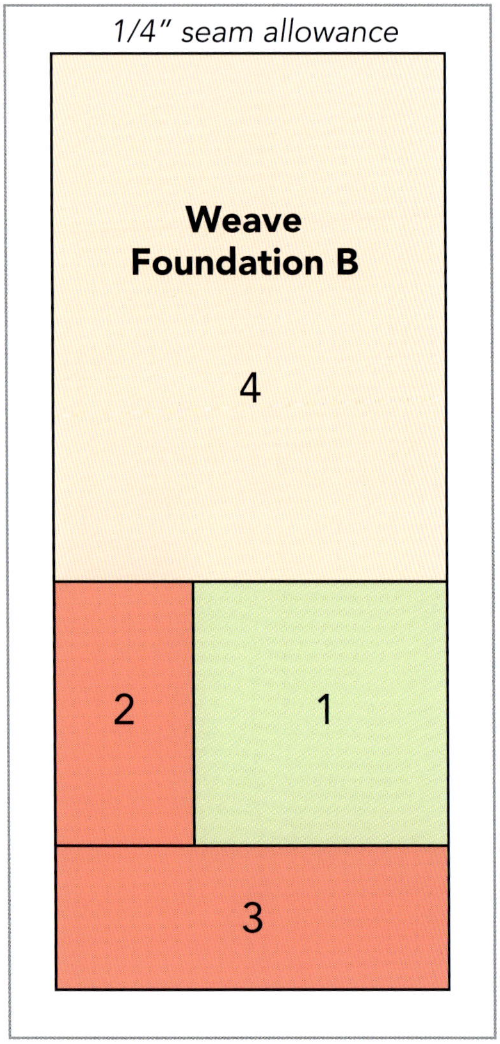

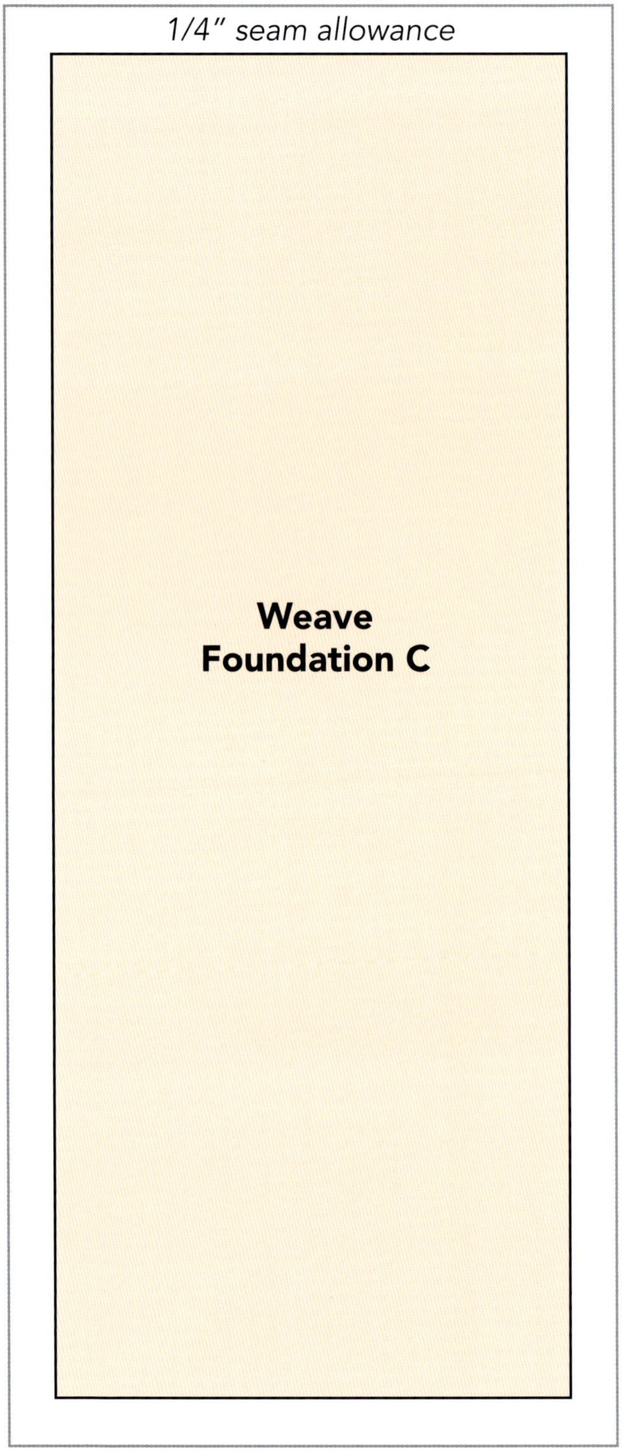

1 inch

Print Check

Foundations must print at 100 percent. When printing, choose none, actual size or 100 percent. Double-check the accuracy of your printout by measuring the 1″ print check with a ruler.

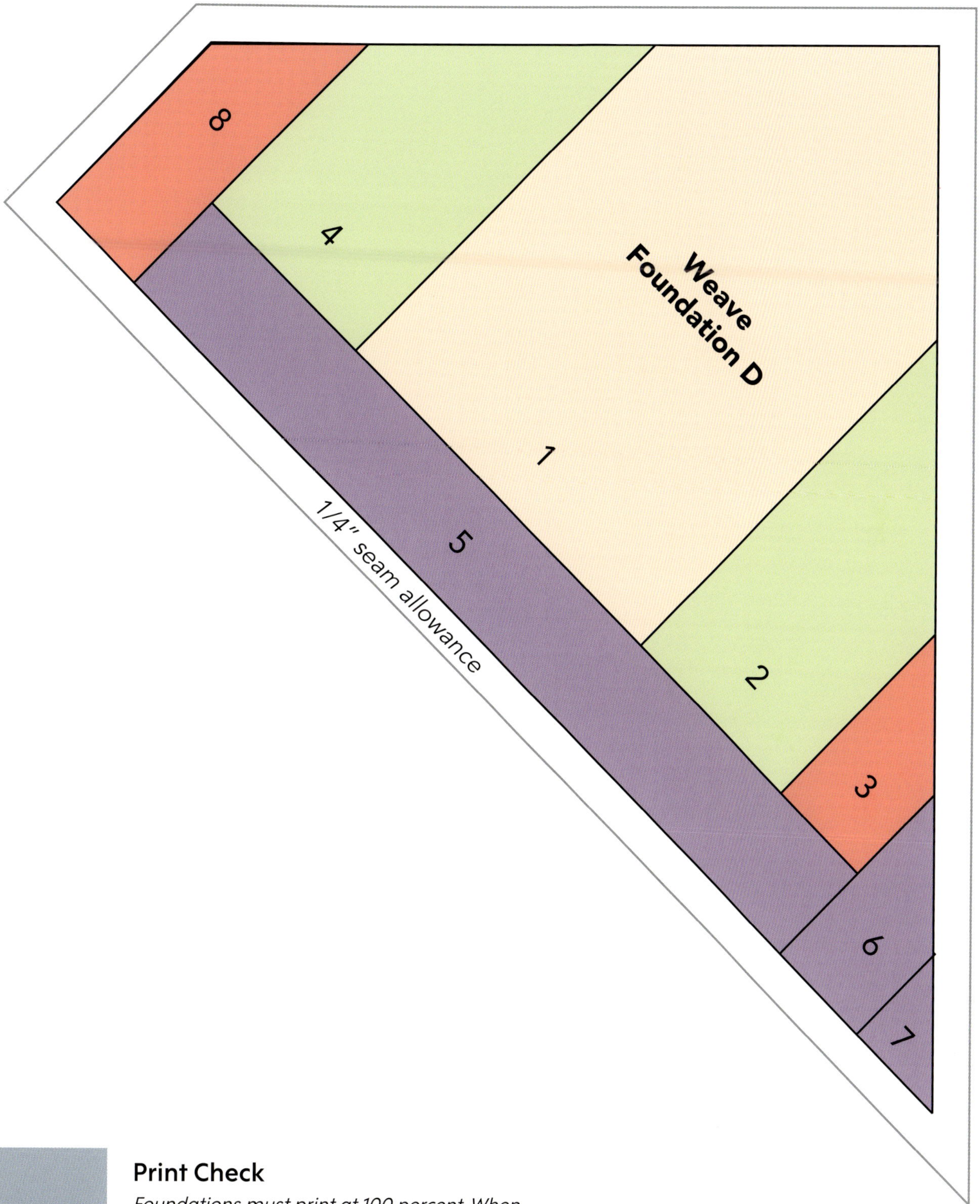

1 inch

Print Check

Foundations must print at 100 percent. When printing, choose none, actual size or 100 percent. Double-check the accuracy of your printout by measuring the 1″ print check with a ruler.

PATTERN *for* *BIRD ON A BRANCH* QUILT

Quilt size: 20½" × 15¾"

Designed and pieced by Dana E. Jones, quilted by Rita Meyerhoff

This charming quilt is a great gift for those who love birds. At 20½" × 15¾", it will fit a small wall space. The design was inspired by a photo of a European robin by Lars Nissen that was available copyright-free from Pixabay.

MATERIALS AND CUTTING (Requirements are based on 40" fabric width)

Fabric	Yardage	Pieces to cut
Light orange	Scrap	B1
Dark orange	fat ⅛ yard	A10, C8, E2
Dark brown	fat ¼ yard	C5, D5, F2, F3, I1, I4, J1
White	Scrap	C1
Greenish brown	Scrap	C2
Brown	Scrap	C6, C7
Light brown	Scrap	A2, A3, A4, A5, A6, A7, A8
Medium brown	Scrap	C4
Light gray	Scrap	A9, A12
Dark gray	fat ⅛ yard	B3, D1, K1
Rust	Scrap	B2
Black	Scrap	A1, B7
Background (blue)	1 yard*	A11, A13, A14, A15, B4, B5, B6, B8, C3, D2, D3, D4, D6, E1, F1, F4, F5, G, H, I2, I3, J2, J3, K2, K3, K4, K5, K6
Backing	½ yard	
Batting	28" × 23"	
Binding	¼ yard *(regular quarter, not fat quarter)*	

**Additional fabric will be needed if background is an ombre fabric as in the photo of Bird on a Branch.*

Notions: Foundation paper and Add-A-Quarter and Add-An-Eighth rulers. If you plan to make cutting templates, you will need a fine-point permanent marker; a clear, flat ruler; and freezer paper or template plastic.

Techniques used: Foundation paper piecing, machine piecing

Assembly

1. Wash, starch, and press fabric. Print copies of all the foundations on pages 146–152 on your favorite FPP paper.

2. For foundations H, I, and K, tape the sections of foundations together, aligning the dots and dotted lines as shown. See Step 2: Joining Foundations, page 145.

   Cut out all the foundations along the outside of the ¼" seam allowances or up to ¼" beyond that. Adding the extra ¼" beyond the seam allowances can help you be sure your fabric pieces fully cover the seam allowances, and it can make it easier to trim your foundations once they are pieced.

3. Determine which pieces you want to make cutting templates for. Make these cutting templates following guidelines in the chapter 5 subsection, "Create Cutting Templates: Efficient Fabric Use, Sewing on Grain," page 102. Cut out the templates.

4. Cut the fabric pieces for the foundations. Recommendation: Label each piece as it is cut. Each label should include the foundation letter and the piece number. Create a bag or envelope for each foundation and organize the cut pieces by foundation.

   If you are not using cutting templates, cut the pieces the following sizes. These sizes are generous for ease in piecing.

A1: 1½" × 1½"
A2: 1" × 1"
A3: 1½" × 1"
A4: 1½" × 1½"
A5: 1¾" × 1½"
A6: 1½" × 1½"
A7: 1½" × 1½"
A8: 2" × 1½"
A9: 2½" × 2¾"
A10: 2" × 2"
A11: 1" × 1"
A12: 3½" × 2"
A13: 1½" × 2"
A14: 2½" × 1½"
A15: 1½" × 1¾"

B1: 5" × 2½"
B2: 4½" × 2"
B3: 5" × 2"
B4: 2" × 1¼"
B5: 2¼" × 1½"
B6: 4" × 2¼"
B7: 2½" × 1½"
B8: 1½" × 1½"

C1: 2½" × 2½"
C2: 3" × 3½"
C3: 2" × 1½"
C4: 4" × 4½"
C5: 3" × 2"
C6: 3¼" × 2"
C7: 3¼" × 2"
C8: 3½" × 3½"

D1: 6" × 2½"
D2: 2" × 2"
D3: 2" × 2½"
D4: 4½" × 2"
D5: 3" × 2½"
D6: 3" × 1½"

E1: 1½" × 2¼"
E2: 1½" × 2"

F1: 6½" × 7"
F2: 4½" × 2"
F3: 5" × 2"
F4: 3" × 2"
F5: 4½" × 2"

G: 6½" × 7½"

H: 22" × 5"

I1: 5½" × 2"
I2: 7½" × 2"
I3: 14" × 13"
I4: 12" × 2"

J1: 9" × 2"
J2: 6½" × 1½"
J3: 7¼" × 2½"

K1: 3½" × 2½"
K2: 2" × 2"
K3: 4" × 2"
K4: 4½" × 2½"
K5: 7" × 6"
K6: 15" × 6"

5. Piece all the foundations. Trim the foundations with ¼" seam allowances around all the outside edges of the foundations.

6. See Step 6: Unit Assembly and Bird on a Branch Assembly, page 145, then join the foundations in the following order:

   - Join foundations A and B. Set aside.
   - Join foundations C and D.
   - Join foundation E to foundations C/D.
   - Join foundations A/B to foundations C/D/E.
   - Join foundation F to foundations A/B/C/D/E.
   - Join foundation G to foundations A/B/C/D/E/F.
   - Join foundation H to foundations A/B/C/D/E/F/G.
   - Join foundation I to foundations A/B/C/D/E/F/G/H.
   - Join foundation J to foundations A/B/C/D/E/F/G/H/I.
   - Join foundation K to foundations A/B/C/D/E/F/G/H/I/J.

7. Layer the backing, batting, and quilt top. Baste. Quilt as desired. Bind the quilt.

Step 2

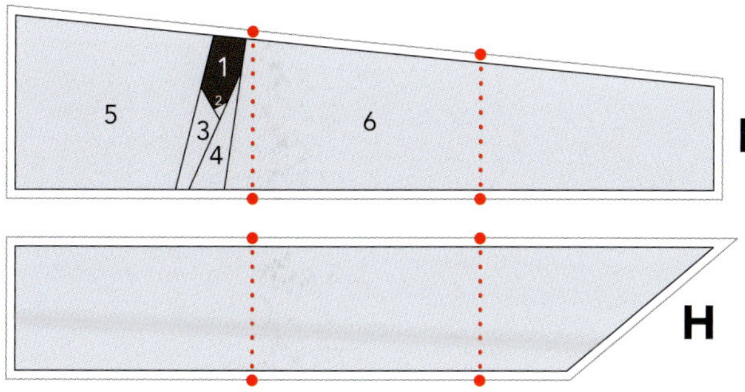

Joining Foundations

Tape FPP sections together, aligning dots and dotted line.

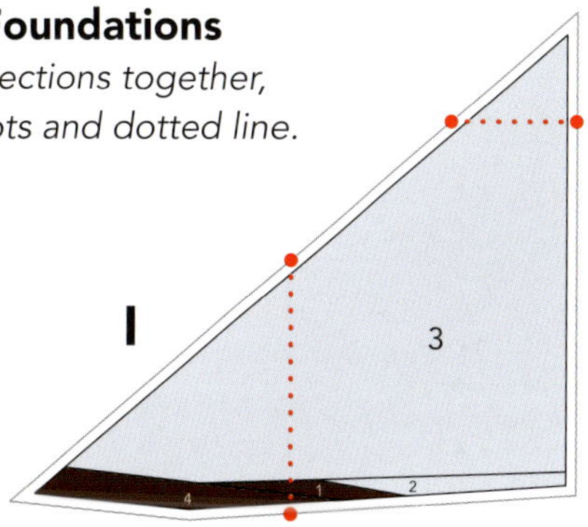

Step 6

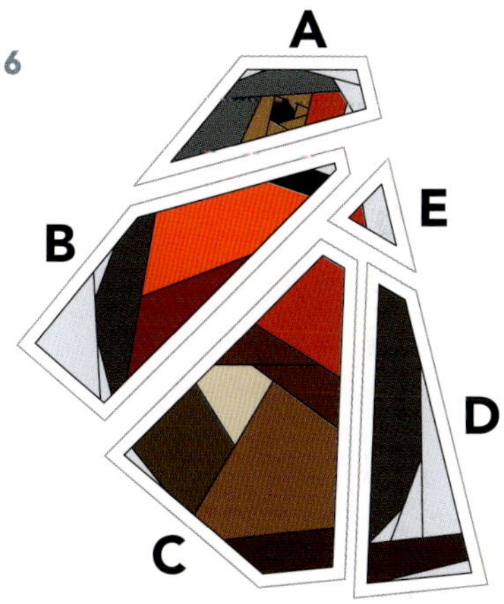

A/B/C/D/E
Unit Assembly

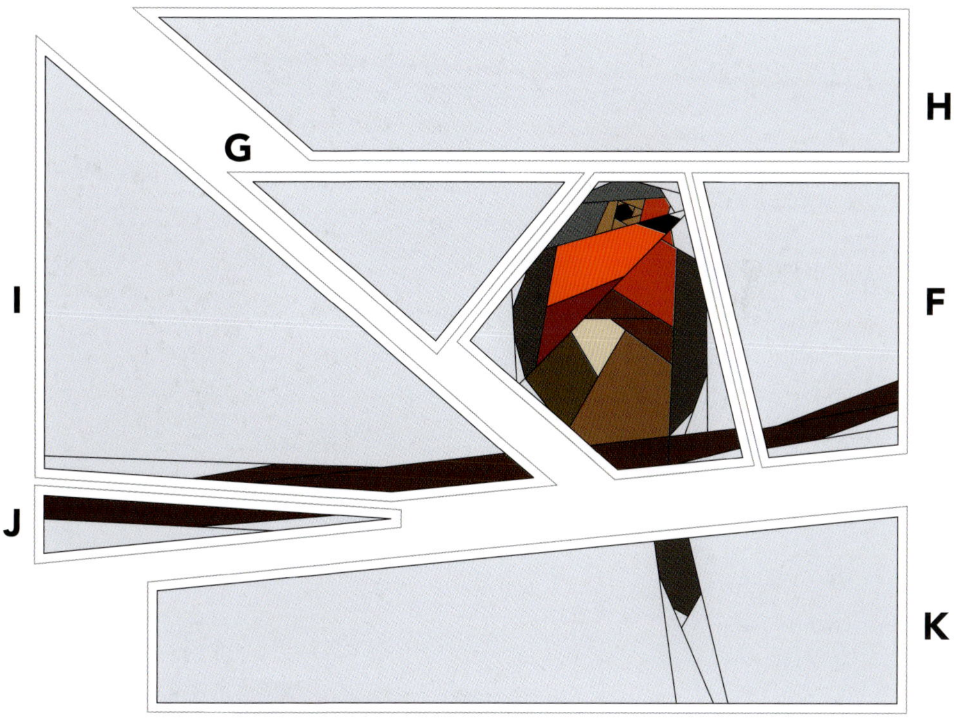

Bird on a Branch Assembly

Photocopied at 125% square will be 1 inch

Print Check

Photocopy the patterns at 125% to make them full-size. Use the reference square above to ensure correct scaling.

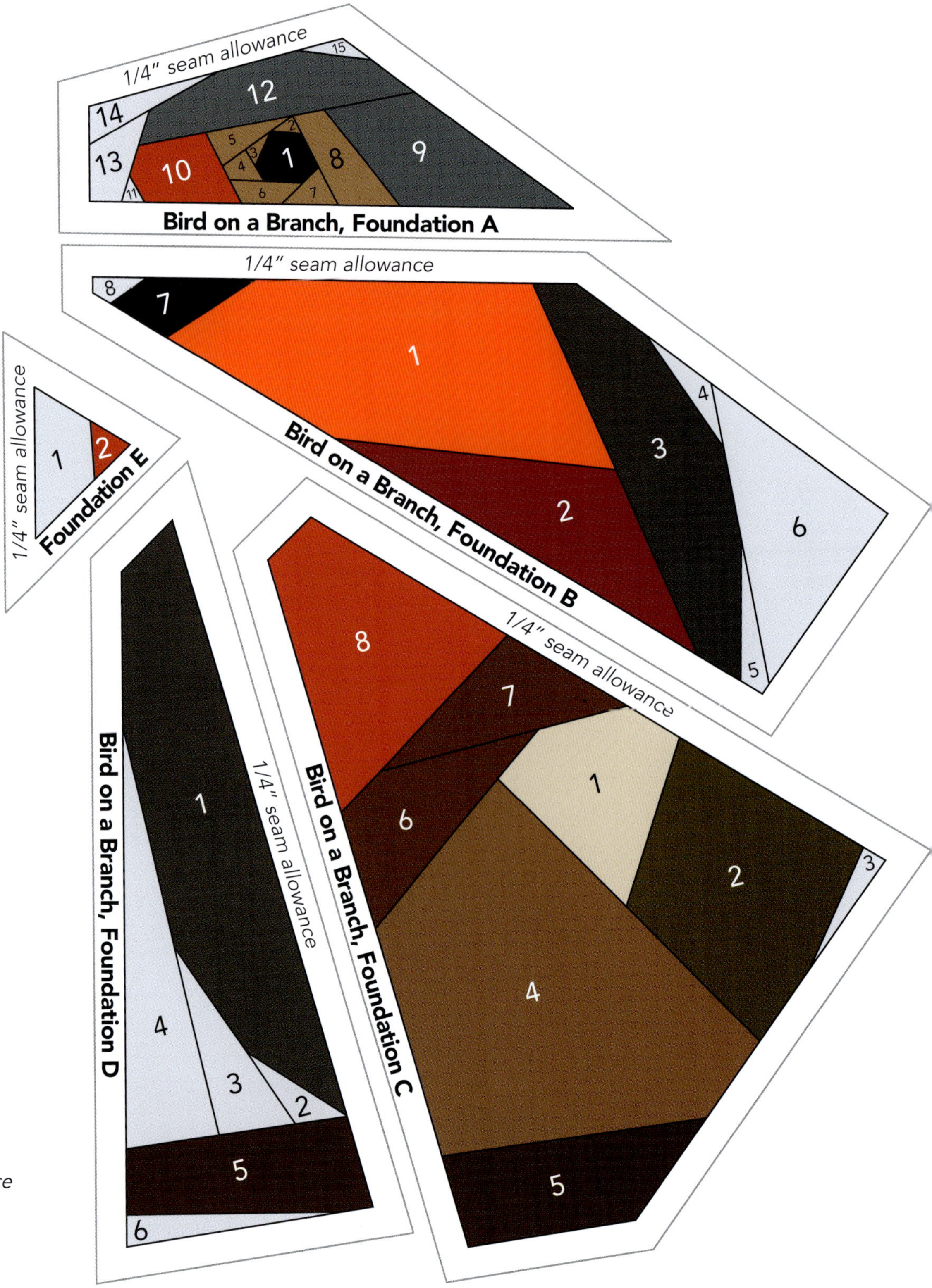

Photocopied at 125%
square will be 1 inch

Print Check

Photocopy the patterns at 125% to make them full-size. Use the reference square above to ensure correct scaling.

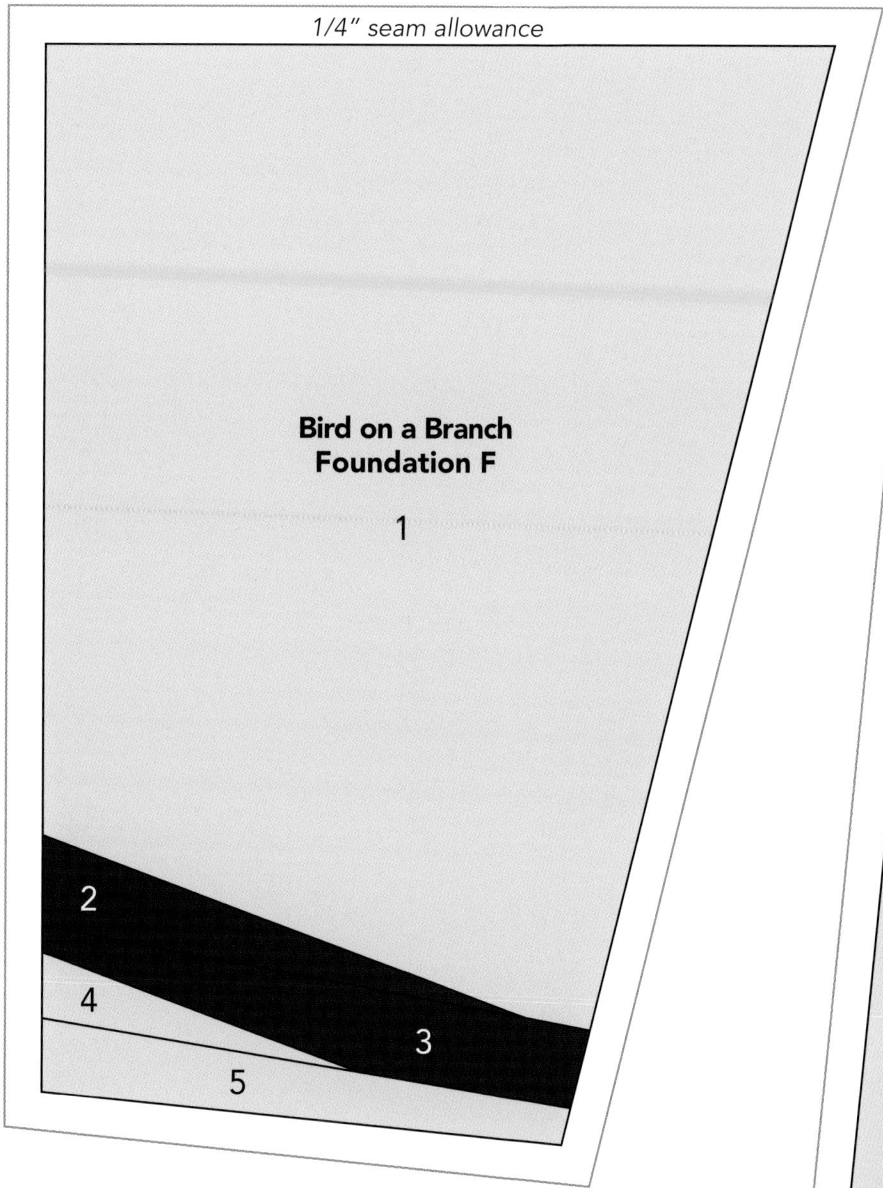

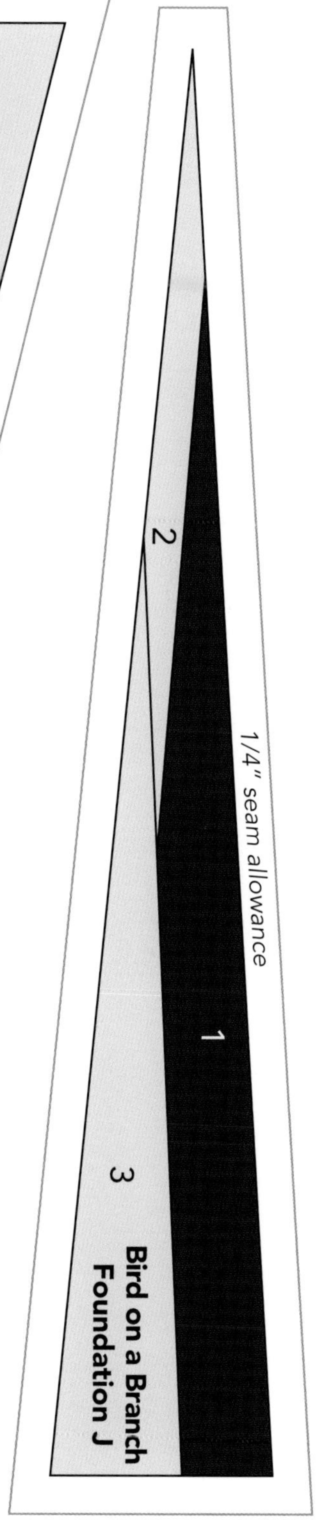

Photocopied at 125%
square will be 1 inch

Print Check

Photocopy the patterns at 125% to make them full-size. Use the reference square to ensure correct scaling.

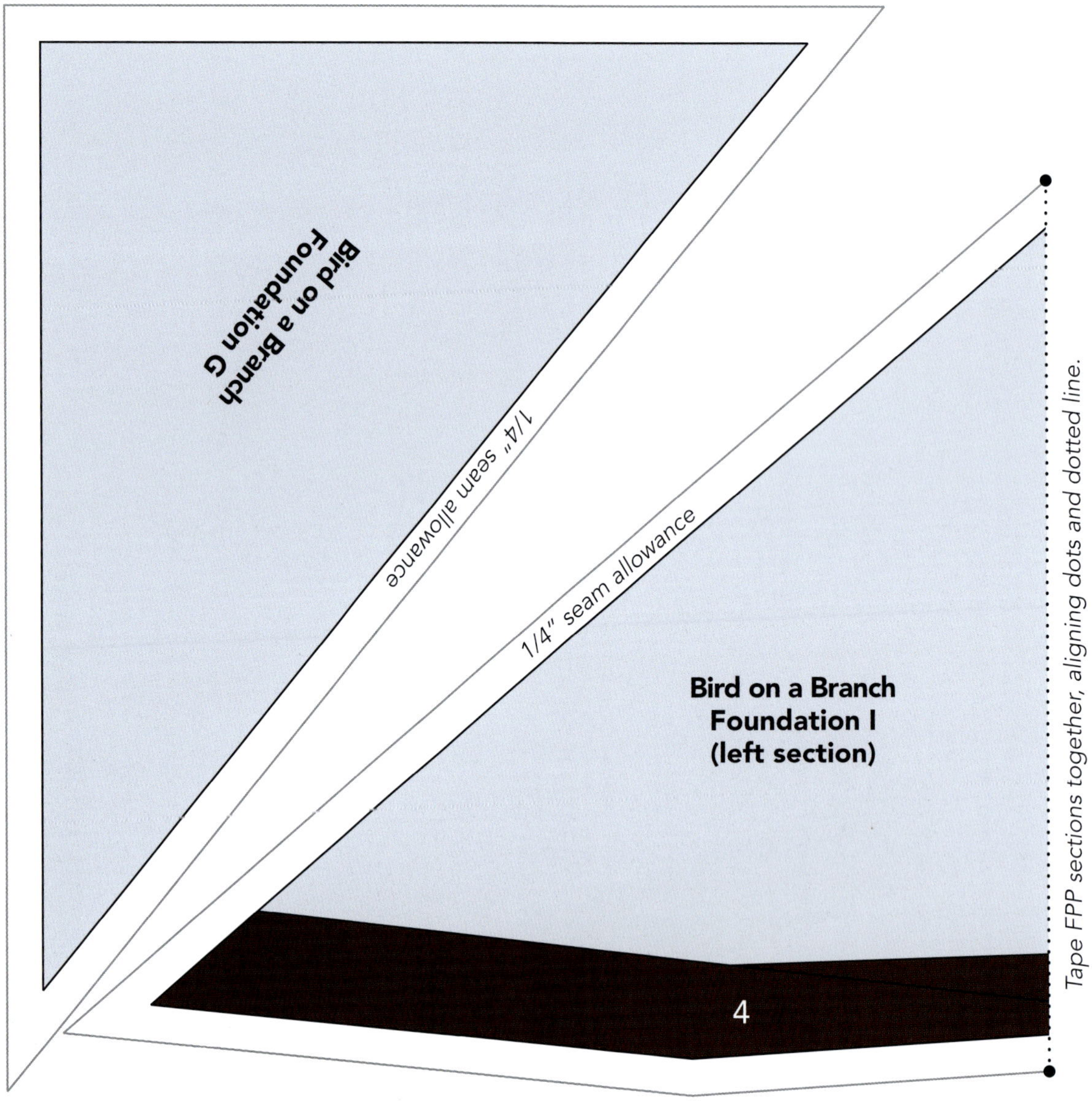

Photocopied at 125% square will be 1 inch

Print Check

Photocopy the patterns at 125% to make them full-size. Use the reference square to ensure correct scaling.

Photocopied at 125% square will be 1 inch

Print Check

Photocopy the patterns at 125% to make them full-size. Use the reference square above to ensure correct scaling.

Tape FPP sections together, aligning dots and dotted line.

Tape FPP sections together, aligning dots and dotted line.

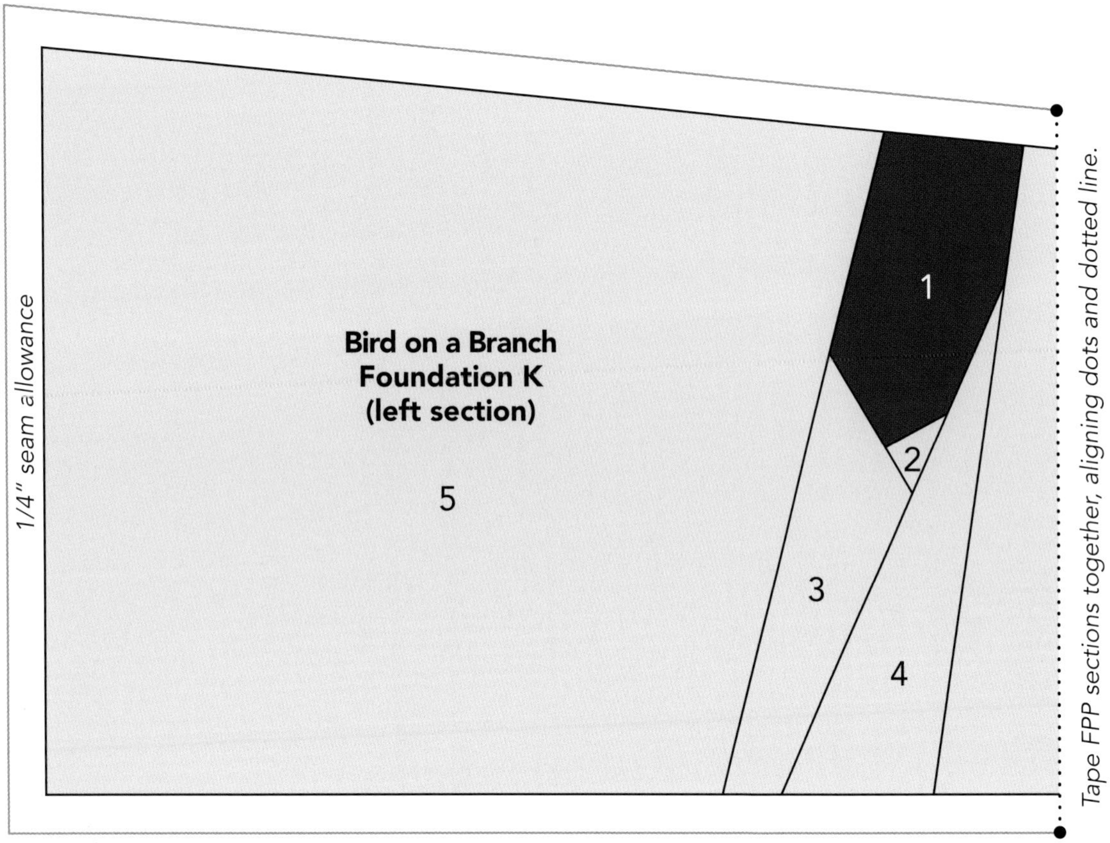

Photocopied at 125%
square will be 1 inch

Print Check

Photocopy the patterns at 125% to make them full-size. Use the reference square above to ensure correct scaling.

Photocopied at 125% square will be 1 inch

Print Check

Photocopy the patterns at 125% to make them full-size. Use the reference square above to ensure correct scaling.

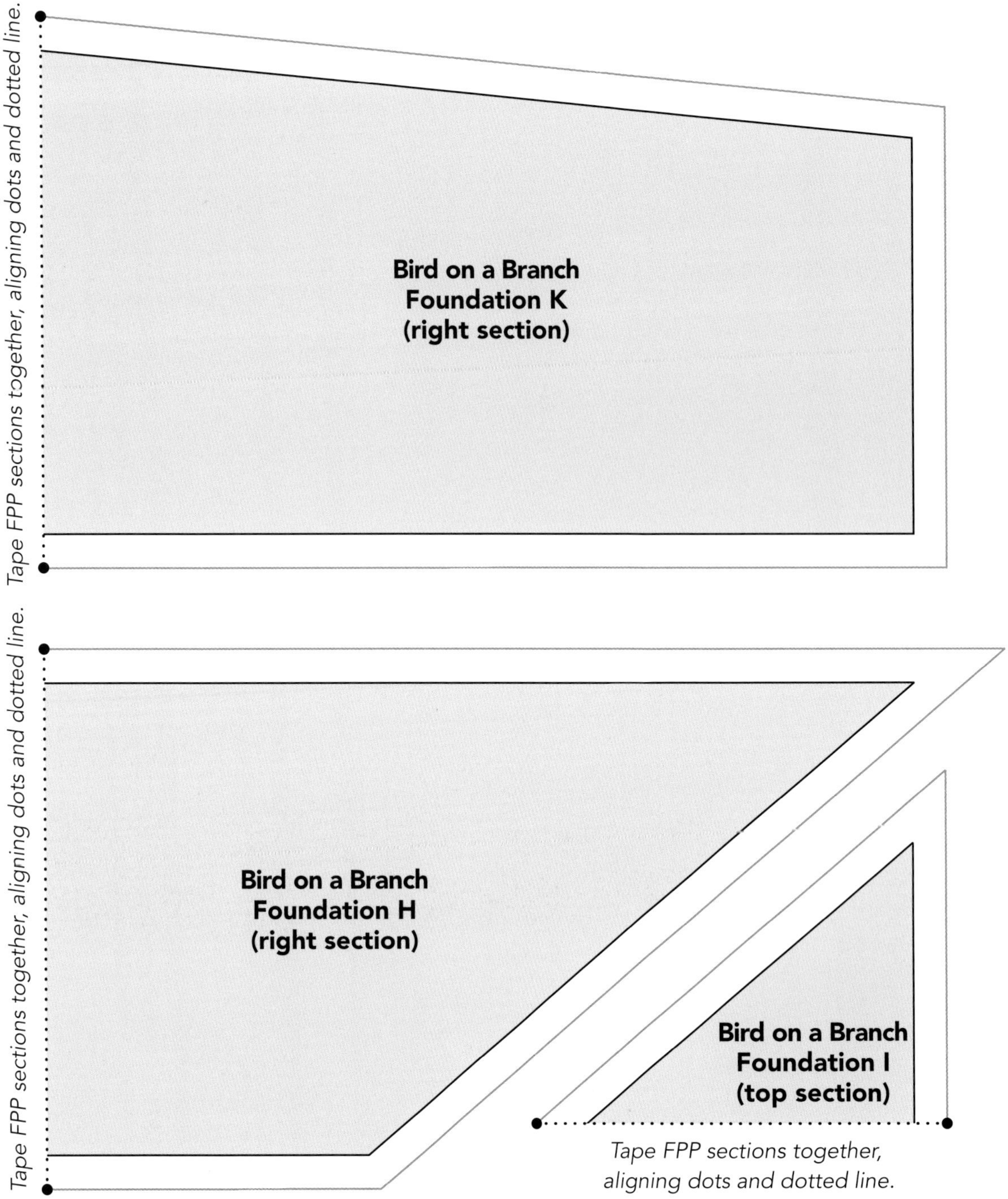

Photocopied at 125%
square will be 1 inch

Print Check

Photocopy the patterns at 125% to make them full-size. Use the reference square to ensure correct scaling.

▲ Cutting pieces for *Avs & Orange*. See quilt on page 111 and foundations for the blocks on pages 131-133.

In developing my Paper Police rules for designing for foundation paper piecing, I stand on the shoulders of many talented quilters, some I've met in person, some I've taken classes with, and some I've met through their books and quilts. I admire the ability of Margaret Rolfe, Carol Doak, Irene Berry, and some of my students to capture the essence of an object in a few strokes and designs that require just one or two foundations. I aspire to having this skill, though I'm inclined to believe you are born with it, and I wasn't. I was born with a love of detail. I'm attracted to folks who share this focus, quilters such as the late Ruth B. McDowell, Sarah Elizabeth Sharp, Juliet van den Heijden, Anita Grossman Solomon, Judy Niemeyer, Jacqueline de Jong, Sarah Pitcher, and some of my students. I'm inspired by Cynthia England, who, it is important to say, is not a foundation paper piecer but rather a picture piecer. Her construction method is uniquely hers—and is great fun. Her design process has much overlap with FPP design, and her book, *Picture Piecing: Creating Dramatic Pictorial Quilts* (England Design Studio, 2002), proved a valuable resource to me as I was learning to design for FPP. Another valuable resource was Ruth B. McDowell's *Piecing: Expanding the Basics* (C&T, 2010).

The quilt world is filled with talented women and men who encourage us along the way. I thank Rita Meyerhoff, Teri Lucas, Jenny Lyon, Debbie Wendt, Cheryl Phillips, ZJ Humbach,

agement and friendship that has brought me to this point in my quilting, and who I know will continue this journey with me.

My thanks to those at quilt shops and guilds who have believed I could teach, beginning with Colleen Nunes, former owner of Quilters Crossing in West Nyack, New York. My thanks to Kris Persun at Holly's Quilt Cabin in Centennial, Colorado, who agreed to see if we could fill a class on how to design for FPP in 2019. We filled that class.

Thanks to all at Schiffer Publishing for their support of this book and their hard work in bringing it to fruition. This includes production editor Karla Rosenbusch, designer Christine Stuermer, cover designer Lindsay Hess, and especially acquisition and developmental editor Kaylee Schofield, who worked with me from perfecting my book proposal through editing and design to publication. Her professionalism, organizational skills, and humor made the journey from idea to book enjoyable.

The first time I attended a national quilt show, I discovered Cherrywood Fabrics. It was love at first sight. I was blown away by the richness of the colors of this hand-dyed fabric and the texture, which looks like suede. I bought a few fat quarters. Over time, I've used Cherrywood in a number of my quilts, and I've built up my stash. When I needed to select fabric for many of the illustrations in this book, I turned to that stash. Of course, there

needed. My thanks to Karla Overland, CEO of Cherrywood, head dyer, and quilt designer, for providing that fabric (https://cherrywoodfabrics.com). Karla also provided photos of fabric swatches used as backgrounds in this book. They are from Cherrywood's Colorado bundle, a nod to my home state.

Thanks to Jacob Wallace, David Chambers, and Sean Tracey at Assist Art Services in Littleton, Colorado, for their expert work on many of the illustrations and photographs.

Thanks and kudos to my students who pushed me to write this book and who have shared their designs in its pages. It was through teaching that clarity about my Paper Police rules and best ways to share them emerged.

Thanks to my family and friends who were convinced this book would be published even before I was, and who were sounding boards when needed. I thank my sister, Wendy Jones, who began quilting even as I was writing this book; my BFF and International Quilt Festival roommate and coconspirator Janet Messanelli Bozzone; and Andrew Fogle, who encouraged me to take time away from the book to breathe deep and gain insight when I felt overwhelmed. Hugs to Jake and Kitsune, my two rescue pups, who were faithful companions through this process, and to Steve Sky, who cared for them and my house when I neglected both in favor of quilting and writing this book.

BIBLIOGRAPHY

Anderson, Alex. *Paper Piecing with Alex Anderson.* 2nd ed. Lafayette, CA: C&T, 2011.

Bakker, Maaike. *Cups and Saucers: Paper-Pieced Kitchen Designs.* Updated ed. Bothell, WA: Martingale, 2011. Patterns available from www.ateliermaaikebakker.nl.

Beam, Carolyn, Paula Stoddard, Diane Volk Harris, Denise Starck, and Amy Rullkoetter, eds. *Quiltmaker's 1,000 Blocks: A Collection of Quilt Blocks from Today's Top Designers.* Cincinnati: F&W Media, 2015.

Brackman, Barbara. *Encyclopedia of Pieced Quilt Patterns,* 3rd ed. Bowling Green, OH: Electric Quilt Company, 2020.

Doak, Carol. *300 Paper-Pieced Quilt Blocks.* Woodinville, WA: Martingale, 2004.

Doak, Carol. *Easy Machine Paper Piecing: 65 Quilt Blocks for Foundation Piecing.* Woodinville, WA: Martingale, 1994.

Doak, Carol. *Show Me How to Paper Piece: Everything Beginners Need to Know.* 2nd ed. Lafayette, CA: C&T, 2022.

England, Cynthia. P*icture Piecing: Creating Dramatic Pictorial Quilts.* Houston, TX: England Design, 2002. Available on jump drive from www.englanddesign.com.

Hall, Jane, Barbara Barber, Carol Doak, Caryl Bryer Fallert, et al. *The Experts' Guide to Foundation Piecing: 15 Techniques and Projects.* Lafayette, CA: C&T, 2006. Available as print on demand from www.ctpub.com.

Huff, Jaynette. *Needles and Notions: Paper-Pieced Patterns with a Sewing Room Theme.* Bothell, WA: Martingale, 2012.

Jones, Dana E. *Pagtinabangay: The Quilts and Quiltmakers of Caohagan Island.* Gilpin County, CO, 2015. Available from www.danajonesquilts.com.

Kinman, MJ. *Crack the Color Code: Add Drama to Your Designs Using the Secrets of Color Interaction.* Louisville: MJ Kinman, 2025. Available from https:mjkinman.com.

Kinman, MJ. *Gemstone Quilts: Creating Fire & Brilliance in Fabric, Step by Step.* Lafayette, CA: C&T, 2020. Patterns available from https://mjkinman.com.

Mahoney, Nancy. *Learn to Paper Piece: A Visual Guide to Piecing with Precision.* Bothell, WA: Martingale, 2016.

McCormick, Carolyn Cullinan. *No-Stress Paper Piecing: 13 Project Using Flannel or Cotton.* Iola, WI: Krause, 2007. www.cmdesignsonline.com.

McDowell, Ruth B. *Piecing: Expanding the Basics.* Lafayette, CA: C&T, 1998. Available as print on demand from www.ctpub.com.

McDowell, Ruth B. W*hen Quilters Gather: 20 Patterns of Piecers at Play.* Lafayette, CA: C&T, 2003.

O'Dell, Mike. Legit Kits foundation paper-piecing patterns. www.legitkits.com.

Pitcher, Sarah. Pitcher's Boutique foundation paper-piecing patterns. www.pitchersboutique.com.

Rolfe, Margaret. *A Quilter's Ark: More Than 50 Designs for Foundation Piecing.* Bothell, WA: Martingale, 2013.

Schwartz, Liz, and Stephen Siefert, eds. *Foundation Pieced Nature Quilts: Designer Edition.* Newport, VA: Zippy Designs, 2002.

Solomon, Anita Grossman. *Make It Simpler Paper Piecing: Easy as 1, 2, 3—a Pinless Fold & Sew Technique.* Lafayette, CA: C&T, 2003.

Sharp, Sarah Elizabeth. *Adventures in Paper Piecing & Design.* Lafayette, CA: C&T, 2018.

Van der Heijden, Juliet. *Animal Quilts: 12 Paper Piecing Patterns for Stunning Animal Quilt Designs.* Blue Ash, OH: F&W Media International, 2017.

Wilkin, Kitty. https://nightquilter.com, Instagram @nightquilter. Paper Pieced Lupine Pattern: https://payhip.com/nightquilter.

INDEX

ABOUT *the* AUTHOR

WHEN DANA E. JONES TOOK HER first foundation paper-piecing class, she was hooked. She loved the precision of the process. Even before she'd finished the project for that first class, she began designing her *Peace Cranes Over Hiroshima* quilt. She had no idea what she was doing, but in the end, she created a design she loves, a design that students across the United States and beyond have embraced and made their own.

As she created more designs for FPP, her Paper Police rules emerged. Dana loves organization almost as much as she loves quilting, so she sought ways to simplify these guidelines toward sharing them with others.

While Dana enjoys many styles of quilting, from making traditional blocks to improv quilting to art quilting, FPP remains her first love. Not one to follow others' patterns, it was a given she'd learn to design for FPP.

Dana is a former editor of *Quilters Newsletter* magazine and the *Studio Art Quilt Associates Journal,* and author and publisher of *Pagtinabangay: The Quilts and Quiltmakers of Caohagan Island,* the story of quilting on a 13-acre island in the central Philippines. This book combines Dana's fascination with fiber and art; her commitment to justice for all people; and her work as a journalist devoted to telling stories that don't make it into mainstream, for-profit media.

As a photojournalist, Dana has been writing and editing since high school, when she landed a part-time job with her hometown newspaper in Libertyville, Illinois. In the 1970s and early 1980s, she worked for newspapers in Illinois, Colorado, Florida, and Alaska. After a short stint in community-college public relations, she found working within the United Methodist Church to be a place to tell stories of women, children, youth, people of color, and others whose stories often go untold. She was editor of United Methodist Women's national magazine, *Response,* for 16 years.

A 1974 graduate of the University of Illinois' journalism school, with a minor in home economics, Dana also studied business management at Webster University in St. Louis and theology at McCormick Theological Seminary in Chicago. She completed close to 30 hours of fine-art instruction at Belleville Area College, now Southwestern Illinois College, where she was named one of the college's top 50 students during its first 50 years. She was selected as the United Methodist Outstanding Communicator of the Year in 2005, and as artist in residence at the Gilpin County Public Library in Colorado in 2012. She has won numerous awards for her writing, editing, and artwork.

Dana's quilts have been exhibited at Rocky Mountain Quilt Museum in Golden, Colorado, and as part of the American Quilt Study Group's 2018 traveling exhibition, *200 Years of Solid Color Quilts.* Dana's quilt for the AQSG exhibition, *In Gina's Footsteps,* was featured on the cover of the exhibition book.

Dana owes her long career in journalism to high school English teacher Mary Lou Humes, who selected her to edit the high school newspaper and took her to numerous journalism workshops. She owes her love of design and typography to Professor Glenn Hanson, who taught for many years at the University of Illinois. She owes her love of quilts to her paternal grandmother, Gertrude Jones, who made sure that all of her grandchildren slept under covers of love pieced from remnants of her house dresses.

Dana and her husband, Andrew "Andy" Fogle, live at 9,200 feet in Gilpin County, Colorado, northwest of Denver. They share their home with their two pups, Jake and Kitsune. Dana enjoys hiking, kayaking, paddle boarding, swimming, photography, and RVing with her tiny Rpod travel trailer. She has just 14 more U.S. national parks to visit to reach her goal of visiting all 60+ parks.